"It [Britain] is the master-piece of Nature, perform'd when she was in her best and gayest humour; which she placed as a little world by it self, by the side of the greater, for the diversion of mankind."

William Camden; Britannia (1586), *trans. Gibson.*

THE PERSONALITY OF BRITAIN

AMS PRESS
NEW YORK

PHYSICAL MAP OF EUROPE.

The overprint indicates the regions (or direction) from which invaders of the Island of Britain (except the Romans) have come, the chief cultures or nations concerned, and probable sea routes. The dates indicate the beginnings of invasions, and are approximate. No attempt is made to show the continental range of widespread cultures. Broken arrow-lines indicate the principal routes by which Mediterranean culture reached Central and Western Europe in early times.

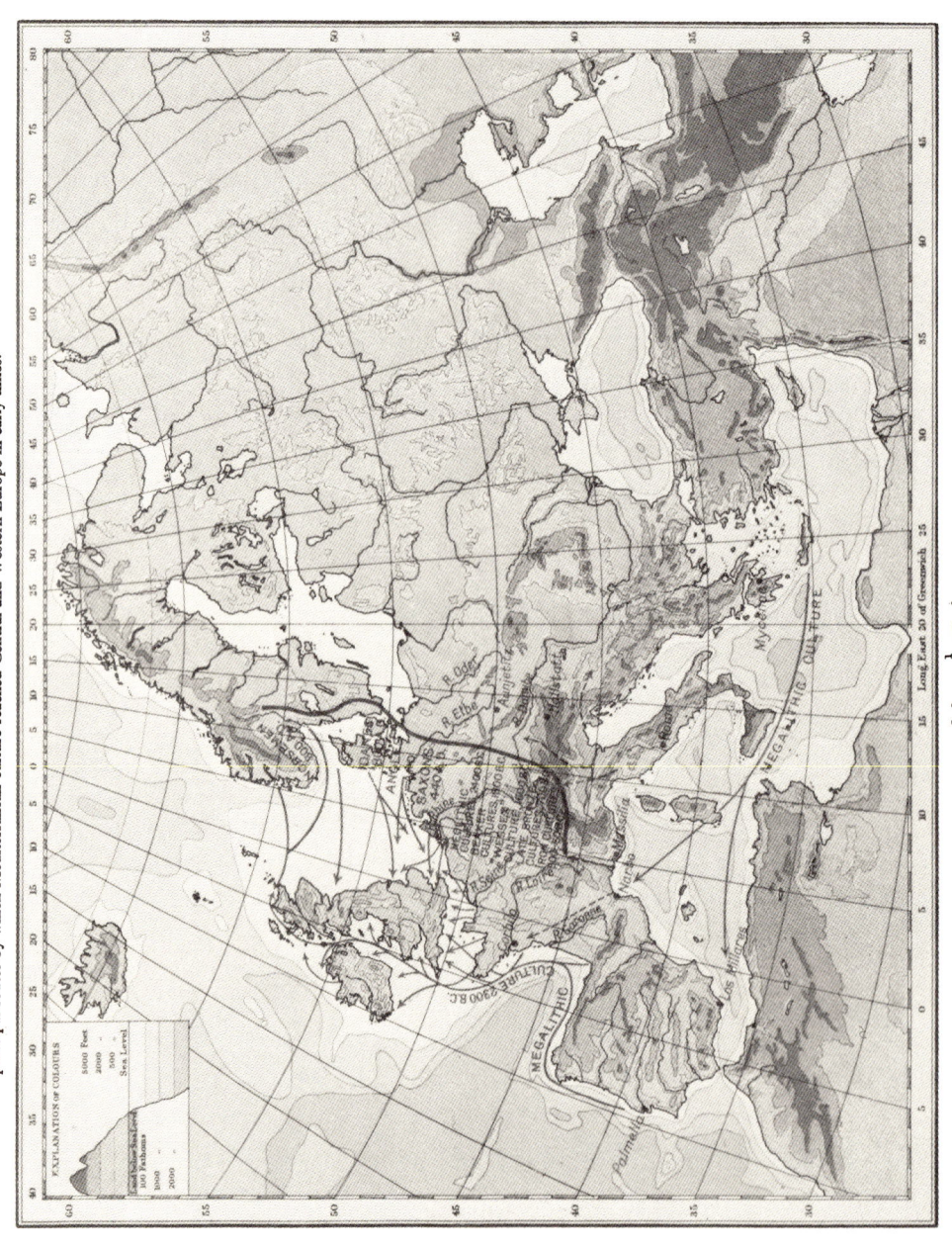

PERSONALITY OF BRITAIN, MAP A.

AMGUEDDFA GENEDLAETHOL CYMRU
NATIONAL MUSEUM OF WALES

THE PERSONALITY OF BRITAIN
ITS INFLUENCE ON INHABITANT AND INVADER IN PREHISTORIC AND EARLY HISTORIC TIMES

BY

SIR CYRIL FOX, PH.D., P.S.A., F.B.A.

WITH NUMEROUS DISTRIBUTION MAPS
INCLUDING A SERIES SPECIALLY PREPARED
BY LILY F. CHITTY, F.S.A.

FOURTH EDITION
(SECOND IMPRESSION)

CARDIFF
PUBLISHED BY THE NATIONAL MUSEUM OF WALES
1947

PRICE: SEVEN SHILLINGS AND SIXPENCE

Library of Congress Cataloging in Publication Data

Fox, Cyril Fred, Sir, 1882-1967.
  The personality of Britain, its influence on
inhabitant and invader in prehistoric and early historic
times.

  Reprint of the 2nd issue of the 4th ed. published in
1947 by the National Museum of Wales, Cardiff.
  Includes bibliographical references and index.
  1. Anthropo-geography—Great Britain.   2. Great
Britain—Antiquities.   I. Chitty, Lily Frances.
II. Title.
GF551.F6   1979   914.1'02   78-27272

First AMS edition published in 1979.

Reprinted from the edition of 1947, Cardiff, from an original in the collections of the University of Oregon Library. Trim size and text area have been slightly altered in this edition. Original trim size: 21 × 26 cm; text area: 16 × 21.5 cm.

MANUFACTURED
IN THE UNITED STATES OF AMERICA

PREFACE

(TO THE FIRST EDITION)

This study of Britain as an environment for Man represents a discourse to be given at the International Congress of Prehistoric and Protohistoric Sciences in London in August of the present year, and has been prepared with that object in view.

It is published by the National Museum of Wales because it provides (*inter alia*) a convenient summary of a variety of influences, internal and external, which helped to mould the successive cultures of the Highland Zone; and because it surveys the relations of the Zone (which includes Wales) to the rest of Britain, to Ireland, and to Western Europe generally.

Since the work deals with Wales as an integral part of the Island of Britain, it may (it is hoped) be found a useful handbook for students and others visiting the Archaeological Galleries, placing the Welsh antiquities therein displayed in their true perspective as elements and manifestations of widespread cultures.

Many of the type-objects of which distribution maps are figured will be found in the Museum.[1] For example: beakers, bronze axes, bronze daggers, gold lunulae, foodvessels, encrusted urns, currency bars, British coins, brooches in the Archaeological Gallery; gold torcs on the Balcony: Ogham inscriptions in the Entrance Hall.

Three coloured maps are included, in order to illustrate as effectively as possible the physical factors which influenced the destiny of Man in Britain. The first shows the position of Britain in relation to the Continent, and the contiguity of their lowland zones; the second shows the form and relief of the British Islands; while the third illustrates, on a larger scale, and therefore in greater detail, the form and physical structure of Southern Britain. Each map has a suitable overprint. For the provision of the first map the Council has to thank an anonymous donor.

The Council is much indebted to the following authors and publishers for permission to reproduce illustrations:—Professor V. Gordon Childe, F.S.A.; Dr. R. C. C. Clay, F.S.A.; Mr. O. G. S. Crawford, F.S.A.; Mr. G. C. Dunning; Mr. E. Estyn Evans, M.A., F.S.A.; Mr. W. F. Grimes, M.A.; Mr. Christopher Hawkes, B.A., F.S.A.; Mr. E. T. Leeds, M.A., F.S.A.; Sir George Macdonald, K.C.B., LL.D.; Mr. J. N. L. Myres, M.A., F.S.A.; Mr. C. G. Stevens, M.A.; Dr. R. E. M. Wheeler, M.C., F.S.A.; His Majesty's Stationery Office; The Editor, "Antiquity"; The Oxford University Press; the Royal Society of Edinburgh, and The Society of Antiquaries of London: and to the Controller of the Stationery Office, Dublin; the Cambrian Archaeological Association; the Hampshire Field Club; the Royal Archaeological Institute, and the Wiltshire Archaeological Society for the loan of blocks.

CYRIL FOX,
Director.

July, 1932.

---

[1] Illustrations of these objects were added to the Essay when the Third Edition was published.

PREFACE
(TO THE FOURTH EDITION)

This edition of the *Personality of Britain* has been prepared in accordance with a decision of the Council to maintain, as far as possible, the existing publications of the Museum during the War.

The author would have liked to experiment in the re-writing of a great part of the Essay; the advance in archaeological knowledge since it was first published (in 1932) has been remarkable, and has shown that the historico-geographical phenomena in which he was interested were in many cases more complex than then appeared to him probable. While much of the recently acquired data can be incorporated by emendation or by addition—as was done in 1938 when the third edition was printed—the total volume of new knowledge is now such as to demand re-assessment of the significance or relative importance of many facts or inductions set out a decade ago. Thus a fresh approach might be of advantage. The author's commitments and duties, however, make this course impossible for him; moreover, Miss L. F. Chitty, whose help, renewed on the occasion of each edition, has been invaluable, could not undertake under present conditions a number of new distribution maps. All, then, that can be offered to the reader is a reprint brought factually up to date, with some expansion, and with a measure of general revision of those portions of the text which are affected by recent research. There are also a few changes in the map series: Miss Chitty has prepared one of Wales in the Bronze Age, and has assisted in the revision of two others; the map of flat bronze daggers has been re-drawn, and the overprint of the coloured " Map A " recast. Plate X and Figure 34 in the third edition have been withdrawn; three maps, previously published elsewhere, have been included.

The work of the author's contemporaries on which much of the textual change is based, is acknowledged in footnotes; in this Preface he wishes to express his indebtedness to the first modern study of the prehistory of Britain as a whole—Professor V. Gordon Childe's *Prehistoric Communities of the British Isles* (1940)—and to two important works of wider range, *The Dawn of European Civilization* (second—re-written—edition 1939) also by Professor Childe, and Mr. C. F. C. Hawkes' *The Prehistoric Foundations of Europe* (1940), which enable the author to deal allusively with the wider European relationships. Note has also been taken of the new knowledge of the vegetational history of Britain attained by pollen analysis, a technique associated in this country principally with the name of Dr. H. Godwin of the Botany School, Cambridge, and practised by Mr. H. A. Hyde, Keeper of Botany in the Museum, on Welsh sites. Lastly, the monumental work of Mr. A. G. Tansley, *The British Islands and their Vegetation* (1939) requires mention, affording as it does a detailed survey of the climatic and structural, as well as the vegetational background to our prehistory and history, so briefly treated in the Essay. The author is greatly obliged to Miss Chitty, and to Mr. and Mrs. C. F. C. Hawkes, for reading his proof sheets and making constructive criticisms and comments; he also has good reason to renew his thanks, incorporated in the text of previous editions, to his colleagues Mr. H. A. Hyde, Mr. Colin Matheson and Dr. F. J. North, for their assistance. The Index has been compiled by Lady Fox.

The Council is much indebted for permission to reproduce illustrations new to this edition to Professor V. Gordon Childe and the *Society of Antiquaries of London* (Figure 9), to Mr. Stuart Piggott and the *Prehistoric Society* (Figure 6), and to the *Cambrian Archaeological Association* (Figure 8).

CYRIL FOX,

June, 1943. *Director.*

CONTENTS

	Page
LIST OF ILLUSTRATIONS	7
CHRONOLOGICAL TABLE	9
INTRODUCTION	10

THE POSITION AND FORM OF BRITAIN, AS AFFECTING INHABITANT AND INVADER .. 15
- Geographical factors influencing Eastern distributions .. 15
- Geographical factors influencing Western distributions .. 21
- Changes of level in Southern Britain .. 24

THE STRUCTURE OF BRITAIN, AS AFFECTING INHABITANT AND INVADER .. 28
- Structural contrasts in Britain .. 28
  - (*a*) The Highland Zone .. 29
  - (*b*) The Lowland Zone .. 29
- The effect of structural differences .. 32
  - The importance of the Lowland Zone .. 38
  - The characteristics of the Highland Zone .. 40
- Physical aspects of the relation of Ireland to Britain .. 42
- Deposits of copper, gold and tin in the British Isles, exploited in prehistoric times .. 44

THE CLIMATE, FLORA, AND FAUNA OF BRITAIN, AS AFFECTING INHABITANT AND INVADER .. 51
- CLIMATE .. 51
  - Climatic changes .. 51
  - Influence of the climate .. 53
- FLORA .. 53
  - Modifications resulting from climatic changes .. 54
  - Relation between vegetation and human distribution .. 54
  - Significance of the " damp " oakwood .. 55
- FAUNA .. 62
  - Biotic influences on Man's distribution .. 63

THE GENERAL DISTRIBUTION OF POPULATION IN BRITAIN IN PREHISTORIC TIMES, AND ITS SIGNIFICANCE .. 64
- (*a*) In the Lowland Zone .. 64
- (*b*) In the Highland Zone .. 69
- The relation between elevation and human settlement .. 73

LONG-TERM CHANGES IN THE DISTRIBUTION OF POPULATION AND THEIR CAUSES .. 77
- The effect of climatic changes .. 77
  - (*a*) In the Lowland Zone .. 77
  - (*b*) In the Highland Zone .. 78

CONTENTS—*continued*

	Page
The effect of increasing population in Early Britain	78
Areas of " easy " and of " difficult " settlement	78
The exploitation of richer soils	82
The " valleyward " movement	83
The change in the economic centre of Lowland Britain	83
Changes in the " southern trade "	83
SUMMARY	84
Chronological outline	84
Propositions	86
EPILOGUE: THE PERSONALITY OF BRITAIN	90
APPENDIX	94
(Note on the Liver-Fluke as a factor in human distribution: by Colin Matheson, M.A., B.Sc.)	
INDEX	95

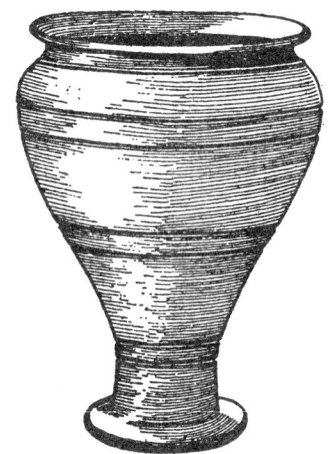

PEDESTAL URN. Scale ⅓. (See Fig. 4.)

BRITISH GOLD COINS: (1) Uninscribed debased stater; (2) Coin of Cunobelin, minted at Camulodunum. ⅓. (See Fig. 37.)

LIST OF ILLUSTRATIONS

Cover
The Routes of Traders and Invaders

Coloured Maps

Map A.	Physical Map of Europe, with overprint	*Frontispiece*
Map B.	Physical Map of the British Isles, with overprint	*Facing page* 28
Map C.	Physical Map of Southern Britain, with overprint	*At end*

Plates

Plate		
I.	Distribution of Neolithic Pottery of Types "A" and "B"	
II.	Distribution of Beakers in Europe	
III.	Distribution of Beakers in Southern Britain	
IV.	Distribution of Foodvessels in the British Isles	
V.	Distribution of Encrusted Urns in the British Isles	
VI.	Distribution of Flat Axes in the British Isles	Between pages 94 and 95
VII.	Distribution of Cast-flanged Axes in the British Isles	
VIII.	Distribution of Cordoned Urns in the British Isles	
IX.	Distribution of Finds of the Late Bronze Age in Wales	
X.	Distribution of Socketed Axes, Breton type and Yorkshire type, in Britain	
XI.	Distribution of Finds of Objects of Early Iron Age "C" in East Anglia	
XII.	Distribution of Viking Settlements in Western Britain	

Illustrations in Text

Fig.		Page
1.	Distribution of Megalithic Monuments in the British Isles	12
2.	Distribution of Beakers in the British Isles	13
3.	Distributions of hoards containing "Winged" Axes in Britain and Western Europe	16
4.	Distribution of Pedestal Urns in Britain and Western Europe	17
5.	Distribution of Iron Age "A" Culture in Southern Britain	18
6.	Distribution of "B" Beakers in Southern England	20
7.	Distribution of Megalithic Monuments in Western Europe	21
8.	Map illustrating sources of Non-socketed Sickles found in Britain	23
9.	Distribution of Double-looped Palstaves in Britain and Western Europe	24
10.	Coastline of Great Britain and Ireland shortly before separation from the Continent	25
11.	Distribution of Iron Age "B" Culture in South-Western Britain	30
12.	Distribution of Fine Celtic Metal-work and Chariot Burials	31
13.	Political and Cultural Divisions of Early England	34
14.	Anglo-Saxon Burial Places, A.D. 450–650, in England	35
15.	The Civil Districts of Roman Britain	36
16.	The Military Districts of Roman Britain	37
17.	Plan of Silchester, Hampshire	38
18.	Plan of Tre'r Ceiri, Caernarvonshire	39
19.	Distribution of Ogham-inscribed Stones in the British Isles	43
20.	Distribution of Flat riveted Knife-daggers in Southern Britain	46
21.	Distribution of Flint Daggers in Southern Britain	47
22.	Distribution of Gold Lunulae in the British Isles and Western Europe	48

LIST OF ILLUSTRATIONS—continued

Fig.		Page
23.	Distribution of Gold Objects of the Middle Bronze Age in the British Isles	50
24.	Distribution of Gold Objects of the Late Bronze Age in the British Isles	50
25.	Chart illustrating Distribution of Rain in the British Isles during 1930	52
26.	Distribution of Finds and Remains attributed to the Bronze Age in the Cambridge Region	56
27.	Distribution of Finds and Remains attributed to the Roman Age in the Cambridge Region	57
28.	The Cambridgeshire Dykes	59
29.	The Frontier Dykes of Wales	60
30.	Offa's Dyke in Herefordshire	61
31.	Distribution of Chambered Cairns in Caithness and Sutherland	72
32.	Distribution of Flat Axes, Moulds and Halberds of the Early Bronze Age in Scotland	74
33.	Distribution of Pictish Symbols in Scotland, sixth–seventh century A.D.	75
34.	Distribution of Hill-forts in North Wales, in relation to the mountain mass	76
35.	Distribution of Finds of the Anglo-Saxon Pagan Period in the Cambridge Region	80
36.	Distribution of Settlements in the Cambridge Region at the close of the Anglo-Saxon Period as evidenced by Domesday Book	81
37.	Distribution of Currency Bars and of British Coins	85
38.	Type-objects: Bronze Age Pottery	91
39.	Type-objects: Early Bronze Age—lunula, daggers, halberd	92
40.	Type-objects: Bronze Age Axes	93

TAIL PIECES

Pedestal Urn (p. 6), British gold coins (p. 6), Encrusted urn (p. 8), Currency bar (p. 89),
Pictish symbols (p. 94), Ogham script (p. 94).

Encrusted urn: Late type. ¼. (See Pl. V.)

TABLE GIVING THE CHRONOLOGICAL SEQUENCE, RELATIVE LENGTH, AND APPROXIMATE DATES (IN BRITAIN)[1] OF THE CULTURE PERIODS OR PHASES TO WHICH REFERENCE WILL BE MADE

2500	Neolithic Age	Neolithic "A," from c. 2400 B.C. Megalithic and Long Barrow cultures, c. 2300–1700 B.C.[2] Neolithic "B," from c. 2200 B.C. or earlier.	Plate I. Figs. 1, 7, 31.
2250			
2000			
1750	Bronze Age	Early Bronze (Beaker Period), c. 1900–1600 B.C.[3]	Map C. Plates II to X. Figs. 2, 3, 6, 8, 9, 20, 21, 22, 23, 24, 26, 32; also 38 to 40.
1500		Middle Bronze "A," 17th cent.–14th cent. B.C. (overlaps)	
1250		Middle Bronze "B," c. 1400–1000 B.C.	
1000		Late Bronze, c. 1000–500 B.C.	
750		L.B. I, traders and migrants. L.B. II, "Urnfield" folk, 8th cent. B.C.	
500			
B.C. 250	Early Iron Age[4]	Hallstatt La Tène I } c. 500–250 B.C. "A" La Tène II, c. 250–75 B.C. "B" La Tène III, c. 75 B.C.–50 A.D. "C"	Plate XI. Figs. 4, 5, 11, 12, 34, 37.
0			
A.D. 250	Roman Period	43 A.D.–c. 450 A.D.	Figs. 15 to 18, 27.
500	Dark Ages	Anglo-Saxon Pagan Period, c. 450–650 A.D.	Plate XII. Figs. 13, 14, 19, 28 to 30, 33, 35, 36.
750		Viking Raids, 793–1066 A.D.	
1000		Domesday Record, 1086 A.D.	

[1] These dates are mainly applicable to the Lowland Zone of Britain. For the prehistoric chronology in Wales, see the Museum *Guide to the Prehistoric Collections*, by W. F. Grimes; and for the problems involved in the correlation of Highland and Lowland Zone cultures, V. Gordon Childe, *Prehistoric Communities*, pp. 7–11.

[2] To a large extent absorbing Neolithic "A" and "B," and overlapping the "Beaker" period. For the chronology of Neolithic culture elements, see Childe, *Dawn of European Civilization*, 2nd Ed., Table III; and C. F. C. Hawkes, *Prehistoric Foundations*, Table V; and cf. Jacquetta Hawkes, *Antiquity*, 1934, Table, p. 41; Piggott, *Proc. Prehist. Soc. East Anglia*, VII, 1934, p. 373 ff.

[3] The divisions of the Bronze Age are substantially those of Fox, *Arch. Camb. Reg.*, 1923, p. 20; the main nomenclature, that of the official *Handbook* issued for the 1st International Congress of Prehistoric Sciences, London, 1932. In the Beaker period, B2 and also B1 migrants are pre-subsidence, c. 1900, A migrants post-subsidence, c. 1800. Middle Bronze "A" is represented by foodvessel cultures mainly in northern and western Britain and by the "Wessex" culture in southern Britain. Middle Bronze "B" represents the fusion of Lowland and Highland cultures into a fairly uniform insular cremation culture typified by the overhanging-rim urn.

[4] The continental classification (Hallstatt-La Tène), as C. F. C. Hawkes has emphasized, is not directly applicable to Britain, and his three major groupings, in part regionally, in part chronologically distinct, are now generally recognized (*Archaeology in England and Wales*, p. 153 ff). Iron Age "A" is based on the Continental Hallstatt, but incorporates La Tène elements; Iron Age "B" represents one form or another of continental La Tène II culture, and the results of their interaction; Iron Age "C" represents La Tène III (Belgic) culture and its fusion with earlier elements.

Introduction

In this brief Essay I shall endeavour to express the character of Britain in prehistoric and early historic ages, and to indicate the effect of the environment she afforded on the distribution and fates of her inhabitants and her invaders.

Man (*Homo sapiens*) entered a more or less recognizable "Britain" on the heels of a temporarily retreating ice-sheet in Upper Palaeolithic (Aurignacian) times, possibly as much as 20,000 years ago. Britain then formed part of the continental land mass of Europe, and—possibly with interludes of insularity—so continued until Mesolithic times, determined geo-chronologically for northern Europe at from *c.* 8300 to 2500 B.C., during which culture phase the final separation took place (p. 26).

My survey, being concerned with Britain as an island, commences with the first considerable movement of men into the country after that event. This movement, dated to about 2400 B.C., is epoch-making, in that it marks the introduction of a food-producing economy, in contrast to the earlier food-gathering economies. The Mesolithic folk survived side by side with the newcomers, but they did little, so far as is known, to influence their crafts.

The continental background to invasion may now claim some attention. The compelling urge, in the case of invaders who arrived in prehistoric times, is a matter of inference, not of knowledge; one invasion we can with reason attribute to expanding demand in a populous community for land for stock-raising and tillage; another to fear of warlike and aggressive neighbours; a third to the stimulus of adventure among warrior peoples; and a fourth to that of profit among energetic trading and colonizing groups. Climatic change imperilling livelihood in the homeland undoubtedly operated, in one case at least. It was peoples situated for the most part, as we shall see, in the middle and lower Rhinelands, northern France, and the west Alpine region who moved west into Britain; in such geographical settings a sea crossing seems to have consistently afforded fearful or restless folk a line of least resistance or greatest opportunity.

These are proximate factors leading to invasion; the underlying cause, in most cases, may well have been tension, social and economic, induced by the surge of Europe upwards from barbarism. It is now well known that the sources of our civilization—urbanization based on stock-raising, agriculture, and metallurgy—are in south-west Asia and Egypt. Thence, from the fourth millennium onwards, knowledge of these novel social arts and crafts spread westward and northward through the mountain barriers into central and western Europe by routes some of which are shown on Map A, and to Mediterranean coastlands and islands as far as Spain. Farmers, traders, and prospectors in search of copper ores, alluvial gold, and (later) tin, seem to have shared in a movement which was uneven in time and space; desired commodities, desirable land, are irregularly distributed, and a Europe hitherto unexplored and unexploited provided many physical obstacles. Certain features in the expansion thus indicated exercised a controlling influence on the early history of Britain. One was the rapid spread by sea westward from the Aegean (in particular from Crete) in the middle of the third millennium, of colonizing groups united by a potent religion, a cult of the dead, inspired by Egypt and expressed in the construction of large stone tombs designed for collective burial (Map A). These Mediterranean seamen—or more probably adventurous dwellers on the western coasts of Spain and Portugal whom they taught and in turn inspired—opened up (about 2300 B.C.) an Atlantic route to the north which ultimately extended to the "amber coast" of Jutland, in partial collaboration with folk similarly equipped who had reached western France overland. Britain lay athwart their track.

Another event of importance to Britain was the establishment in central Europe of secondary centres of civilization based on farming and a flourishing bronze industry; the cemetery of Aunjetitz, in Bohemia (Map A), is the type-station of an early phase (*c.* 1800–1450 B.C.). The freedom of commerce which made these societies possible created also trans-European trade routes east and west, north and south; particularly important is the Elbe–Brenner " amber" route from Jutland to north Italy, which lessened the importance of the Atlantic traffic, and so of Britain, in the developing pattern of European culture.

But none of these changes affected the importance of the Mediterranean region. As Minoan Crete decayed, the brilliant Mycenaean culture blossomed in Greece, and from 1600 B.C. onwards its achievements in art and life influenced the whole of Europe; thenceforward the continental primacy in organization, wealth and cultural progress continued to be held by one or other of the central Mediterranean societies.

Certain other basic features of the European progress towards civilization, as it affected Britain, may briefly be stated. One feature is that the simpler techniques of the new order, stock-raising and agriculture, tended to outstrip, in their overland (and possibly oversea) expansion north and west, knowledge of the mysteries of metal-working; the first waves of invaders that broke on Britain's shores after her insulation thus possessed a Neolithic economy. So slow was the Eastern (and Mycenaean) achievement in reaching the margins of Europe, that nothing comparable with the city state, its crown and flower, was established in Britain until a few generations before the Roman conquest. Another feature is that, situated as Britain is beyond the bounds of France, contact with any Mediterranean civilization in early times was either very tenuous or indirect; that is, she received impulses to cultural advance whether by invasion or trade, whether by sea or land, almost entirely from the secondary centres of European civilization, to two of which reference has already been made. The last feature that needs to be mentioned here is that, other things being equal, the further a continental society is from the Mediterranean the more barbarous (or the less civilized) it will be; the geographical position of any one group of Britain's invaders is thus of paramount importance, for on this will depend whether a particular invasion lowers, or raises, cultural standards hitherto existing.[1]

We may now concentrate on our proper theme, the island of Britain. We can, of course, without any research, realize certain aspects of Britain in the distant centuries with which the survey mainly deals. We can see, as the shipmen who brought the megalithic culture saw, the height and range of the western bastions, as where the great scarp of the Cuillins flanks Skye; and we can, like them, enter deep estuaries which reflect blue hills and green forest on mile after mile of their mirrored surfaces. Britain to-day, as then, presents every type of hill outline and valley contour, of ravine and mountain scarp; her lowlands then as now, were well watered and tempting alike to the keeper of sheep and the tiller of the ground. But the differences, as we shall see, are profound; the present coastline of the whole country, and not that of the Channel only, is to a large extent the creation of the forces of nature within our period. Most of our arable fields were moreover dense forest, most of our meadows marshlands. Thus my task offers difficulties at the outset. The most convenient line of approach is to find out, by the study of distribution maps, where in this island early Man actually lived and laboured; in the process of determining, stage by stage, what conditioned his activities here, we shall, I hope, attain the ends in view.

The first map (Figure 1) illustrates the distribution of a familiar group of ancient structures—megalithic tombs and long barrows mainly of the Neolithic Age[2]. They show a close-set grouping in southern England, on western peninsulas of Wales and Scotland, and in northern Scotland; the only large groups in eastern England are in Lincolnshire and

---

[1] In connection with this and the preceding paragraphs the distribution maps in Childe, *Dawn of European Civilization*, 2nd Ed., and Hawkes, *Prehistoric Foundations of Europe*, should be consulted.
[2] Stone circles and alignments are excluded, as originating in all probability in the Early Bronze Age, and menhirs as being mostly undateable.

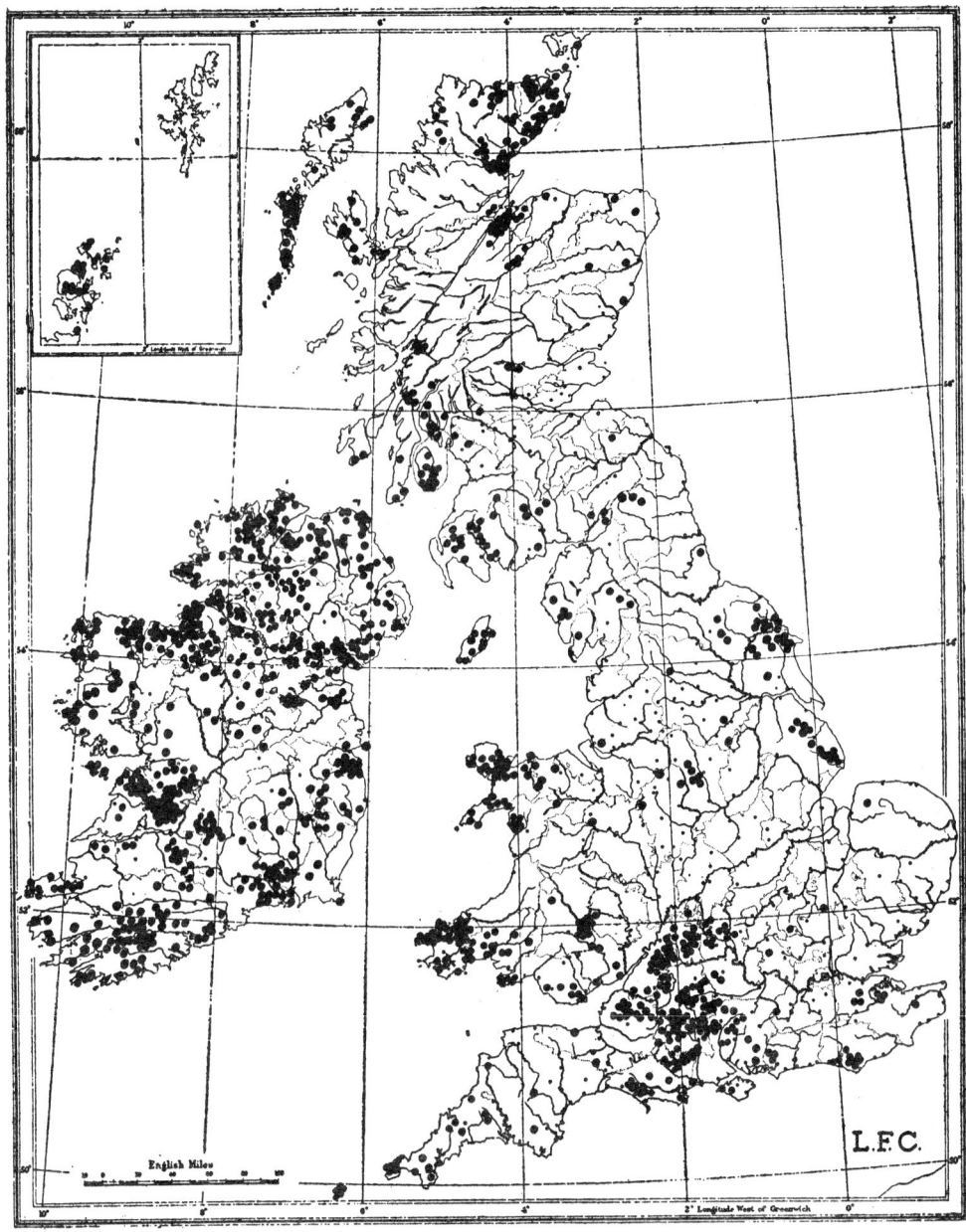

FIGURE 1.—DISTRIBUTION OF MEGALITHIC MONUMENTS (CHAMBERED CAIRNS, DOLMENS AND LONG BARROWS) IN THE BRITISH ISLES. Omitting stone circles, alignments, and menhirs. (Pages 11, 14, 21, 22, 32, 44.)

By L. F. Chitty and C. Fox, revised with additions by L. F. Chitty (1938): making use, *inter alia*, of Collingwood, *Cumb. and West. A.A. Soc.*, N.S. XXXIII (1933), pp. 168, 171–3; *O.S. Megalith Maps of Wessex, The Trent Basin, and South Wales*; Crawford, *O.S. Professional Papers*, N.S., 6 & 8, and unpublished information, also *Long Barrows of the Cotswolds* (1925); M. E. Cunnington, *Wilts. Arch. Mag.*, 38 (1914), 379–414; Curwen, *Archaeology of Sussex*, Fig. 13; Elgee, *Early Man in N.E. Yorkshire*, pp. 40–53, and map; Grimes, *Proc. Prehist. Soc.*, 1936, 106–39; Childe, *Prehistory of Scotland*, Map I; Borlase, *Dolmens of Ireland*, checked for N. Ireland by M. Gaffikin and Estyn Evans in *Irish Naturalists' Journal*, V (1935), 242–50, Pl. 17; Grahame Clark, Prehist. of Isle of Man, *Proc. Prehist. Soc.* (1935), 78–81, Fig. 7.

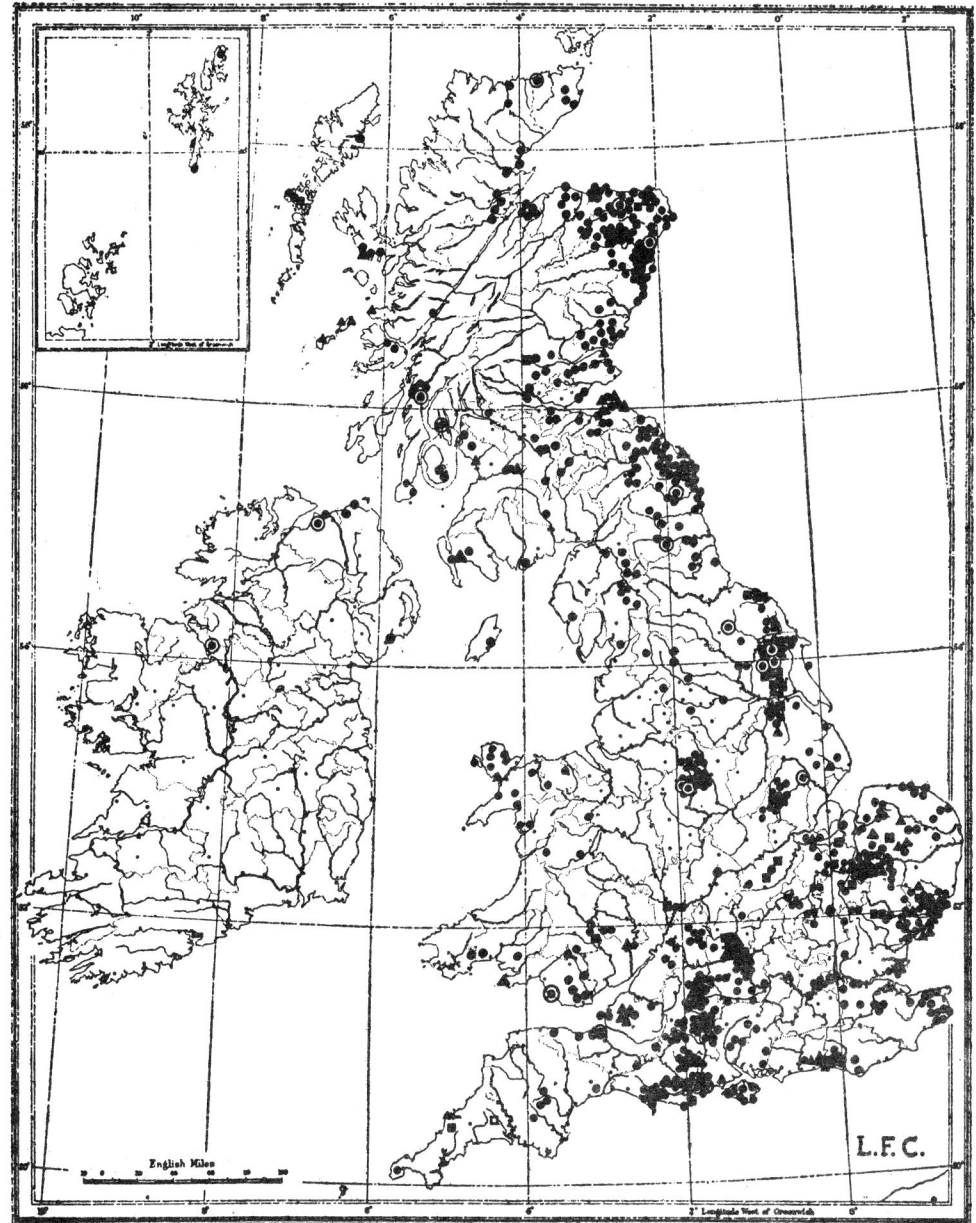

FIGURE 2.—DISTRIBUTION OF BEAKERS OF THE EARLY BRONZE AGE IN THE BRITISH ISLES.
(Pages 14, 16, 28, 32, 41, 64n.; Beakers are illustrated in Fig. 38, 1-3.)

By L. F. Chitty and C. Fox, revised with additions by L. F. Chitty (1938); using, *inter alia*, Abercromby. *Bronze Age Pottery* and Fox *Arch. Camb.*, 1925. p. 1 ff.; C. W. Phillips *Arch. Journ.*, XC (1933), 123–5, Pl. V, and XCI (1934), 153; E. M. Clifford, *Proc. Prehist. Soc.*, 1937, 159–62, map; Calkin, *Proc. Bournemouth N.Sc.S.*, XXVIII (1935-6), 48–53, Table I and Map; Dunning, *Proc. I.o.W.N.H.A.S.*, II (1933), 292–8, with map; Grimes, *Proc. Prehist. Soc. E. A.*, VII (1932), 92–3; Childe, *Prehistory of Scotland* (1935), Map II; M. E. Crichton Mitchell, *Proc. Soc. Ant. Scot.*, LXVIII (1933-4), 132–89; Chitty, *Antiq. Journ.*, XIII (1933), 259–65; Estyn Evans and Megaw, *Proc. Prehist. Soc.*, 1937, 29–42, disproving Mountstewart beaker.

● Beaker,   ■ Handled beaker.   ◉ Group of 3 or more.   ▲ Settlement.

Yorkshire. The pronounced western trend of this distribution is emphasized by the dense occupation of Ireland, and by the site marks on the smaller islands—Scilly, Man, the Hebrides and Orkneys. The second map (Figure 2) shows an equally familiar group of objects—beakers of the Early Bronze period, illustrated in Figure 38, 1–3. The chief fact that impresses us on this map is that the distribution is as markedly eastern as the megalithic is western, areas blank on the former map being densely occupied—East Anglia and the Fenlands, Northumbria, eastern Scotland, for example; the only intensive overlaps are on the Yorkshire Wolds and in Wessex. If we take a third group, in this case of much later sites, cemeteries of the Anglo-Saxon Pagan period, *c.* 450–650 A.D. (Figure 14, after E. T. Leeds), we find them strictly limited to, and evenly distributed over, the whole of the eastern half of southern Britain.[1]

The first question that arises is how these different distributions are to be explained. Must they be considered in isolation, or are there underlying and constant factors to be taken into account in framing any rational explanation of them? In these pages the existence of such dominating factors will be made manifest, and the part each may have played in shaping Man's life as expressed in his choice of occupation sites, and in the fate of his successive cultures, will be estimated.

That the reader should not be misled or confused, two points must be established before the argument proceeds. The one is that the Essay is concerned to establish principles and not to present the prehistory of Britain; consequently examples illustrating a particular or recurrent phenomenon are selected, without respect to chronology, throughout the whole range of our prehistory and early history.

The other is that in pursuit of its aim, a given distributional situation may be, as here, expressed in the simplest terms available, stripped of those complexities which make the pattern of human life and activity so interesting, and which it is the business of the prehistorian and historian to elucidate. Figure 1, for example, isolates an outstanding feature of the Neolithic culture, while ignoring other aspects (e.g. Neolithic pottery of types "A" and "B" and causewayed camps) which show that the culture as a whole had a variety of sources. Again, while it is stated that the figure includes both long barrows and chambered cairns, no attempt is made to deal with the problems that the presence of these different elements present; it is irrelevant to the point under discussion. Figure 2, in its turn, shows the full range of the "beaker" invasion, but ignores its variety; the phenomenon may be described as the intrusions at different points on our coast of groups of folk having similar culture, intrusions which cover a considerable period of time. "A," "B1" and "B2" beaker folk represent the main differentiations.

It is true that some of the massed maps show, by a variety of symbols, the diversity of material which goes to build a culture pattern; but usually it is the resultant pattern only which is relevant to my purpose. When detail is important to the argument, a special map is provided, as in the case of Neolithic pottery (Plate I) and of B beakers (Figure 6).

The theme of the Essay when worked out covers, in the distribution maps, a wide range of time fairly fully; a list of the maps arranged chronologically is given on page 9, and a brief chronological summary of the prehistory of Britain on pp. 84–86.[2]

---

[1] It should be noted that, while these three groups of objects are not from dwelling sites, they show sufficiently clearly on such small-scale maps the general range and distribution of their makers.

[2] For a full survey of the prehistory of Wales, see the Museum *Guide to the Prehistoric Collections*, by W. F. Grimes.

The Position and Form of Britain

Geographical position and form suffice to explain, in large measure, the two chief variations in distribution. Let us consider the eastern group first.

The Geographical Factors influencing Eastern Distributions: The position of these islands, alongside western Europe, on the "continental shelf," and separated from the mainland by narrow seas, is such as to invite invasion from almost any point on five hundred miles of the European coastline from Brittany to the Elbe-mouth and beyond, as is seen on Map A. Invasion emanating therefrom is favoured by the indentation of our coastline (Map B). The broad slow-moving rivers flowing into the North Sea—the Trent and Ouse opening into the Humber estuary, the Fenland rivers—Welland, Nene, and Great Ouse, opening into the Wash; the winding channels of the East Anglian rivers—Waveney, Orwell, Stour, and Colne; the Thames; all afford good harbourage and many provide access into the very heart of Britain. The south coast inlets and estuaries, and harbours such as those at Christchurch and Weymouth, provide equally easy entry for invaders.[1] Though Caesar was content with an open beach for his raiding galleys, earlier seafarers were probably more careful. It is relevant to add that the southern part of the North Sea and the English Channel being "drowned" river valleys, the configuration of the opposite coast conforms to the British, while the lateral valleys on both sides provide convenient and opposite estuaries, e.g. the Rhine-mouth and the Thames.

Britain presents (Map A and Cover) two fronts to the long coastline of the continent referred to above; the southern, to the Channel zone from Brest to Calais; the eastern, to the North Sea zone, comprising portions of present-day Belgium, Holland, Germany, and Scandinavia. Bearers of new cultures approaching either zone have of course shown a tendency to make the shortest (Straits of Dover) crossing of the narrow seas, and distributions focused on the continental angle—Kent and Thames estuary—frequently occur. This is well shown in E. Estyn Evans' distribution map (Figure 3) of winged axes[2] of the Late Bronze Age, and in Hawkes' and Dunning's map of the pedestal-urn cremation-culture—Iron Age "C" (Figure 4). In both the points of departure were probably the Somme and the Seine estuaries. The classic examples of the use of this crossing are the Roman raids (55–54 B.C., Deal beach), the Roman conquest (43 A.D., Richborough, Thanet), and the Saxon intrusion (*c.* 449 A.D., Thanet). Allowing for this tendency to cross by the Straits, it might be supposed that the distribution of a given culture within the eastern half of Britain is likely to indicate from which of the two continental zones the invaders responsible for it came. Some facts point to this. The Western Neolithic (Neolithic "A") culture is known to have come from northern France, while the affinities of the so-called Neolithic "B" culture—which is probably mainly Mesolithic—lie in the Baltic region. The *primary* settlements of the former are concentrated in the Wessex-Sussex-upper Thames districts, where alone the "causewayed camps," an integral part of the culture, are found;[3] the *primary* settlements of the latter, on the other hand, are on the east coast spreading inland up the Thames,[4] the rivers of the Wash, and the Trent (Plate IA and B, based on Stuart Piggott).

---

[1] It is said that a man in a small open boat proceeding from Normandy to a south coast port with a favourable wind need not be more than three hours out of sight of land.

[2] These are an element of the West Alpine culture-complex dating 700 B.C. or earlier. See this author in *Antiquity*, 1930, pp. 157–172.

[3] E.g. Knap Hill, Robin Hood's Ball and Windmill Hill (Wilts.), Maiden Castle (Dorset), Hembury (Devon), the Trundle, Combe Hill and Whitehawk (Sussex), Abingdon (Berks.). See E. C. Curwen, *Antiquity*, 1930, pp. 22–54.

[4] "The 'B' culture was essentially that of eastern England; 'A' of the south and south-west." Stuart Piggott in *Proc. Prehist. Soc. East Anglia*, 1934, p. 375.

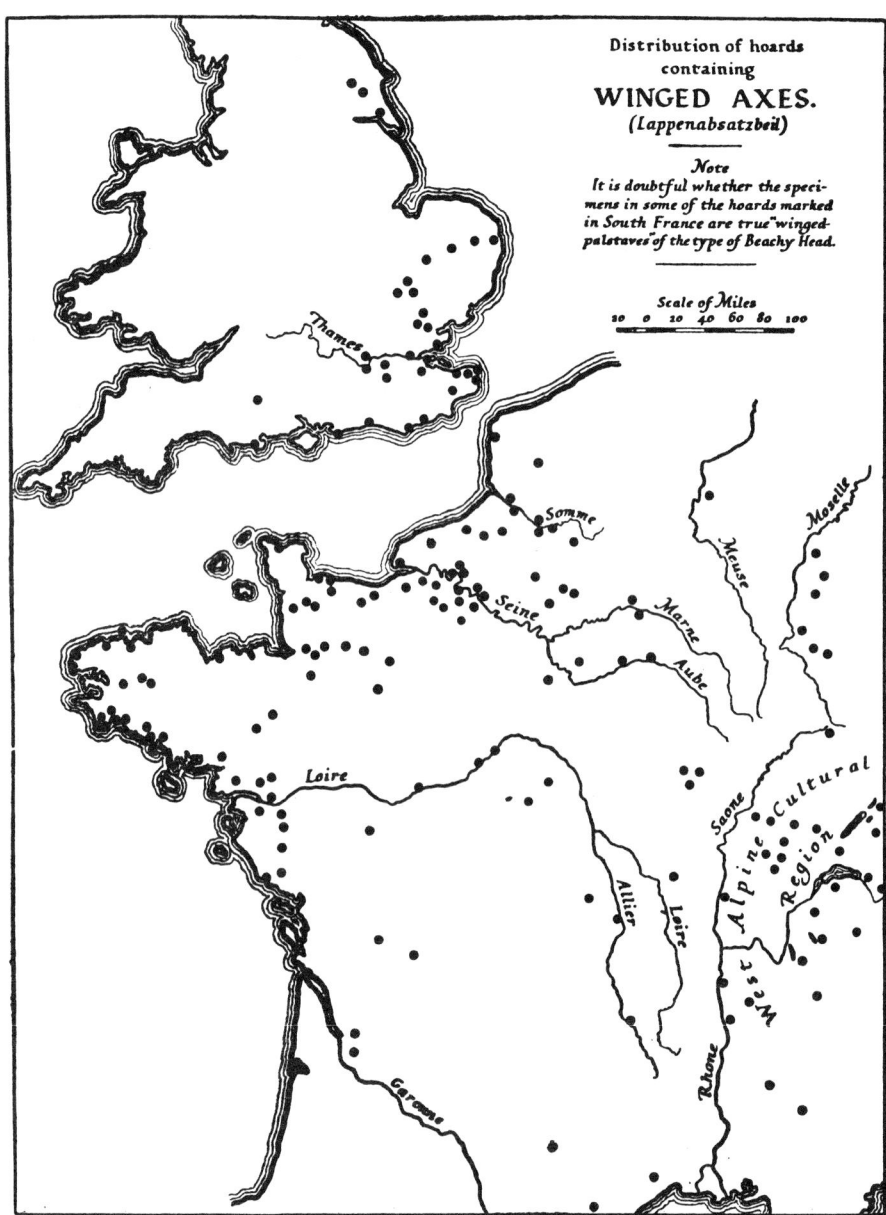

FIGURE 3.—DISTRIBUTION OF HOARDS CONTAINING "WINGED" AXES OF THE LATE BRONZE AGE.
(Page 15. Illustrated in Fig. 40, 5.)

After E. Estyn Evans, "The Sword-bearers," *Antiquity*, 1930, p. 159.

Again the extent of the beaker distribution on the east coast, from Kent to Aberdeen (Figure 2) indicates the more northerly zone as the chief source, and this indication is confirmed by the close similarities recognized to exist between the beakers of the Low Countries and those of East Anglia. Plate II shows the European distribution of beakers; the majority of our beaker folk, those using B2 and A types of pot (Figure 38), came from the Rhinelands.

Similar pressures were also at work later, for the Anglo-Saxon mass migrations are known to have come from the North Sea zone in the fifth century A.D., and the weight of their invasion fell on the east coast of Britain (Figure 14).

But the more we study our early invasions the less dependable as a working hypothesis is the distinction suggested above. For a very interesting reason: the breeding ground of those cultures which had most influence on southern and eastern Britain lay deep in western Europe, mainly round the middle and upper Rhine and the Alpine fringe, as is indicated on Map A. Now whether these cultures spread down the Rhine or across northern France; whether they were carried to eastern England from the Rhine mouths, or to southern England from the mouths of the Seine and Somme; or whether (if the continental diffusions north-westwards were more general than particular) the decision to cross the Channel came from

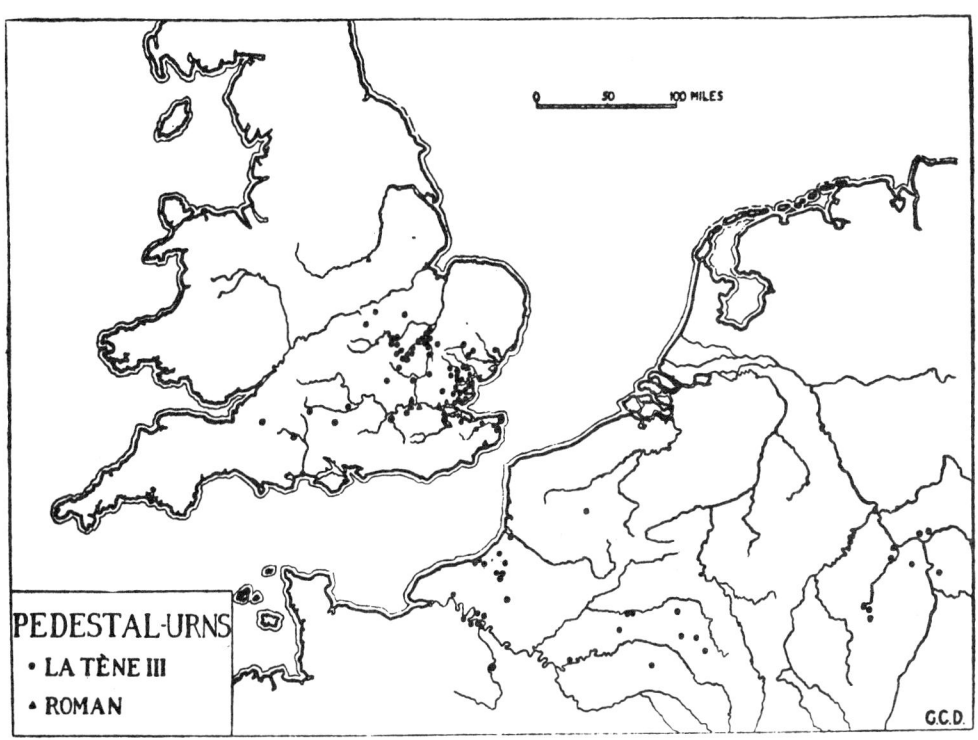

FIGURE 4.—DISTRIBUTION OF PEDESTAL-URNS, MAINLY OF THE LA TÈNE III PERIOD (IRON AGE "C" CULTURE).
(Page 15. Illustration on p. 6.)
After Hawkes and Dunning, "The Belgae of Gaul and Britain," *Archaeological Journal*, Vol. 87, 1930, Fig. 7, p. 189.

the dwellers by one estuary rather than another; depended on what—in this connection—we may almost call chance. And indeed there is evidence suggesting that in the folk movements which (aided by commercial expansion) established the Late Bronze Age, and those which established the Iron Age, in Britain, bearers of similar cultures from time to time pushed across the North Sea into east coast estuaries and across the Channel into south coast ports. The grouping of settlements of the "Deverel-Rimbury" folk of the 8th century B.C. on the Essex coast, and on the Hampshire-Dorset coast, for example, is thus explicable.[1] A distribution

[1] Preston and Hawkes, *Antiq. Journ.*, 1933, p. 436 ff, and map, p. 441. See also C. M. Piggott, *Proc. Prehist. Soc.*, 1938, p. 181, and Figs. 10 and 11; and C. F. C. Hawkes in *P.P.S.*, 1942, pp. 27 ff.

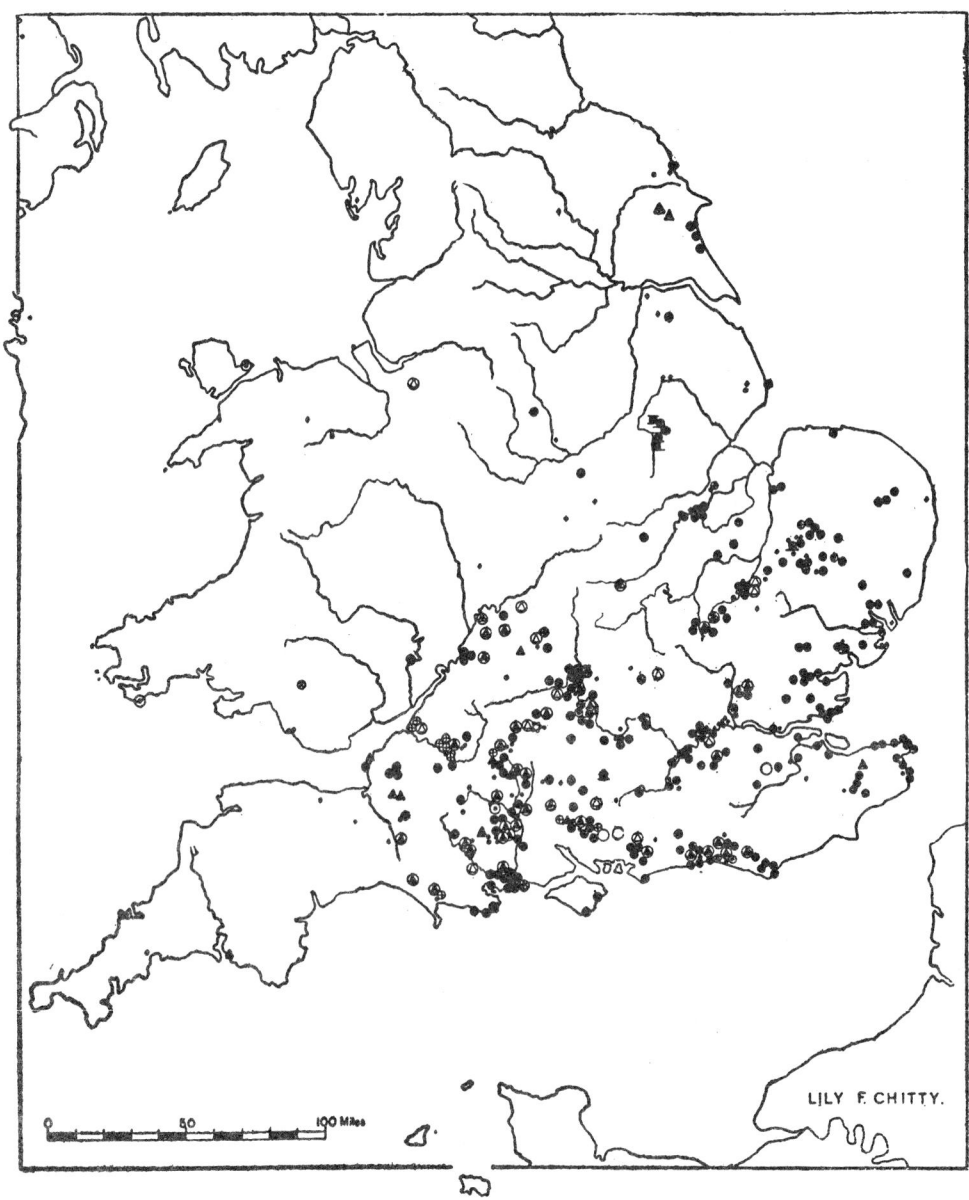

FIGURE 5.—DISTRIBUTION OF IRON AGE "A" CULTURE IN SOUTHERN BRITAIN. (Pages 19, 33.)

By L. F. Chitty (1938), making use of, *inter alia*, Hawkes, Myers and Stevens, "St. Catherine's Hill," *Proc. Hampshire Field Club*, Vol. XI (1929), p. 162, Fig. 18; Hawkes, *Antiquity*, V (1931), 60–97, Map, Fig. 63; Ridgeway & Smith, *Proc. Soc. Antiq.*, XXI, 97–118; Dunning, *Arch. Journ.*, XCI (1934), 269–95, map and schedule.

○ Swan-neck or ring-headed pin. ● Do., in hoard. ♦ Hallstatt brooch. ◊ Other bronzes. ● La Tène I brooch. ● Do., in hoard. ● "A" pottery (mainly from settlement sites). ⊕ "A" pottery in barrow, primary burial. ═ "A" pottery with burial, not in barrow, or secondary. ⊗ "A" pottery containing bronze implements; also Llynfawr hoard. ■ Iron socketed axe. ◉ Hill-forts and camps dated by "A" pottery. ⓐ "A" pottery found, but not proving date of defences. ▲ "A" pottery antedating defences. O Hill-fort assigned to "A" culture.

map of Iron Age "A" culture (Figure 5) illustrates a cognate process and provides weighty evidence of similar character. The main concentrations are in southern Britain; but coastal finds, indicative of widely ranging movements by sea, occur.[1] Thus it was not beyond the seafaring capacities of invaders, if obstacles were put in the way of landings on the coast opposite to their port of embarkation, to sail a considerable distance in seach of unhindered entry. The settlement of the tribe known as the Parisii, in the third century B.C., may be a case in point; they came to eastern Yorkshire from the valleys of the Marne or Seine in northern France. The direct evidences of the peculiarly aristocratic civilization associated with this group are confined to this region and a few other sites in eastern Britain (p. 34).

Inadequacy of sea transport probably accounts for the smallness of the numbers concerned in such movements as these; it is an important factor to bear in mind, for it tends to give a unique character to the ultimate expression of any culture derived from the continent, in Britain. Britain is vulnerable enough, but her culture at any given period tends to show a number of variant elements, rather than an extension beyond the sea of a stable, definite, continental complex. The early phases of the Iron Age illustrate this point. No greater contrast could be imagined than that between the peasant cultures established in south Britain at sites such as All Cannings Cross and the art-loving, militarist, horse-breeding civilization of east Yorkshire. Another aspect of this phenomenon is noted by Childe: the Neolithic "A" culture, he says, "exhibits a marked insularity when compared with its continental counterparts."[2]

The paucity of numbers concerned in invasion tends to slow down the diffusion of a given culture in Britain—indeed, profound changes may take place in a culture-complex before the expansion of a people is complete. This was the case with the Anglo-Saxons; their pagan cemeteries (Figure 14) cover a period of 200 years, but the expansion of the nation within the island continued for centuries after the change in religion and burial customs.

In general, the effect of the vulnerability of Britain to invasion is that she has always tended to present successive strata of culture, and a very mixed population, the latest arrivals being dominant, and the novel culture more strongly marked in the eastern and southern part of the island than in the western. In East Anglia, for example, Neolithic man was supplanted by the beaker folk, who—after a long interval—were followed by peoples having Late Bronze culture, and these by iron-using Celts; the latter (after Romanization) were replaced by Angles, and Angles were replaced by Danes. In each case we may suppose that the upper class of the conquered, after decimation, was merged in the subject classes. A recent survey of East Anglia shows how infiltration by way of the estuaries and rivers took place in successive prehistoric periods.[3] One of the maps illustrating this survey is here reproduced (Plate XI).

There is a succession of well-marked cultures with continental affiliations the British distribution of which is more or less confined to Wessex, and the probable or certain source the extreme west of the Channel zone—the Brittany peninsula.

An important element of the beaker folk, those using the B1 type of pot very close to the classic forms originating in Spain, using also occasionally "West-European" tanged daggers of copper, are held to have come thence. The Wessex distribution is shown in Figure 6, after Stuart Piggott.[4] It is interesting to re-examine Plate II in this connection.

[1] Plymouth, St. Austell, Harlyn Bay in the south-west; Merthyr Mawr, Stackpole, Clynnog, Din Silwy on the Welsh coasts.
[2] *Prehistoric Communities*, p. 41.
[3] *Proc. Prehist. Soc. East Anglia*, 1933, pp. 149–164.
[4] There is no general distribution picture of all the variant types of beaker in Britain at present available. But J. G. D. Clark, *Antiquity*, 1931, map on p. 419, and W. F. Grimes, *Proc. Prehist. Soc. East Anglia*, 1931, maps on p. 346, may be consulted with advantage.

While our B2 and A beaker users probably represent the last stages of a long migration from the eastern end of the Pyrenees, either up the Rhone valley or across the Alps, to the Middle Rhine and Holland,[1] the B1 folk may reasonably be held to have issued from the more westerly migrants who had reached Brittany by sea.[2] It was a shorter route than the other, but in fact they seem to have reached our shores no earlier than the easterly B2 migrants; for indeed they had halted for some while in Brittany, whence they brought over (*inter alia*) the ideas which produced the megalithic alignments of Avebury.

Again there are strong arguments in favour of Piggott's view that the rich and aristocratic culture which, in the 17th century B.C., ushered in the Middle Bronze Age in southern Britain, and which had drawn its elements widely from across land and sea, was mainly fashioned in Brittany, finding in Wessex a region giving scope for its potentialities.[3] It is also probable that an important element of the neolithic complex, the Long Barrow culture of Wessex, Lincolnshire and Yorkshire,[4] was fundamentally Breton in origin.

In an earlier paragraph the contribution of commerce to the establishment of a new culture in Britain was hinted at. It is sometimes difficult to distinguish archaeologically

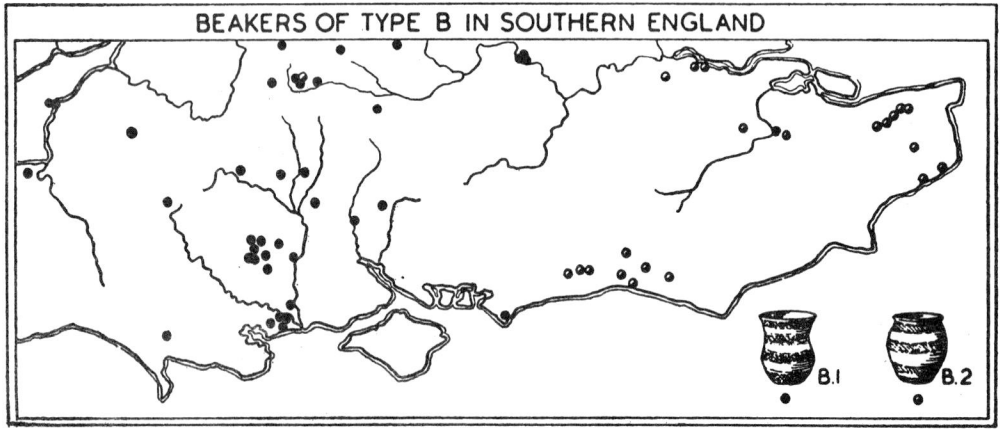

FIGURE 6.—DISTRIBUTION OF "B1" AND "B2" BEAKERS IN SOUTHERN ENGLAND.
(Pages 19, 20.)
After Stuart Piggott, *Proc. Prehist. Soc.*, 1938, p. 56, fig. 1.

between the effects of commercial infiltration and of invasion; but it is fundamental that we should so distinguish. About 1000 B.C. there began a new phase in the history of Britain, when bronze was cheap, a knowledge of advanced metallurgical techniques widespread, the range of working tools extensive, and the striking sword a familiar weapon. That immigrant swordsmen from the Continent initiated this change was the obvious and generally accepted explanation, and it is certainly partly correct; but the scarcity in southern Britain, until the 8th century B.C., of new pottery forms which can be correlated with the novel bronze types makes it difficult to sustain as a general proposition.[5] That we are observing for the most

[1] See Hawkes, *Foundations*, p. 257.
[2] This being so, the absence of early (B1) forms on the western coasts of Britain, e.g., in South Wales is certainly surprising. For late B1 forms see Fox, *Archaeologia*, Vol. 89, pp. 100–04.
[3] *Proc. Prehist. Soc.*, 1938, pp. 52 ff.
[4] Piggott, *Antiquity*, 1937, pp. 441–55; *Proc. Prehist. Soc.*, 1937, pp. 173–5. For the distribution picture in Britain, see Childe, *Prehistoric Communities*, Fig. 10. Features of one Lincolnshire barrow appear to derive from the Cotteswold chambered cairns: Hawkes, *Foundations*, p. 270.
[5] The comparatively slight intrusion of peasantry who cultivated the Sussex downlands in L.B. I, about 1000 B.C. is discussed by Hawkes, *Proc. Prehist. Soc.*, 1935, pp. 45–57. The "Deverel-Rimbury" invasion (initiating L.B. II) provides most of the new pottery forms.

part the intrusion of metal merchants and of itinerant unattached craftsmen bringing in an improved technique of bronze founding—which was by their means spread rapidly and widely throughout Britain—now appears highly probable.[1]

The Geographical Factors influencing Western Distributions: We may now consider the causes governing a western distribution of invading cultures as illustrated in Figure 1. While

FIGURE 7.—DISTRIBUTION OF MEGALITHIC MONUMENTS IN WESTERN EUROPE. (Page 22.)
Based (1938) on V. G. Childe, *Dawn of European Civilization*, Map III and Map IV; N. Aberg, *Das Nordische Kulturgebiet in Mitteleuropa während der jungeren Steinzeit*, Map V; Forde, "Early Cultures of Atlantic Europe," *American Anthropologist*, 1930; and (for Britain) Figure 1 of this essay.

folk to whom the sea was a barrier to be overcome would (as we have seen) tend to occupy eastern and southern Britain, to those to whom the sea was a highway a different area of these islands offered itself. To early navigators, following the Atlantic costs of Portugal, Spain,

[1] See Crawford, *Ant. Journ.*, 1922, p. 27 ff and Fox, *Archaeology of the Cambridge Region*, 1923, pp. 57, 61, 318, for the older view; for the newer, Hawkes in *Proc. Prehist. Soc.*, 1935, pp. 57-59, foreshadowed in *Arch. in Eng. and Wales*, 1931, pp. 131, 145; also Childe, *Prehistoric Communities*, pp. 8, 168-71, 187-8.

and France, the first landfall in Britain is Cornwall, and convenient refuges are afforded by harbours and estuaries on either side of Lands End, and on the coasts washed by St. George's Channel and the Irish Sea. From this sea a deep-water channel which skirts the Western Isles has been used from early times as a sea-way to northern Britain; it was in some measure sheltered from the dangers of the north Atlantic by the Hebridean Islands.

Maps A and B illustrate the route; by it, in part from Spain, in part from Atlantic France, the megalithic culture reached Britain; its use explains the European distribution of the monuments (as shown in Figure 7); the massing of evidences of the culture in Caithness, the Orkneys and Shetlands (Figures 1 and 31) may in large measure be due to the importance of the peninsula and the adjacent islands as affording the last opportunity for sea-going boats to water and revictual prior to the crossing of the North Sea. When the route was in frequent use by Norsemen in Viking times (Plate XII) nearly 3,000 years later, Caithness (and the adjacent islands) again became important for similar reasons; they were the first landfall.[1] Some peoples have, however, found the straths of northern Scotland in themselves desirable occupation sites; Childe has shown that the flourishing Broch culture of the first century A.D. and later represents a late use of the Atlantic route by hardy seamen and settlers who " reproduced the warlike (Iron Age " B ") maritime economy of Cornwall."[2]

H. J. Fleure emphasizes the presence of a stalwart dark broadheaded people " along routes of coastwise sailing and perhaps also across bases of peninsulas "—the west of the British Isles, Orkneys, the Norwegian coast—spreading from the eastern Mediterranean. The type illustrates in his view not only the megalithic movement but an oft-repeated tendency for southern folk to make use of this traffic lane.[3]

When the western sea route was fully open, Britain was in the path of the expansion of Mediterranean culture. Under such conditions, indeed, the standard of culture in western Britain was likely to be higher than in eastern Britain. Higher or lower, there is a tendency, based on geography and reinforced by factors we shall consider later, for eastern and western Britain to be influenced by different streams of culture and to show differential development.

The use of the western sea route is not confined to long-distance movement. We have seen (p. 19) that Brittany has been a jumping-off ground for invaders from the continent, and that such invaders tended to concentrate in Wessex. But this is not the whole story. The cultural development of Devon and Cornwall has been profoundly influenced by Brittany, and to restless folk with seafaring instincts dwelling on bays and estuaries in Finistère and Morbihan (and southwards to the Loire), the whole of western Britain lay open (Map A and Cover). A great part of our megalithic culture was derived thence and the influence of migrants from the region on later cultures in the west, especially on the shores of the Bristol Channel, is now becoming increasingly manifest. It is possible that elements of the " Wessex " Bronze culture already referred to came oversea to south Wales,[4] and part of the Iron Age " B " culture (p. 33) was probably also derived from Brittany. A recent study suggests that even inland folk, compelled to migrate in prehistoric times, might obtain transport to Britain from Atlantic ports. Figure 8 illustrates (*inter alia*) the probable sea route taken by the users of a certain type of bronze sickle, 700 B.C. or earlier, from the Lake of Constance on the Alpine fringe, to Somerset.[5]

[1] And so played a prominent part in the politics of the Viking Age: cf. *Heimskringla*, ed. Monsen (1932), p. 312, ¶ 96, and index, Caithness.
[2] *Prehistoric Communities*, p. 245.
[3] *Journ. Roy. Anthrop. Inst.*, Vol. 48, p. 155 ff, esp. p. 157. See also this author's *Races of England and Wales*, p. 54.
[4] W. F. Grimes, *Proc. Prehist. Soc.*, 1938, pp. 119–120.
[5] Another probable instance of the use of the same route will be found in *Antiq. Journ.*, 1939, pp. 375–376 (Fox).

The commercial use of the western sea route in Late Bronze Age times presents features of interest. Figure 9, after Childe, shows the range of the double-looped palstave; " it reveals not only the centre of dispersion " in north-west Spain, but " leaves little doubt that the British examples are the result of direct overseas trade with the Peninsula."[1] Incidentally it suggests coastal trade up the English Channel to northern Europe in a way no

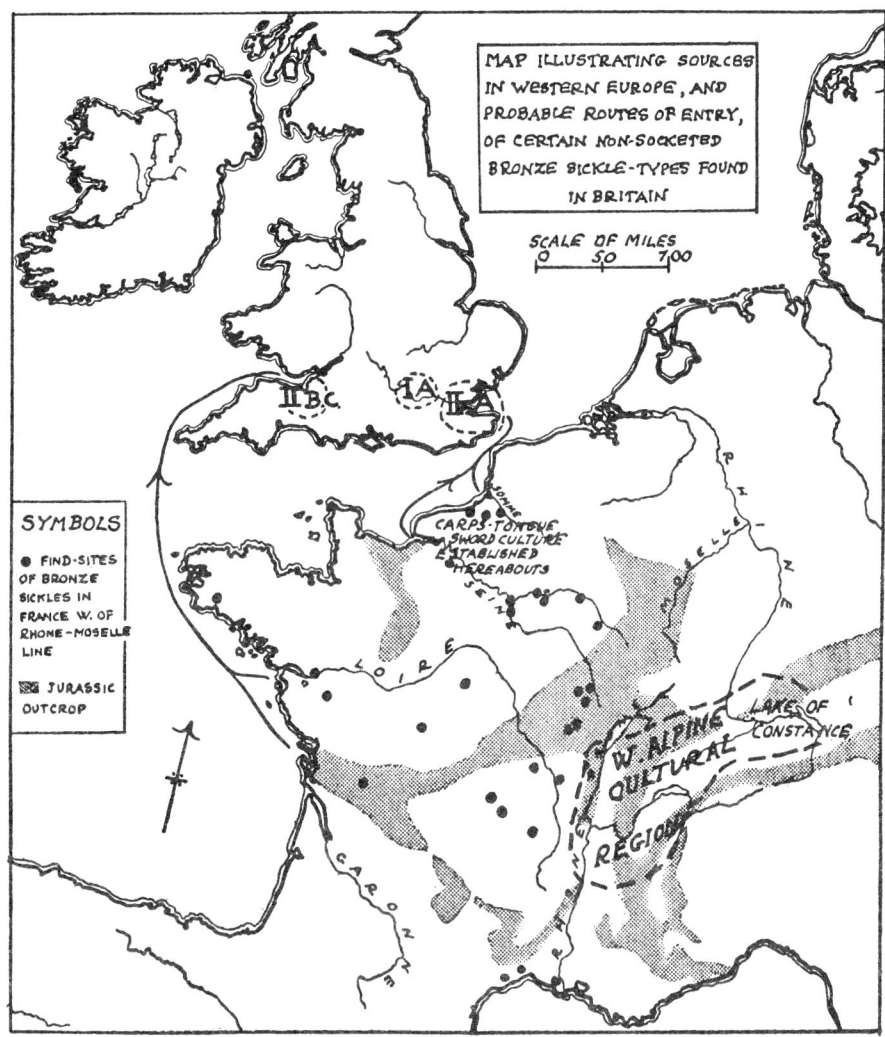

FIGURE 8.—Map of western Europe illustrating sources of non-socketed bronze sickles found in Britain. (Page 22.)
After Cyril Fox, " The Non-Socketed Sickles of Britain," *Arch. Camb.*, 1941, p. 154, Fig. 6.

early distributions do. Plate X (A), a distribution map of square-sectioned socketed axes, shows the Breton traders frequenting ports along the whole of the south coast of Britain; as doubtless did the Veneti, from the same harbours, five or more centuries later. Furthermore, sea trade to the Bristol Channel and the coasts of Wales (as well as to Ireland) was revitalized in the sixth century when Hallstatt culture was spreading over western

[1] *Antiq. Journ.*, 1939, p. 321.

Europe; trade and settlement are indeed inextricably intermingled where Cornish tin and Forest of Dean iron are concerned. The Llyn Fawr hoard, in Glamorgan, has provided evidence suggesting that the first iron-workers in Britain may have established their forges in the west.[1]

One question raised in this section has not yet been adequately answered. While it is easy to see that the users of the seaways in the third millennium would tend to colonize western Britain, it is less easy to understand why they should attempt to reach Scandinavia and the amber region by the dangerous Pentland Firth: the English Channel and the North

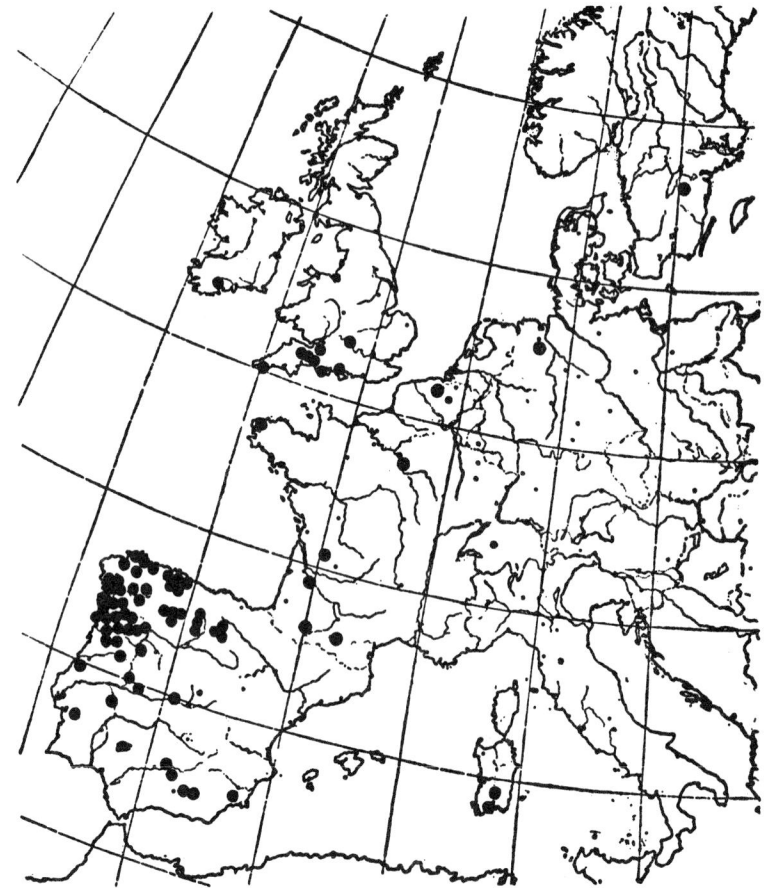

FIGURE 9.—DISTRIBUTION OF DOUBLE-LOOPED PALSTAVES OF THE LATE BRONZE AGE. (Page 23.)
For illustration see Fig. 40, 4.
After V. Gordon Childe, *Antiq. Journ.*, 1939, p. 322.

Sea would appear to offer a safer and shorter route. The positive evidence that this route was used is of the scantiest; a distributional argument against it is provided by the megalithic monuments of Kent, which are typologically related not to Atlantic France but to northern Germany. When we seek for the cause of the neglect, certain possibilities emerge.

Changes of Level within the Prehistoric Period in Southern Britain: We have hitherto assumed that throughout the Neolithic, Bronze, and Early Iron Ages, Britain was an island of much the same size and outline as at present. But though this is true for the most recent phases

[1] C. Fox, in *Antiq. Journ.*, 1939, pp. 387–390.

under investigation, it is not entirely true for the whole period. Excavations for docks or harbour improvements have revealed at many points old land surfaces, some below the level of the lowest tides; and at many places on our coasts storms which remove the covering of beach reveal black peaty earth with bones of animals thereon, and with tree stumps rooted therein, between the tide levels.

We have, indeed, preserved to our own times in these deposits remains of ancient forests with their inhabitants. Clement Reid in 1912 wrote that at the beginning of the phase represented by these forests the " greater part of England stood fully 70 feet above its present level, for the oldest deposit we deal with is a land surface . . . 60 feet below tide level ";

FIGURE 10.—THE COAST LINE OF GREAT BRITAIN AND IRELAND SHORTLY BEFORE SEPARATION FROM THE CONTINENT. (Pages 25, 27.)
By F. J. North (1932).

and his conclusions have been but little modified by subsequent research.[1] Britain was then, of course, linked to the continent by a land bridge. The map, Figure 10, kindly prepared for me by Dr. F. J. North, shows the coastline of Britain when the land was from 70 to 100 feet higher than it is now. The outline is drawn along the 100-foot submarine contour, with allowances on the one hand for the scour of the tides, and on the other for the creation

---

[1] Clement Reid, *Submerged Forests*, 1912, p. 106. Recent researches indicate a greater extent of submergence, in the East at all events; peat deposits (*moor-log*) having been dredged up from the floor of the North Sea at depths ranging from 100 to 170 feet. H. Godwin, *New Phytologist*, 39, p. 396.

of sandbanks—a rough and ready, but reasonably accurate method of graphically indicating the extent of the change in form and area.

The date when subsidence began, that is when the lowest of our submerged forest beds was dry land, cannot yet be accurately determined. Clement Reid in 1913 suggested 3000 B.C. for the conditions shown on the map,[1] but recent research in Britain and on the continent tends to throw back the date very considerably. The problem assumes special importance in connection with the land-bridge. P. Ullyot[2] on certain zoogeographical grounds fixes the time when Britain was finally and definitely cut off from the continent early in the Boreal phase. L. Dudley Stamp, in his "Geographical Evolution of the North Sea Basin,"[3] holds that the final separation took place during the Boreal-Atlantic transition (p. 51). There is archaeological evidence bearing on the problem; the dramatic discovery of a bone harpoon of Maglemose type dredged up in material from an ancient land surface 25 miles off the coast of Norfolk in 1932,[4] strongly points to a Maglemose culture distribution stretching from Denmark to Britain along the dunes fringing a diminished North Sea.[5] Thus, the break-through would be subsequent to the expansion of this culture, which flourished in Boreal time. It should be added that the deepest peat deposits on the North Sea floor examined by H. Godwin and others[6] were Boreal. If we suggest a date about 5000 B.C. it would accord with the available evidence.

We may now consider the problem of the date at which subsidence ended. In the west of Britain conditions seem to have been stable for at least 2,000 years. The well-known Glastonbury lake dwellings were built on peat deposits adjoining the Bristol Channel shortly before the Christian era, and there has been no change here in the relative levels of land and sea since.[7] On the other hand, worked flints have been found in the forest-bed peats between the tide marks in north Devon and south Pembrokeshire, and a deposit Neolithic or later, in a peat bed at Barry, Glamorgan, *circa* 5 feet below mean tide level.[8] More definite is the recent discovery of fragments of two beakers of B1 type in a pit partly eroded by the sea and situated between the tidemarks south of Brean Down, Somerset.[9] Thus subsidence would appear to have ended in the region of the Bristol Channel some time between the dawn of the Bronze Age and the Early Iron Age.[10]

In the east the problem has been re-opened by J. G. D. Clark and other members of the Fenland Research Committee. A section through the peat and clay deposits at Peacock's

---

[1] *Submerged Forests*, p. 120.

[2] "A Note on the Zoogeographical History of North Western Europe," *Proc. Prehist. Soc.*, 1936, p. 169 ff; see also 1938, pp. 230–231.

[3] *Journal du Conseil International pour l'Exploration de la Mer*, XI, 1936, esp. p. 158 ff and Figs. 12 and 13. See also F. E. Zeuner, "The Origin of the English Channel," *Discovery*, 1935, p. 196 ff.

[4] British Maglemose Harpoon Sites, H. and M. E. Godwin, *Antiquity*, 1933, p. 36 ff, esp. pp. 46–47. Cf. J.G.D.C., in *Proc. Prehist. Soc.*, 1936, p. 239.

[5] See the distribution map of the Maglemose culture, *The Mesolithic Settlement of Northern Europe*, J. G. D. Clark; and cf. Tansley, *The British Islands and their Vegetation*, Fig. 40, p. 156.

[6] H. Godwin, *loc. cit.*, p. 396.

[7] See H. Godwin on "Correlations in the Somerset Levels," *New Phytologist*, 40, 1941, pp. 108–32, esp. p. 119 (clay overlying these sites is probably due to river flooding). The conclusion is confirmed by the discovery of an Iron Age settlement site, 200 B.C. or earlier, in sand dunes at Merthyr Mawr, Glamorgan, on the opposite side of the Channel. Fox, *Arch. Camb.*, 1927, pp. 44–66.

[8] C. Reid, *op cit.*, p. 53. Having regard to the tidal range in the Bristol Channel this might indicate a subsidence of + − 20 feet. This observation is correlated with others in the area by H. Godwin, *New Phytologist*, 39, p. 320, Fig. 5.

[9] *Antiq. Journ.*, 1938, p. 172.

[10] F. J. North, *Evolution of the Bristol Channel*, pp. 53–57. An investigation of peat at East Moors, Cardiff, tends to confirm this dating.—H.A.H.

Farm in the southern Fens near Ely,[1] Cambridgeshire, disclosed Neolithic "A" remains at a depth of 15 feet below ordnance datum, while an Early Bronze Age layer was only 6 feet below datum; this indicates rapid subsidence in the third millennium, which was nearing its end in the Early Bronze Age. When the Neolithic living floor, then, was occupied, the mean sea level in the North Sea in relation to the land mass would appear to have been some 25 feet lower than at the present day.

This conclusion depends on two assumptions: that the phenomenon was general, and not due to "tilt"—local and irregular earth movements; and that the damping down of the tidal flow into an enlarged "Wash" by sand dunes, storm beaches, or salt-marsh, was not excessive.

Both assumptions would appear to be justified by observations made on the Essex coast. Hazzledine Warren in 1912[2] described pottery and flint implements picked up from time to time near Clacton, at Dovercourt, and other sites on partially submerged land surfaces. These sites have since been reinvestigated; the occupation level extends below the "lowest level of spring tides," its time-range extending from late Mesolithic through Neolithic "A" to "B2" beaker.[3] The absence of "A" beaker sherds suggests that the occupation ceased suddenly, and at about 1800 B.C. The authors consider that the "sequence of events on the Essex coast and in the Fen basin was substantially synchronous." Thus we cannot suggest a less extent of subsidence on the Essex coast than the 25 feet of Peacock's Farm. Here the access of tidal sea cannot have been unduly restricted; and we observe that there was no appreciable "tilt" in the subsidence of south-eastern England, since two places over 50 miles apart yield similar results.[4]

We must therefore conclude that from Neolithic "A" times onwards to the coming of the "B2" beaker folk, a period of perhaps 500 years, south-east England was some 25 feet higher than it is to-day. We may also accept with but little modification Clement Reid's dictum of 1912, "about 3,500 years ago we get back to the period of unchanging sea level in which we are still living."[5]

Having regard, then, to the shallowness of the North Sea and to the existence of broad belts of shallow water at the eastern end of the English Channel (Figure 10); also to the effect of tidal scour and land erosion accompanying subsidence, we are justified in picturing the Straits of Dover in megalithic times as being much narrower than at present—the broken ends of the Kent-Artois chalk ridge within everyday sight of each other—and the adjacent part of the North Sea as being extensively occupied by marshy flats, and sandbanks exposed at low tide. Here, then, enters the possibility envisaged on an earlier page: such shallow, seas (with strong tides) are notoriously dangerous to mariners, and the route to Scandinavia and the Baltic may for this reason have been rejected, or but little used, by the adventurers settlers and pioneers who used the Atlantic traffic lane to Britain.[6]

---

[1] *Antiq. Journ.*, 1935, p. 284 ff; esp. Pl. XLVI. H. Godwin and M. H. Clifford's recent important studies of the Fenland deposits should be consulted, *Philos. Trans. B.*, Vol. 229, 1938, pp. 323-406.

[2] *Journ. Roy. Anthrop. Inst.*, XLII, 1912, pp. 91-127.

[3] *Proc. Prehist. Soc.*, 1936: *Archaeology of the Submerged Land Surface of the Essex Coast*, by S. H. Warren, S. Piggott, J. G. D. Clark, M. C. Burkitt, and H. and M. E. Godwin, esp. pp. 209-210.

[4] Examination of peat from the sea floor off the Norfolk coast at 23.5 feet below datum gives similar results in terms of forest history: Godwin, *New Phytologist*, 39, p. 396.

[5] *Submerged Forests*, p. 115. Attention should be drawn to the fact of subsidence in the Lower Thames area since Roman times (*R.C.A.M.*, London, III, p. 13: F. Adcock, *Discovery*, 1938, p. 195). See also Ordnance Survey Professional Paper, N.S., No. 14, 1932. Further information on this movement, which may be of wider significance since similar data have been obtained from Felixstowe on the one side, and Newlyn on the other, is contained in an authoritative report in *The Times*, Feb. 13, 1939. Minor fluctuations of level have also occurred in the East Anglian Fenlands.

[6] For the opposite view, see C. A. Nordman, *The Megalithic Culture of Northern Europe*, Helsingfors, 1935, esp. pp. 110-111; also G. E. Daniel, *Proc. Prehist. Soc.*, 1941, pp. 23-24.

On the other hand, we can see how easily inland folk such as the Neolithic "A" people could reach southern Britain with their flocks and herds and so initiate an agricultural civilization in these islands; they could ferry across the relatively narrow gap during slack water and calm weather.[1] This applies also to the B2 beaker folk who followed them.[2] Finally, it is clear that we must regard the difficulties of transport attending the invasion of eastern and southern Britain as becoming greater as the centuries passed.

The facts and inferences recorded above have another significance. As a result of subsidence and erosion combined, a large part of that Britain which Neolithic folk knew and utilized is beneath the sea. Settlements tend to take place near a landfall; and the patches of dry ground at the mouths of estuaries, in bays, and adjacent to harbours must have been thickly dotted with the huts and cooking-places of the first agricultural settlers. Most of these have vanished, and any distribution picture of Neolithic settlement must therefore be imperfect. The loss of evidence is probably greater in eastern than in western Britain; but there may have been extensive megalithic occupation of such coastal flats as existed, for example, in Cardigan Bay. The same considerations apply, but of course in a constantly lessening degree, to every subsequent culture. Erosion has resulted in tidal water ebbing and flowing over the site of many a village recorded in *Domesday Book*.

The Structure of Britain

Though the position of Britain in relation to continent on the one hand, and to seaways on the other, and the progressive development of her insularity, explain the distribution of Man's settlements in broad outline, we are not yet in a position fully to account for the limitations and irregularities of that distribution as illustrated, for example, by the beaker map (Figure 2). Why, when beakers are found as far west as Pembrokeshire and Wigtownshire, should nine-tenths of them occur in the eastern half of the island? Why should a vigorous people like the Anglo-Saxons take a century and a quarter to colonize, at any point, the western seaboard of Britain? Scantiness of original numbers seems insufficient to account for the phenomenon in every case. A further stage on the road to a full explanation lies in the physiography of the country, which depends on geological structure.

Structural Contrasts in Britain: Britain includes the widest possible range of geological formation, resulting in great diversity of scenery and character. The older rocks lie to the west and north of the country, the younger to the east and south. The greater part of Scotland consists of igneous and metamorphic rocks—gneiss, schists, granites; in Wales and England north and west of a line from the mouth of the Tees to the mouth of the Exe, there is a great development of Palaeozoic rocks—slates, sandstones, shales, hard and massive limestones. The rest of England is made up of Secondary and Tertiary formations—limestones (generally softer and less compact than those of Palaeozoic age), chalk, sandstones, gravels, sands, and clays.

[1] Cf. Childe, *Prehistoric Communities*, p. 41; Hawkes, *Foundations*, p. 142.
[2] In this connection a recent reminder that the "A" beaker folk must have crossed the southern part of the *North Sea* to eastern Britain should not be forgotten. Hawkes, *Foundations*, p. 277.

PHYSICAL MAP OF THE BRITISH ISLES.

The overprint shows probable sea routes, the natural boundary between the Highland and the Lowland Zones of Southern Britain, certain prehistoric landways, and the physiography of the Lowland Zone. Dots indicate "damp oak" forest; wavy lines fen or marsh.

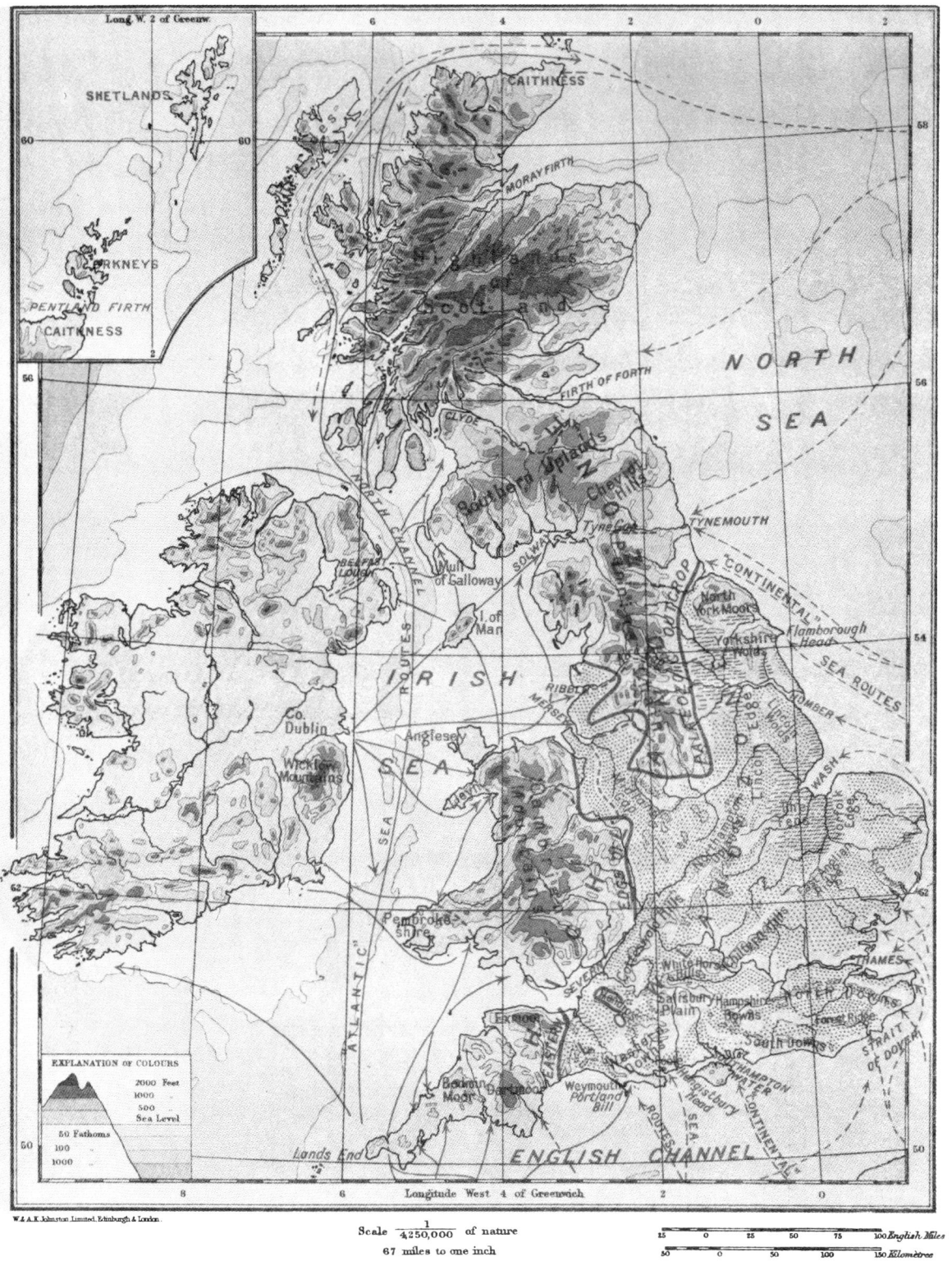

Scale $\frac{1}{4,250,000}$ of nature

67 miles to one inch

PERSONALITY OF BRITAIN, MAP B.

(*a*) *The Highland Zone* : Now the districts composed of the older (harder) rocks tend to be mountainous, while those of the later (softer) rocks are mainly lowland. The outcrops lie (as Map B suggests) in successive belts, the strike of which is N.E.–S.W. A change of physical character, very abrupt in places, marks the passage from the older to the younger rocks; the outcrop of the Palaeozoic forms in fact a natural frontier, in two sections. The first of these sections begins with the high ridge of the Pennine Chain, many of whose summits are over 2,000 feet in elevation, and which extends for 130 miles southward to the Peak district in Derbyshire. There is then a 30 mile break in the Palaeozoic bastions (the Midland Gap) occupied mainly by Secondary deposits, and the second portion of the frontier commences considerably further west and north than the southern end of the first portion. Flintshire, Denbighshire, Shropshire—the Welsh Marches in short—now mark the frontier, which, in north Wales, is indicated by the Clwydian range (nearly 2,000 feet), the Berwyns (up to 2,700 feet), the South Shropshire Hills (1,700 feet) and their north-eastern outpost, the Wrekin. South of Shropshire the Malvern Hills and the Forest of Dean flanking the broad valley of the Severn (itself a considerable obstacle) form the natural boundary between west and east, very striking when seen from the eastern side of the valley. Crossing the Severn estuary, the Mendips and the Quantocks (over 1,000 feet), are Palaeozoic outcrops; Exmoor (Dunkery Beacon, 1,707 feet) forms a hill barrier fronting the Vale of Taunton; Dartmoor, a high plateau some 500 square miles in area with many rocky summits from 1,600 to over 2,000 feet in height, is its southern counterpart. Behind or beyond these frontier hills and mountains lie the Highlands of Scotland (up to 4,000 feet), the Southern Uplands and the Cheviot Hills (up to 2,700 feet). Bordering the Irish Sea are the Lake District massif (Skiddaw and Helvellyn, over 3,000 feet) and the main ranges of the Cambrian mountains, which reach their greatest elevation in north Wales (Snowdon, 3,560 feet) and have extensive tracts over 2,000 feet.

In addition to the lowland of the softer, later rocks, there is of course a certain amount of lowland, intermont and coastal, in the mountainous country of the older rocks. In northern Britain, in particular, an east coastal belt of fertile land below the 500 feet level, from 5 to 30 miles in breadth, is fairly continuous from Durham to Caithness, as is well seen on Map B.

(*b*) *The Lowland Zone* : The wide unbroken extent of the lowland of the Secondary and Tertiary rocks, and its position nearest the continent, renders it far more important than the low-lying areas of the Highland. This point, perhaps, needs elaboration. For the development of individual cultures an adequate economic setting, such as the Lowland Zone provides in full measure, is needed; but the intermont and coastal lowlands of the Highland Zone are for the most part too scattered and too limited in area to provide the necessary economic bases for independent development. Wealth is mainly based on broad tracts of cultivable land, and a numerous peasantry. Such limited lowland areas, then, either illustrate the Highland Zone culture at its best, or, if accessible from the Lowland Zone, reflect lowland zone culture. But see p. 41, where the unique cultures of northern and eastern Scotland, mostly centred on coastal lowland, are referred to.

To the Lowland Zone proper we must now return. In it the hills seldom reach a greater height than a few hundred feet; they have easy rounded contours, and offer no serious obstacles, but they form an interesting pattern.

The key to the understanding of this pattern lies at its centre, the chalk plateau formed by Salisbury Plain and the White Horse Hills; thence extend ranges of low hills in all directions. To the S.W. the Western Downs extend to the sea between Weymouth and Lyme Regis; to the east are the Hampshire Downs, from which extend like two fingers the North and South Downs, whose terminations are marked by white cliffs at Dover and

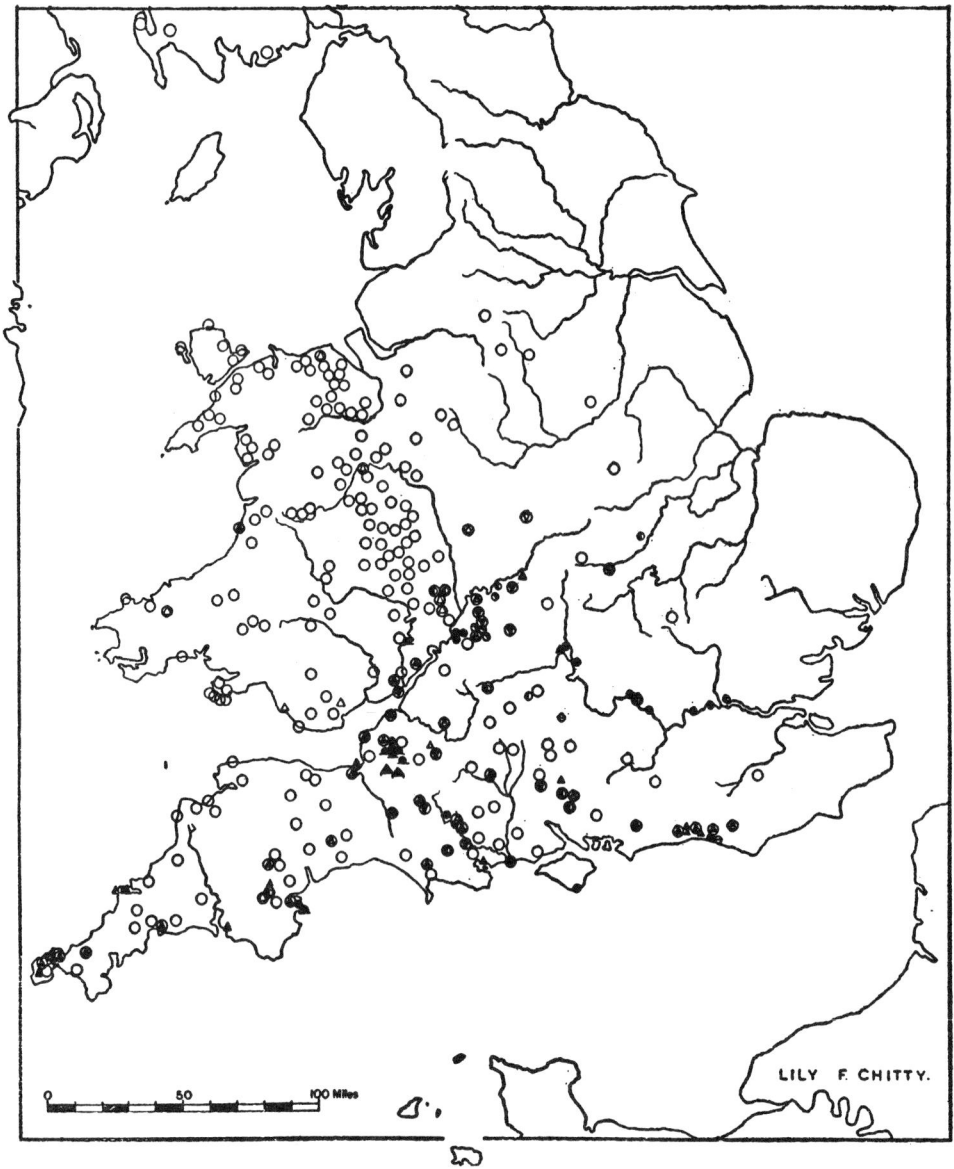

FIGURE 11.—IRON AGE "B"—SOUTH-WESTERN CULTURE: SHOWING ALSO HILL-FORTS WITH INTURNED ENTRANCES. (Pages 33, 36, 50, 58, 73, 82 *n*.)

By L. F. Chitty (1938). See Bulleid and Gray, *Glastonbury* (1911, 1917) and *Meare* (forthcoming); Cf. Hawkes, *Antiquity*, 1931, p. 78, Fig. 9; Leeds, *Arch.*, LXXVI (1927), 205-40; Radford, *M. Sarmento Festschrift* (1933), 320-31, and map. For maps of Inturned Entrances, see Chitty, *Liverpool Annals A.A.*, XXIII (1936), 107-11, Fig. 3, and *Arch. Camb.*, 1937, 129-50; for "Duck" Pottery, Leeds, *op. cit.*, Fig. 11; Donovan and Dunning, *Bristol and Glos. A.S.*, 58 (1936), 160-4, Figs. 3-5. For Currency Bars, R. A. Smith, quoted under Fig. 37.

◐ Currency bars, 1 or 2. ⊚ Hoard of do. ● Scroll pottery and related "Glastonbury" ware. ◉ "Duck" pottery. ⊖ "B" influence on pottery. ⊥ Cave occupied. ⩓ Lake village. ▲ Unfortified settlement. ⊥ Cemetery. ⊛ Camp of primary S.W. culture; entrance inturned. ⊕ Do. "B" superimposed on "A" culture. ⊕ Do. probably "B" origin. O Camps with entrances inturned or closely related forms: culture non-proven. ⊘ Do. entrance *not* inturned, *or* form unknown. ⊛ Camp with inturned entrance of "A" culture.

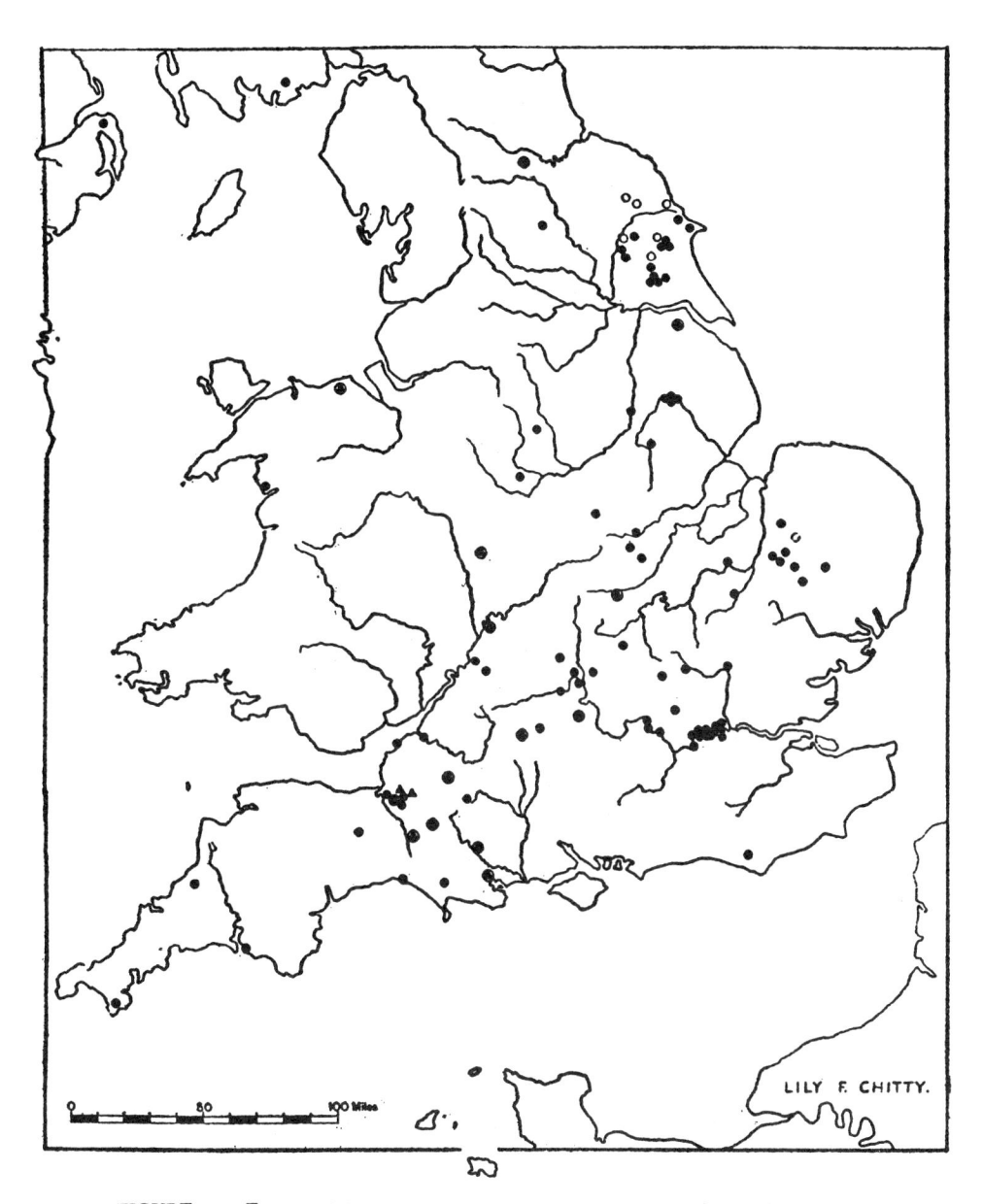

FIGURE 12.—FINE CELTIC METAL-WORK EXCLUDING BELGIC AND OTHER LATE EXAMPLES.
(Page 35.)

By L. F. Chitty (1938), using, *inter alia*, *Early Iron Age Guide*, B.M. (1925); Leeds, *Celtic Ornament* (1933); Kendrick and Hawkes, *Archaeology of England and Wales* (1932), 188–91; Hawkes, *Arch. Journ.*, XC, 1933, 150–5.

● Object of fine Celtic metal-work.   ● Hoard of fine Celtic metal-work.   O Chariot burial with which no fine metal-work was associated.   ⊛ Found in a hill-fort.   ▲ Found in a lake-dwelling.

Beachy Head respectively. Between these fingers of chalk downland lie sandy ridges within, and bordering, the Weald of Sussex; Hindhead, the Ragstone Ridge, and the Forest Ridge. On the north side of the central plateau there extend, north-eastwards, two parallel ridges. The easterly chalk ridge forms the Chiltern Hills and the East Anglian Ridge; this fades out in Norfolk, just reaching the sea at Hunstanton, but reappears in Lincolnshire and Yorkshire respectively as the Lincoln Wolds and the Yorkshire Wolds; terminating at Flamborough Head, a well-known landmark of the chalk. The westerly ridge forms the Cotteswold Hills, limestone, fading out in the Northampton Uplands; reappearing—as Lincoln Edge—on the flank of the Vale of Trent, and—as the North York Moors—on the sea's margin, overlooking the Vale of York, and forming the cliffs adjoining Whitby and Robin Hood's Bay. If to the realization of this radial structure, this raised pattern, is added an appreciation of its background, the four major extents of low-lying land, centred on the four deep estuaries of lowland Britain, the reader is in possession of all the relevant factors. These are the southern group of river valleys centred on Southampton Water, the Thames valley, the complex of rivers draining through the Fenland into the Wash, and the Ouse-Trent system converging on the Humber estuary.[1]

Lastly, it is to be noted that, while there is practically no building stone for the "dry" walls of hill forts or for megalithic monuments in the lowland save on the limestones (Corallian and other subdivisions of the Jurassic) which extend from Dorsetshire to Yorkshire, the denudation of overlying Tertiary rocks has provided, on Salisbury Plain[2] and the Berkshire Downs, residual masses of sandstone, sarsens—just the right kind of monoliths for early man's constructions, and their existence made the grandeur of Stonehenge and Avebury possible.

The Effect of Structural Differences in Britain: We are now in a position to proceed with the analysis of our distribution maps. If the reader will turn to the megalithic map (Figure 1), he will see that geological structure provides an explanation of the major features of the distribution. The igneous and metamorphic rocks of Cornwall and Devon forming much high moorland did not tempt Man, but the chalk downs of Salisbury Plain and the limestones of the Mendips and the Cotteswolds did; he ventured on to the limestones of the southern Peak and occupied the chalk of Lincolnshire and Yorkshire; the distribution in Wales, in Galloway, the Clyde region, Skye, the Hebrides and Caithness (Figure 31) shows that in the west and north he preferred the islands, sea plains, and coastal foothills, and hardly ventured on to the inland plateaux. Only one important aggregation is not yet fully explicable on a geological basis: that in the Black Mountains of Brecknockshire.

Thus the typical distribution based on the western seaways, while mainly in the Highland Zone, shows extensions into the Lowland Zone, the most important of which are in the south-west: the Salisbury Plain region and the Cotteswold Hills. Both districts are readily accessible by sea from the west (Map B). The former afforded, when all factors are taken into consideration, the best settlement area in Britain in prehistoric times; and was, as we now perceive, a natural meeting ground of continental and "Atlantic" cultural influences. No wonder then that the two most striking monuments of prehistoric times are sited on this upland; no wonder that in the structure of the nobler of them material from the far west (Pembrokeshire) was incorporated.

Turning to the beaker folk (Figure 2), we see that in northern Britain they were mainly concentrated on the narrow east-coastal belt of lowland; in southern Britain, mainly in the Lowland Zone. This latter point is more clearly brought out in Plate III, in which the beakers in southern Britain are plotted on an orographical map.[3] There are a few aggregations on the

---

[1] An interesting map in which the structure of the Lowland Zone is analyzed on a basis of soil characters, with a commentary by S. W. Wooldridge, will be found in *An Historical Geography of England*, ed. H. C. Darby, Fig. 14, p. 95.
[2] For the former presence of sarsens on Salisbury Plain see Reid, *Geology of country round Salisbury*, Memoir Geol. Survey, 1903, p. 68.
[3] Published 1932; not subsequently revised.

eastern margin of the highlands (Northumbria and the Peak district); but the examples deep in the Palaeozoic outcrop are scanty and scattered.

The map of the Iron Age "A" culture (Figure 5), referred to on p. 19, shows a typical Lowland Zone pattern widely and fairly evenly distributed east of the Humber—Bristol Channel line, expanding from southern and eastern bays and estuaries; the Highland Zone apart from a few (mainly coastal) finds, is empty. Undefended agricultural villages and farms, and hillforts of simple type, provide the setting of the culture,[1] which represents the initial Iron Age invasions and intrusions.

With respect to the Anglo-Saxons, whose sixth century cemeteries are plotted on Figure 14, it is significant that the western frontier of their kingdoms at the end of the sixth century A.D. is, from Yorkshire southward, almost exactly aligned on the palaeozoic outcrop (Figure 13, after E. T. Leeds; cf. Map B).[2]

It is easy to understand why the major physical factors should exert so powerful an influence on distribution. Lowland country, with its insignificant hills and easy contours, is more easily overrun by invaders than highland. The difficulties which mountainous country presents to an invader are well known; moreover, the highlander lives a harder life and is less easily conquered, still less easily displaced, than the lowlander. No evidence as to the effectiveness of the physical barrier formed by the Highland Zone could be stronger than that provided by the great Dyke named after King Offa, the frontier between the Celtic peoples of Wales and the Mercian kingdom at the end of the eighth century A.D. The efforts of the Mercians, culminating within this energetic king's prolonged reign of 39 years, resulted in the boundaries of their territory being pressed only a short distance within the natural limits of the Highland (Figure 29).

Certain rock formations and extended outcrops are of great importance in connection with the diffusion of culture within Britain. This is the case with the escarpment referred to in a previous paragraph, extending north-eastward from the Cotteswold Hills; it is composed of Jurassic rocks, and forms a convenient route for trade and traffic between east Yorkshire, the upper Thames valley and south-west Britain.[3] The foodvessel, for example (Plate IV and p. 41), shows a significant diffusion along this outcrop. Such a diffusion, again, provides a major problem in connection with Iron Age " B."

Early Iron Age " B " is a generalized term for the cultures resulting from a number of irruptions from overseas, initiated in the third century B.C.; the intrusive groups are recognized to have been mainly concentrated in two separate areas, the south-west and the north-east.[4] On the characters indicative of the south-western culture-complex (in part due to a developed tin trade) there is general agreement; objects attributable to it are plotted by Miss Chitty on Figure 11. Excluding for the moment consideration of the open-circle symbols on the map, the distribution shows several coastal foci of diffusion, from the Isle of Wight to Lands End, and around the estuary of the Severn. Type sites of a later development in Somerset are the Glastonbury and Meare lake villages. The south-western folk were great fort builders; multiple banks and ditches and elaborately defended entrances are characteristic. Close similarities in technique between Cornish and Brittany forts (cliff-castles) have recently been demonstrated.[5]

---

[1] See Childe, *Prehist. Comm.*, pp. 194–207.

[2] The phenomenon is illustrated from different sets of data by S. W. Wooldridge in *An Historical Geography of England*, Figs. 16 and 17, pp. 112, 125.

[3] For a description of this formation from an archaeological standpoint, see *Arch. Camb.*, 1927, p. 96 ff.

[4] For a convenient and up-to-date summary, with references, see Childe, *Prehistoric Communities*, Chs. XI and XII.

[5] R. E. M. Wheeler, *Antiq. Journ.*, 1941, pp. 265–266; A. S. R. Gordon, Gurnards Head, an Iron Age cliff castle in Cornwall, *Arch. Journ.*, 1940, p. 96 ff. esp. p. 100. The exceptional part played by Brittany in our cultural development both in the Lowland and in the Highland, will have been gathered from frequent

At the present stage of our knowledge complete agreement as to what should be included in a distribution map of the north-eastern " B " culture—attributed to the Parisii and culturally related groups—is probably unattainable. The fine La Tène II metal-work from east Yorkshire, the Witham, the Fenland borders and the lower Thames, martial in character, is

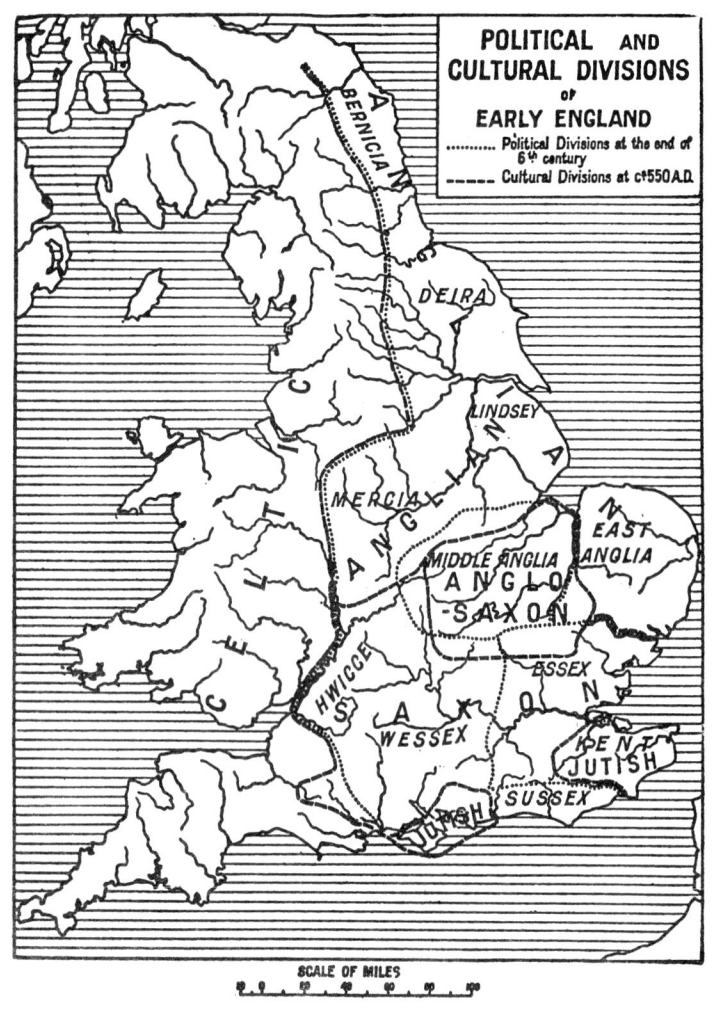

FIGURE 13.—POLITICAL AND CULTURAL DIVISIONS OF EARLY ENGLAND;
(Pages 33, 62.)
After E. T. Leeds, *The Archaeology of the Anglo-Saxon Settlements*, 1913 (Oxford University Press), Fig. 4, p. 39.

references in this essay. This Early Iron Age correlation is held to be due to the technical skill and commercial enterprise of the Veneti. There are two main reasons for Breton vigour and competence. The first is that the key position at the salient angle of the Channel and Atlantic coastal zones renders Brittany, as we have seen, a meeting place for continental and maritime cultures in process of expansion, that is, for landsmen and seamen, and for merchants. From Brittany any invading group could make the short sea journey to Lowland Dorset or Highland Cornwall, or the long sea journey to Wales or Ireland, at will. The second reason is that her character, a well-defined peninsula with numerous harbours, metal ores, and a varied geological structure, has favoured and stimulated progress in a population thus diversified. The evidence suggests that from Brittany Britain has received not mere drifts of folk who having reached the edge of the Continent must needs spill over it into an invisible island, but organized communities well equipped spiritually and technically.

fundamental to this culture. Moreover, finds of non-Belgic art objects along the Jurassic outcrop, and strays in the Highland Zone, are probably also to be associated with it. We have prepared a map (Figure 12) on which this metal-work is shown, together with similar specimens found elsewhere in southern Britain.[1] The concentration of such works of art in

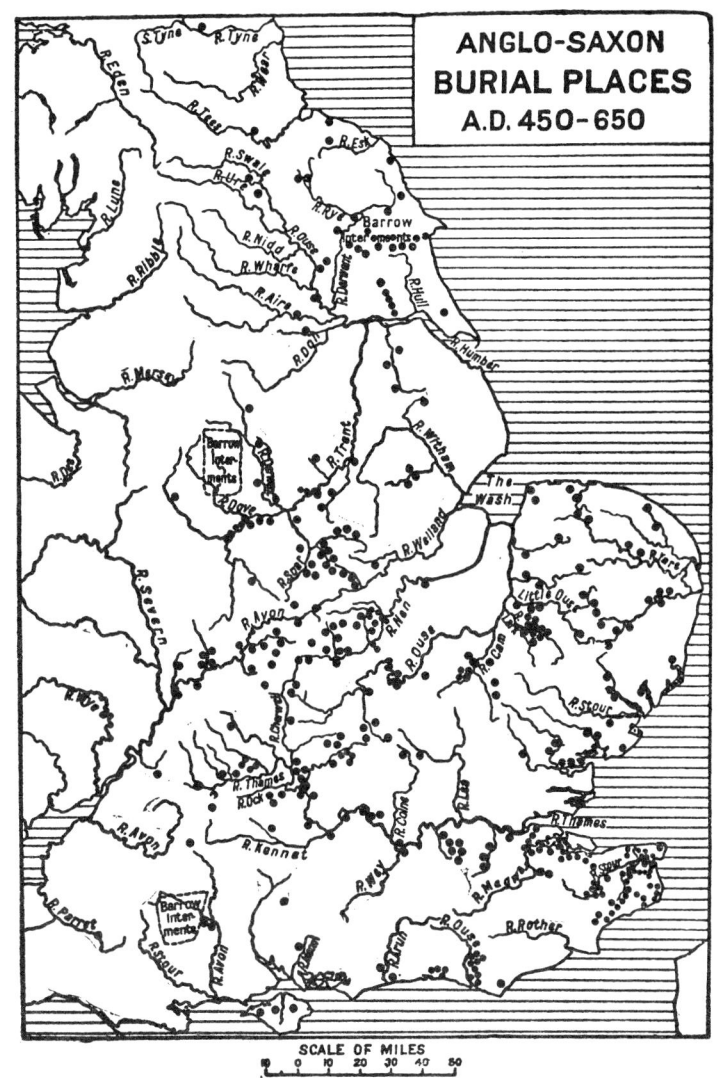

FIGURE 14.—ANGLO-SAXON BURIAL PLACES, A.D. 450–650, IN ENGLAND.
(Pages 14, 17, 19, 33, 79, 81.)
After E. T. Leeds, *The Archaeology of the Anglo-Saxon Settlements*, 1913 (Oxford University Press), Fig. 1, p. 19.

[1] In this map we accept as early, objects described by E. T. Leeds in the first two chapters of his *Celtic Ornament* (1933); also horse-bits of his (*a*) and (*b*) classes, and terrets of types 1, 3 and 4; La Tène II involuted brooches are also included. It should be stated that in Mr. Leeds' view, the culture trend along the Jurassic outcrop is in the opposite direction to that suggested in the text, and is definitely of south-western origin. Text and map are based on ideas tentatively put forward in a paper in *Archaeological Cambrensis* (1927, pp. 67–112), in which the significance of this outcrop " as a link between Yorkshire and S.W. Britain " in La Tène times were stressed (see pp. 94–100).

the focal area of the south-western " B " culture is crucial. Does the diffusion along the Jurassic strata of the art cultivated by the Yorkshire charioteers point to a fusion of the north-east and the south-west cultures, in the west, or was the metal-work of the latter area independently evolved?[1]

To return to Figure 11: the as yet undated forts having inturned entrances, plotted as open circles on this map, and probably representing, in the main, expansion of the south-

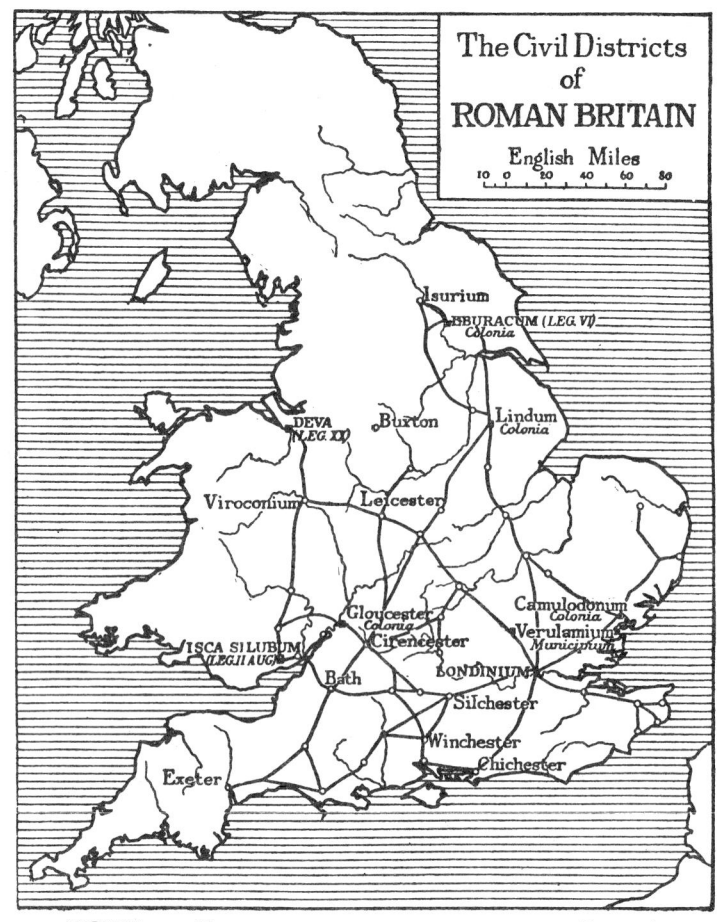

FIGURE 15.—THE CIVIL DISTRICTS OF ROMAN BRITAIN. (Page 38.)
After F. Haverfield and G. Macdonald, *The Roman Occupation of Britain*, 1924 (Oxford University Press), Fig. 20.

C. F. C. Hawkes suggests (*Ant. Journ.*, 1940, pp. 118–121) that the majority of La Tène I brooches should be regarded as representing one facet of the (Eastern) Iron Age " B " invasion-complex of the 3rd century B.C., and not earlier trading activities. I am disposed to agree. If this view be adopted, the representation of the " B " culture would be greatly strengthened, and that of the "A" culture diminished, as reference to the distribution map of these brooches (in *Arch. Camb.*, 1927, p. 68) will indicate. There is no doubt that Iron Age " B " folk from northern France ranged widely in search of suitable country for settlement; they landed in the Tay and Moray Firths in Scotland, as well as on the south coast in Kent and Sussex.

[1] An important advance has recently been made, by J. B. Ward Perkins, in his paper on Iron Age Metal Horse-bits of the British Isles: *Proc. Prehist. Soc.*, 1939, p. 173 ff. The two-link bit is shown to be of S.W. origin, the three-link, of N.E. origin.

western "B" culture,[1] show a remarkable concentration on the Welsh Marches; the pattern provides a new and instructive feature; it shows vividly how penetration of a Highland massif by Lowlanders takes place. The foothills are occupied, and the flanks of the river valleys; the blank areas on the map are the main mountain masses.

Much of this development in Wales is certainly late, and may even be post-Conquest (c. 43–80 A.D.):[2] in this connection it may be pointed out that the effective establishment of

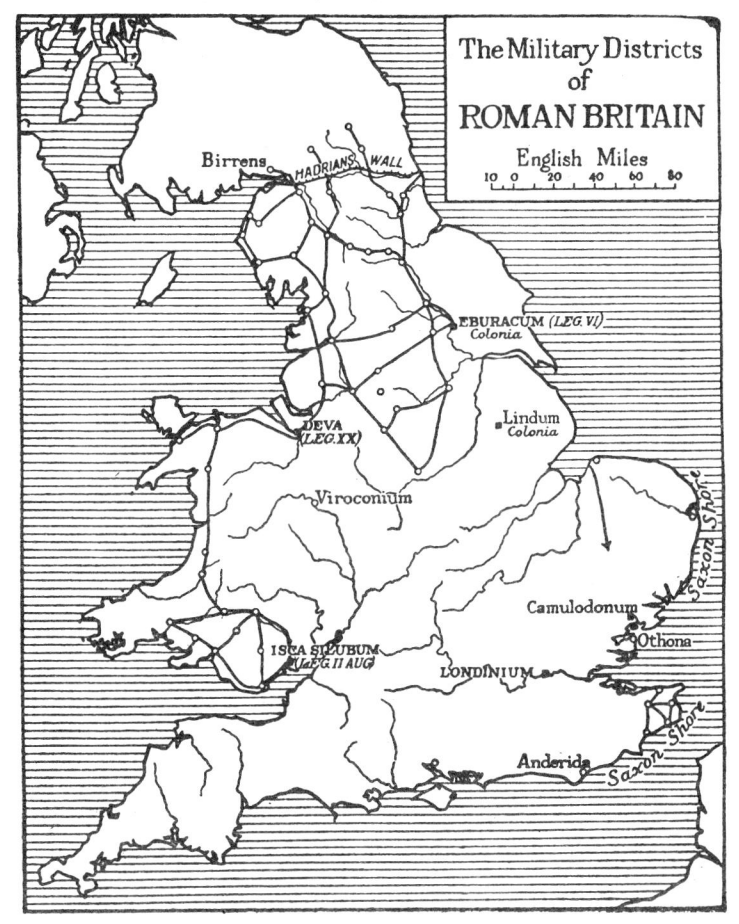

FIGURE 16.—THE MILITARY DISTRICTS OF ROMAN BRITAIN. (Page 38.)
After F. Haverfield and G. Macdonald, *The Roman Occupation of Britain*, 1924 (Oxford University Press), Fig. 21.

Iron Age culture in the northern sector of the Highland Zone was long delayed; the finds in the Brigantian area west of the Yorkshire Ouse and in southern Scotland are for the most part associated with Roman objects, or show intrinsic evidence of contact with Roman culture. In Wales, moreover, the spread of the characteristic defensive technique of Iron Age "B" seems to have outstripped the cultural spread; C. Daryll Forde secured but a handful of potsherds and a bead as a result of four seasons' work on the Pen Dinas hillfort on Cardigan

---

[1] Mr. W. J. Varley informs me that he has found Iron Age "A" pottery in the hillfort of Eddisbury, Cheshire. In this region a diffusion from the east not the south of England is probable.
[2] See Lily F. Chitty, "How did the Hillfort Builders reach the Breiddin?" *Arch. Camb.*, 1937, p. 129 ff., with map.

Bay,[1] and B. H. St. J. O'Neil had a similar experience at Ffridd Faldwyn, Montgomery.[2] These results are illuminating in connection with another distribution map (Figure 37) showing iron currency bars and coinage characteristic of the Iron Age "B" and "C" cultures respectively. Primitive though bar currency may be, neither it nor the coinage effectively penetrated the Highland Zone at any point.[3]

The Importance of the Lowland Zone: The Roman civilization epitomizes the contrast between Highland and Lowland, and illustrates the importance of the latter. It is true that this civilization, in a sense, overstepped the limits of the Lowland, but the junction of Lowland and Highland marks, as Haverfield emphasized, the boundary between the civil and military areas (Figures 15 and 16, after Haverfield and Macdonald). It is well known that effective Romanization was confined to the lowlands. The contrast between contemporary tribal centres such as *Calleva*—Silchester in Hampshire (Figure 17), a civilized country town, and Tre'r Ceiri in Caernarvonshire (Figure 18), a barbarous hillfort, is striking; this contrast must be regarded as an extreme example of a phenomenon necessarily recurrent.

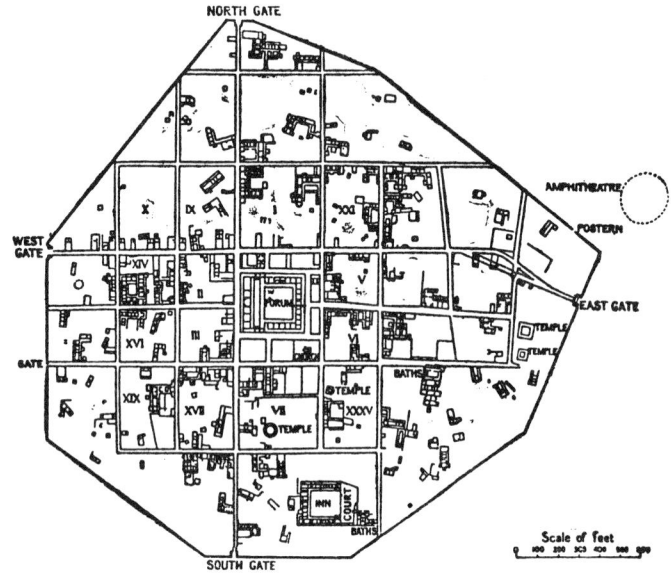

FIGURE 17.—PLAN OF SILCHESTER, HAMPSHIRE, A ROMANO-BRITISH TOWN.
(Page 38.)
After F. Haverfield and G. Macdonald, *The Roman Occupation of Britain*, 1924 (Oxford University Press), Fig. 36.

It is evident that the Lowland nourishes richer cultures than does the Highland; taking Britain as a whole the most important centres of any culture or civilization are likely to be in the south of the island. We have already referred to the indentations of the east and south

---

[1] *Bulletin, Board of Celtic Studies*, VII, 77, 324; VIII, 378. The finds include one sherd with "duck" ornament.
[2] *Arch. Camb.*, 1942, pp. 1–57, esp. p. 21.
[3] There is evidence of varying value that several iron ore-fields were worked by the Celts in southern Britain in the centuries immediately preceding the Roman occupation: among these, the Weald of Sussex, Northamptonshire (wherein Hunsbury—see *Arch. Journ.*, 1936, pp. 95–96—is a classic site) and the Forest of Dean are certain or highly probable. A recent study suggests that this currency was made and distributed in western Britain by elements of the tribe known as the Dobuni, controlling the mines of the latter region. Fox, *Antiquity*, 1940, pp. 427–433, and *Antiq. Journ.*, 1939, pp. 387–389.

coast, the harbours and estuaries which invite invader as well as trader. To this disadvantage —from the native point of view—is added the fact that the areas thus rendered vulnerable are all lowland; and since the opposite coast is similar, lowland fronting lowland, conditions

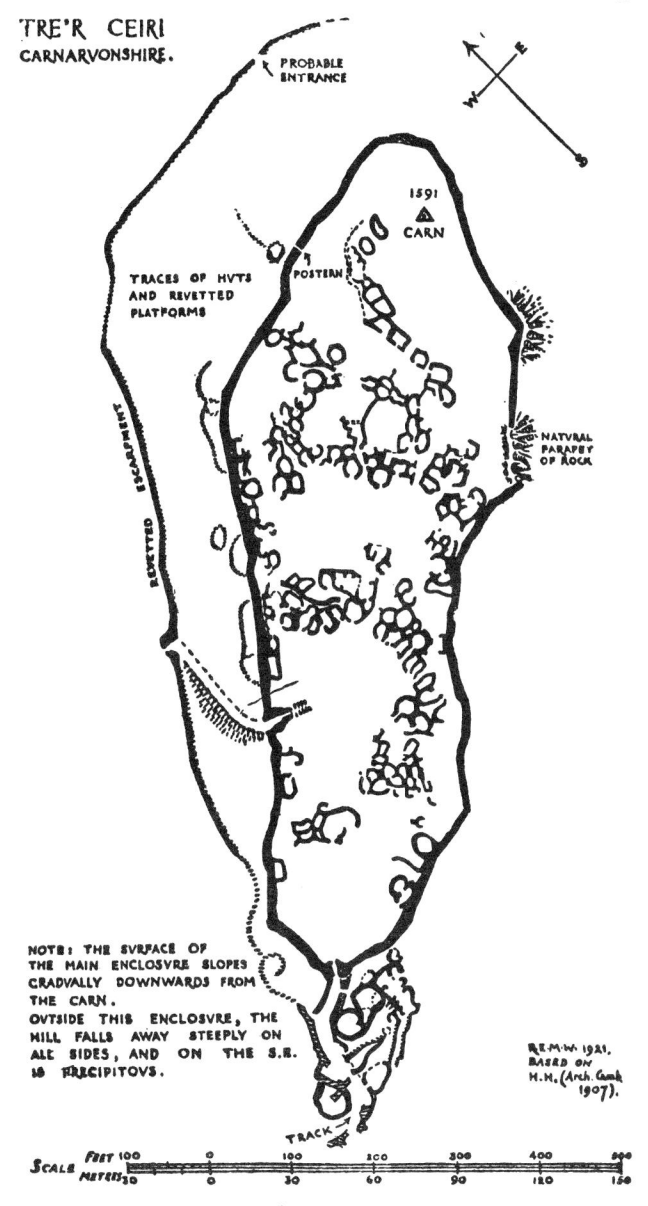

FIGURE 18.—PLAN OF TRE'R CEIRI, CAERNARVONSHIRE, INHABITED IN THE ROMAN PERIOD. (Page 38.)

After R. E. M. Wheeler, *Prehistoric and Roman Wales*, 1925 (Oxford University Press), Fig. 107.

extremely favourable to invasion are set up. It is the tragedy of British prehistory and history, and the key thereto, that the most habitable and most easily conquerable areas are adjacent to the shores whence invaders are most likely to come. (See Map A.)

The tragedy of British history: because a fresh invasion from the east not only paralyzes the older culture by destroying it where it is most flourishing, but tends to cut off the survivals of that culture in the west from the stimulus of contact with Europe. This is well seen, historically, in the fifth-sixth centuries A.D., when the conquest of the British Lowlands by the barbarian Saxon cut off the Celtic Church of the west from effective contact with the general body of Christendom for 150 years; the breach between the Celtic and the Roman Church, so prominent in the ecclesiastical history of the seventh century, is recognized to be due to that isolation.[1]

It should be added that the relative ease with which new civilizations are established in the Lowland Zone does not prevent the partial resurgence of earlier cultures apparently obliterated. Conquering peoples may impose their culture (and their language); but when the invaded country is an island, they are seldom in sufficient numbers to do without the services of the conquered, in slavery or serfdom. Moreover, if it was possible in England of the sixth century A.D. for communities of Britons to maintain themselves in Lowland forests (the Chilterns) or fens (East Anglia), how much more considerable such survivals must have been in prehistoric Britain, the greater part of which was jungle or swamp? Associated, for example, with the exotic Wessex culture of Middle Bronze Age "A" were earlier culture elements not only of the beaker-folk whom the new lords replaced, but also of the Neolithic peasantry. These elements increased in importance, for from them the chief pottery type of the Middle Bronze Age "B" culture, the cinerary urn, was derived.[2]

The Characteristics of the Highland Zone: Confining our attention to the cultures reaching Britain by way of the Lowland Zone, it may be asked if we are to regard the Highland Zone merely as a barrier to cultural advance, and as a region wherein a few strays and adventurous outliers of these lowland cultures precariously exist? I think not, for the Highland has a more positive cultural character than that concept allows. In the Lowland of Britain new cultures of continental origin tend to be *imposed* on the earlier or aboriginal culture. In the Highland, on the other hand, these tend to be *absorbed* by the older culture. Viewed in another aspect, in the Lowland, you get *replacement*, in the Highland, *fusion*.[3] It is true enough that a given culture brought across the narrow seas tends to manifest itself less distinctively in the Highland than in the Lowland, more feebly, and, as we have seen, later. But the power of absorption, the tendency to fusion in the Highland, may at times result in a greater *continuity of cultural character*, or it may provide the west with a cultural character of its own; of these possibilities examples may be given.[4]

Firstly, continuity. There is a wide range of evidence of this, such as the survival of the Celtic language, the persistence in the west of very old racial stocks,[5] and of tribal custom; the importance of kinship and clan in Wales and Scotland. It will here suffice to mention a group of archaeological facts associated with burial: that throughout the Bronze Age burials in Wales tend to show survivals of megalithic custom; that isolated instances of barrow burial are met with long after the introduction of Christianity in Wales; and that the Bronze Age

---

[1] Oman, *England before the Norman Conquest*, 3rd ed., p. 267.

[2] Varley, Jackson, and Chitty, *Prehistoric Cheshire*, 1940, p. 93. Cyril Fox, in *Archaeologia*, 89, pp. 105-7.

[3] See *Arch. Camb.*, 1926, p. 28. E. Estyn Evans points out (*Archaeologia*, 83, 1933, pp. 197-201 and Figs. 1 and 2) that intrusive cultures may not always flood the whole Lowland Zone, and that the line where the resistance of the native culture imposes absorption *may* be in advance of the boundaries of the Highland Zone.

[4] "Continuity and persistence are remarkable features of the life of Wales as revealed by Archaeology." H. J. Fleure, in *Arch. Camb.*, 1923, p. 241. See also this author in *Arch. Camb.*, 1916, pp. 117-118, and 1917, pp. 350-351.

[5] H. J. Fleure, *Races of England and Wales*, p. 103.

custom of depositing white quartz stones on the burial place is carried on in Wales to the present day.[1]

Secondly, individuality. Though the first rush of an invasion, or the pressure of a vigorous and expanding culture, may result in the establishment of an apparently uniform culture in Lowland and Highland, the Highland tends to assert itself and to oust or transform the intruding elements. This is well seen in the Early Bronze Age. The beaker culture (Figure 2) is established along the eastern seaboard of the highlands as well as in the lowlands; but within a few centuries differentiation between the two areas is again apparent, the distinctively northern type of ceramic, the foodvessel, having been evolved. Plate IV shows the distribution; foodvessels have a limited distribution in southern England.[2]

The "outstripping" of cultural by defensive techniques in the Highland Zone in the Early Iron Age, referred to on pp. 37-38, is also explicable in a manner consonant with the ideas expressed in this section. The hillforts of Pen Dinas and Ffridd Faldwyn may not be the work of invaders, but of natives; they may represent a protective reaction, a partial absorption of new elements into the older Highland culture. A close parallel to the process here envisaged is seen in the Middle Ages, when the Welsh princes adopted the mound castle of the Norman invaders.

The shrinkage within historic times of the area in Britain in which Celtic languages are spoken indicates the varying power of resistance to Lowland influences of the several parts of the Highland Zone. The first area to yield its Celtic speech was the southern Scotland-Pennines region; the second, the south-western peninsula (Cornwall). Wales, less accessible than either, has succeeded in maintaining her Brythonic speech. The Highlands of Scotland, as remoted as Ireland from lowland influences, have retained, like Ireland, a different and possibly older stratum of the Celtic language.

While cultural unity as between Highland and Lowland is, then, precarious and superficial, a measure of cultural unity within the Highland Zone not infrequently occurs. The encrusted- and cordoned-urn maps (Pls. V and VIII), discussed below, emphasize such tendency towards unity, since both pottery types are seen to extend from Ross-shire and Aberdeenshire in Scotland to Pembrokeshire in Wales. When unity fails to be manifested in the Highland Zone, the divergence is most striking in Scotland north of the Forth-Clyde isthmus, for physical reasons; the remoteness of this region and its inaccessibility permitted the development of unique cultures. This is especially noticeable in the Early Iron Age and in the Early Christian period, when the Broch culture and the Pictish culture occupy the north and east of the Scottish Highlands respectively (Figure 33, after Childe).[3] The failure of the Roman military organization to extend effective control beyond the Forth-Clyde line is, in essence, an illustration of the same point. It should be noted that the landward inaccessibility of Cornwall, and its accessibility by sea, tends to give a distinctive quality to its culture in all periods.

It may be asked whether the culture of the Highland Zone ever developed sufficient vigour to impose itself on the Lowland Zone. The answer should probably be in the negative. Elements of the Long Barrow culture spread north-eastwards to Lincolnshire and Yorkshire, but its original focus was Wessex, not the Highland Zone. The foodvessel culture was strongly established in east Yorkshire; as we have seen, it never effectively established its hold on southern England. No later evidence can be adduced; the chief

---

[1] For examples of such survivals, see *Arch. Camb.*, 1925, pp. 283 and 288; and 1926, pp. 31-32, and Fig. 6.

[2] This map gives a remarkable picture of the occupation areas of southern Scotland. Cf. Childe, *Prehistory of Scotland*, pp. 89-95.

[3] For a distribution map of the Broch culture, see this author's paper in *Proc. Roy. Soc. Edin.*, Vol. 50, 1930, p. 53; and for his latest views on its origin, *Prehist. Comm.*, p. 244 ff.

centres of Iron Age " B " culture in the south-west, the only likely example, are within the boundaries of the Lowland Zone.

Discussion of the cultural characteristics of the Highland Zone is incomplete until the influence of the neighbouring island has been taken into account.

Physical Aspects of the relation of Ireland to Britain : There are three ways by which new ideas, new cultures, or invaders can reach Ireland : either (1) by the Atlantic route from Spain and western France, or (2) by sea round the north of Britain, or (3) mainly by land, across Britain. Since the importance of the Atlantic route declined, in the Bronze Age, Ireland has not been extensively harried or settled by seafarers from the south. Hallstatt culture, represented (e.g.) by *situlae* and cauldrons, must have reached Ireland by this route about 600–500 B.C. ; but the absence of any such evidence for an Early Iron Age immigration is remarkable.[1] The Viking culture arrived by, and its bearers freely used, the northern sea route in the ninth and following centuries A.D. (Plate XII).

The third alternative has points of some interest. The eastern and north-eastern parts of Ireland are areas where the Bronze culture is seen to be very vigorous, and these parts present good harbours together with expanses of lowland fronting the Irish Sea and Britain, just as eastern Britain presents good harbours fronting the continent (see Map B). Thus it might be expected that close cultural contact between the two islands would ensue, and Ireland be as susceptible to invasion from Britain in her turn as is Britain from the continent. Intrusion has occurred, but not massive invasion. The reason for her isolation is clear ; it is the existence of the Highland Zone of Britain, an obstacle which hinders or prevents access to the shores of St. George's Channel and the Irish Sea. This has saved Ireland from many invasions and has limited and modified others. The beaker culture never effectively reached her ;[2] the Roman effort faded out on the shores of the Irish Sea ; the Saxon conquest never even approached her.

Such cultural influences and invasions as in early times reach Ireland from Britain, then are almost always[3] those of the Highland Zone. Plate V illustrates this. The " encrusted " urn was evolved from the foodvessel in northern Britain, and its strikingly characteristic forms trickled across to the east and north-east coasts of Ireland, by the North Channel, because this was the narrowest seaway, and therefore the easiest crossing.[4] The cordoned or hooped urn—another Late Bronze form—is a highland modification of the overhanging-rim urn so frequently found in British barrows. The distribution map of the type, prepared by Lily F. Chitty (Plate VIII), shows how constant was the relationship between the Highland Zone and Ireland; the patterns on Plate V and on this Plate are in this respect almost identical. The remarkable map of Ireland in the Early Iron Age by J. Raftery, published by Adolf Mahr, which is almost completely barren of finds south of the line Shannon estuary-Dublin, serves to underline this argument.[5] Invaders and cultures of British origin show, then, a tendency to concentrate in Ulster for the same reason that continental cultures show a tendency to concentrate in south-east Britain. This suggests that the aloofness of Ulster from the general life of Ireland has its basis in prehistoric times ; indeed, the island at times presents as marked a cultural duality as Britain does.

---

[1] E. T. Leeds, *Celtic Ornament*, p. 15 ; A. Mahr, *Proc. Prehist. Soc.*, 1937, p. 441 ; Joseph Raftery, *Féil-Sgríbhinn Eóin Mhic Néill*, pp. 272–281.

[2] Recent work suggests that the beaker folk in northern Ireland may represent a more important (ethnic) element than the text indicates. J. McL. May, *Journ. Roy. Soc. Antiq. Ireland*, LXII, pp. 88–89.

[3] Occasionally lowland cultures may filter through that Zone; see J. B. Ward Perkins on contacts between E. Yorkshire and N. Ireland in the Early Iron Age, *Proc. Prehist. Soc.*, 1939, p. 182.

[4] I cannot accept Sir Lindsay Scott's view that the movement is in the opposite direction. V. G. Childe's recent summary of a problem, admittedly not so simple as I had envisaged in 1927, may be consulted. *Prehist. Comm.*, p. 150.

[5] *Proc. Prehist. Soc.*, 1937, p. 405 (Fig. 29).

But Ireland was by no means a sleeping or merely receptive partner in the varied life of these islands in early days; she reveals an active creative life of her own based on the Mediterranean culture which she received by the Atlantic route in Neolithic and Early Bronze Age times and developed. This creative power, stimulated by occasional bearers of new cultures, seafarers and traders, invigorated the Highland Zone of Britain: primarily the

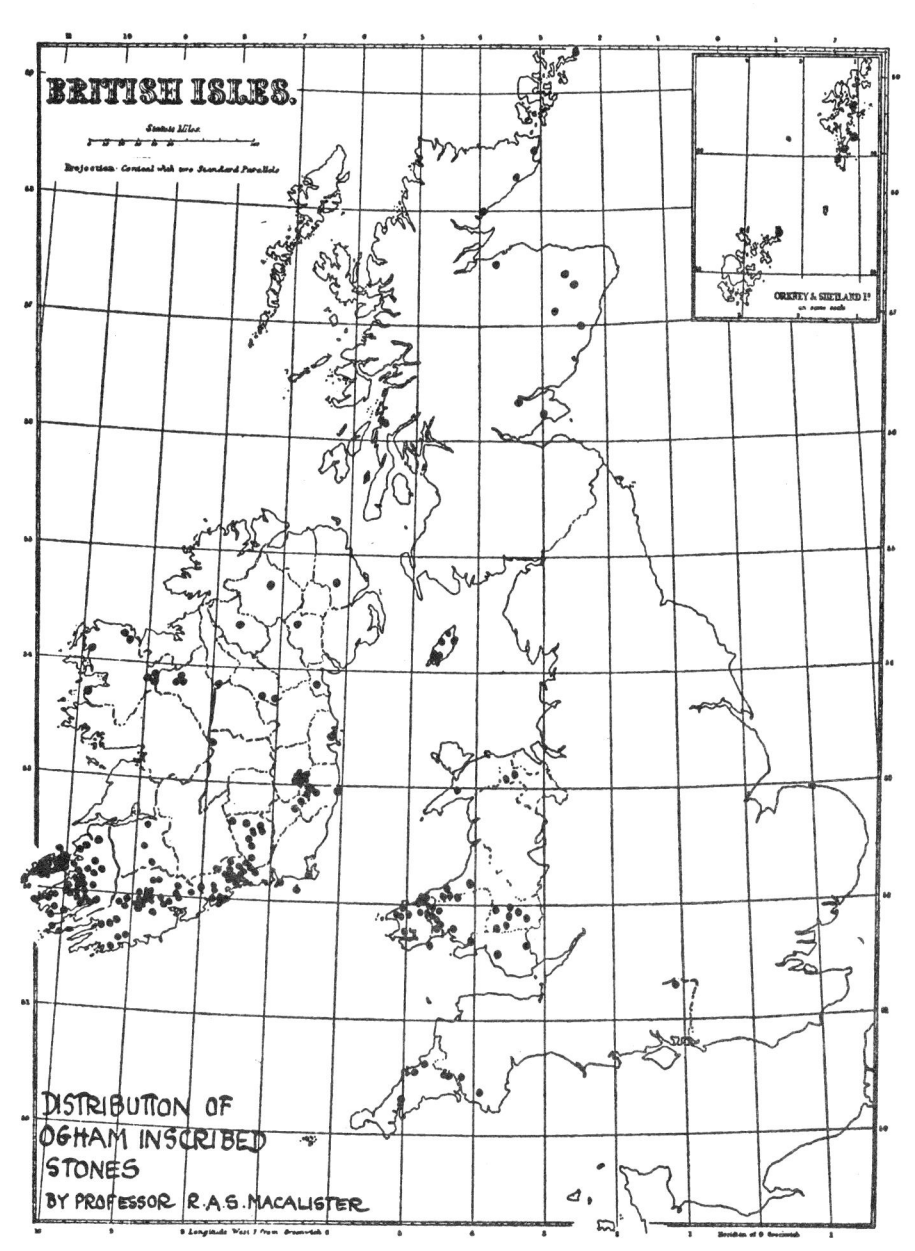

FIGURE 19.—DISTRIBUTION OF OGHAM-INSCRIBED STONES IN THE BRITISH ISLES.
(Page 44. Illustration on p. 94.)
Prepared by R. A. S. Macalister (1932).

opposite coasts of St. George's Channel and the Irish Sea, and south-western Scotland. Sometimes (as in early and middle Bronze Age) the transmission is mainly by way of the Clyde estuary. We may turn again to Plate IV, which shows the distribution of foodvessels of these periods; the typological links between the British and Irish series are strong, and many were forged in Ireland. At other times Wales is chiefly affected, as in the case of the culture associated with Ogham-inscribed stones, which represents a movement of Gaelic-speaking folk and their culture from southern Ireland in the fifth century A.D. Figure 19, illustrating this, has been kindly prepared for me by Professor Macalister.[1] Occasionally the shores washed by the Irish Sea are universally affected, as in the case of the megalithic civilization (Figure 1).

An outstanding feature of these distributions may then be re-stated in a form which gives it general interest: there is a definite tendency for the shores of the Irish Sea to form a "culture province."[2] At the same time, we must recognize that the duality of Irish culture we have referred to has its repercussions; the culture of northern Ireland influences north Wales and northern Britain; the culture of southern Ireland, south Wales and Cornwall.

The interplay of cultures in the area thus defined is well illustrated by the Isle of Man, which, lying at its centre, a halfway house for its sea-borne trade, has received and absorbed, in the Neolithic and Bronze Ages, cultural elements from Ireland, north England, and south-west Scotland.[3]

In furtherance of this survey of Irish cultural connections, reference may be made to the events of the sixth and seventh centuries A.D., when the Early Christian civilization of Ireland extended its influence over the whole of the Highland Zone of Britain; and to those of the first half of the tenth century A.D., when the Kings of Dublin exercised intermittent control over the coastlands of the Irish Sea and Northumbria, holding court at York. The limitation to northern England of this political and military overlordship is noteworthy. Reviewing the whole of the evidence, it would appear that whenever culture centred in Ireland (as distinct from Irish trade) expands, its force is spent in the Highland Zone and in the northern outliers of the Lowland Zone (east Yorkshire). It does not *effectively* reach across the mountain barriers to southern England.

Deposits of Copper, Gold, and Tin in the British Isles, exploited in Prehistoric Times. One aspect of Ireland's relations with Britain remains to be examined.

Considerations set out in the Introduction point to the southern trade, whereby contacts (indirect though they be) with Mediterranean cultures are maintained, as most important for Britain; for by such contacts the ideas[4] permeating a progressive civilization are disseminated as well as goods. Northern trade may provide precious things, amber for example; but the keels that bring it bring nothing else. In the early part of the second millennium the most important objects were metal tools, the most important ideas those relating to metallurgy. Let us consider how both reached us.

Those beaker folk—the "A" beaker people—who about 1800 B.C. came into eastern Britain from beyond the Lower Rhine already knew the flat round-heeled riveted daggers of copper which had lately been developed in Central Europe; but they were too far from the original source of supply to possess any (or many) of these precious weapons. Their culture

---

[1] Having regard to the cultural advance which the possession of a script represents, it is significant (in view of what has been said above) that the main strength of the Ogham culture lies in Southern Ireland, nearest, that is, to the continental sources from which the stimulus towards the creation of its remarkable alphabet must have come.

[2] H. L. Movius, Jr., finds this generalization true of the Mesolithic Period: *The Irish Stone Age*, 1942, p. 210.

[3] Since the above was written (1932) an interesting study of the culture of the Isle of Man, by Grahame Clark, has appeared; it confirms my conclusion. *Proc. Prehist. Soc.*, 1935, pp. 70–92.

[4] Knowledge of arts and crafts, as well as notions. Cf. Childe, *Antiquity*, 1943, p. 25.

was in effect Neolithic, and they rendered this dagger-type in flint (Figure 21, after W. F. Grimes). Apart from the few tanged copper daggers of the older "West-European" type, previously mentioned,[1] the Britain they entered knew no such metal weapons, and in the greater part of the Lowland Zone, where flint was so abundant, the flint dagger remained their characteristic type. But on and near the margins of the Highland Zone the central European dagger is found reproduced in copper and then in bronze; Figure 20 shows the distribution of specimens thought to be early. A demand by the "A" beaker folk for this dagger was, it is held, being met by Irish metal merchants[2]; that is, our early bronze culture came in the main not from the south or east, but from the west. The British Isles indeed provide the outstanding example of the irregular expansion in Europe of the techniques associated with higher civilizations.[3]

This came about because the megalithic folk or those among them who were prospectors discovered, not later than the end of the third millennium, Ireland's precious and accessible riches. The gold-bearing gravels of the streams issuing from the Wicklow Mountains were intensively worked, as were adjacent deposits of copper. Copper ores in Cork and Kerry were probably also exploited. The country was flooded with implements and weapons—flat axes and halberds—of this metal; the prime metallurgical secret must have been disseminated, for though Ireland has virtually no tin these early types are commonly found in bronze also.[4] Now both copper and gold occur in Britain, in Anglesey and Carmarthenshire for example; but there is no reliable evidence that either was mined here until Roman times.[5] Instead, the Irish trade was developed to serve Britain's needs; and through Britain, western and northern Europe.

A remarkable map (Plate VI) prepared by Lily F. Chitty illustrates this influence of Ireland on the development of civilization in Britain about 1900–1600 B.C. Here we have the distribution of flat and hammer-flanged axes of Irish type; the pattern reveals the traffic lanes by which, from ports in the Highland Zone fronting the Irish Sea, these tools reached most parts of the country.[6] A map of one group of these Irish axes—the decorated examples—has since been prepared by Megaw and Hardy.[7] The fruit of laborious study of the type, it shows Britain as an entrepôt for continental trade, the chief southern route (to France) being probably north Wales–middle Severn–Gloucester–Thames valley; the route to the Baltic is less clear, but it was cross-insular, not by sea via Caithness. The distribution of

[1] Three well-known examples in Wiltshire were probably (as Piggott suggests) brought in by B1 beaker folk (*Proc. Prehist. Soc.*, 1938, p. 56), but trade may be held to account for the initial appearance of the type on the Atlantic route, in Ireland and Scotland: Coffey, *Bronze Age in Ireland*, Fig. 3, p. 9; and Childe, *Prehistory of Scotland*, Fig. 23, p. 98.

[2] In this matter I follow Piggott (*Proc. Prehist. Soc.*, 1938, pp. 59–60) and Hawkes (*Foundations*, pp. 278–280). The essential contribution of the "A" beaker folk was the demand for the new type, which the Irish industry alone could supply. Where the invaders did not penetrate, as in Ireland itself, the demand did not arise: the type is thus very rare in museum collections in Ireland, though the copper blade figured by Coffey (*op. cit.*, p. 8) may be an early Irish rendering. The concentrations on my map then are no guide to source, but represent areas of effective demand. Compare Piggott's map of Baltic amber distribution in Britain c. 1600 B.C. (*loc. cit.*, Fig. 16, p. 81) for which such an interpretation is inevitable.

(Late examples of these daggers dating from Middle Bronze Age "A" and after have been omitted from the map; they were doubtless made in this country, in the rather different conditions created by the arrival and diffusion of the "Wessex culture.")

[3] Childe, *Dawn*, 2nd ed., p. 321.

[4] R. A. S. Macalister, *Archaeology of Ireland*, pp. 55, 91.

[5] For the sites of deposits then worked see *An Historical Geography of England*, Fig. 10, p. 69.

[6] E.g., from north Ireland into Scotland via the Clyde and Galloway; and to Yorkshire via the Ribble-Aire gap; from the Dublin area by two routes across north Wales and Shropshire to the Cotteswolds and S. England. The type lasted long in Scotland, and moulds (showing local manufacture) have been found in the N.E. (see Fig. 32 in this Essay, and Childe, *Prehistory of Scotland*, p. 97).

[7] B. R. S. Megaw and E. M. Hardy, *Proc. Prehist. Soc.*, 1938, p. 280, map, Fig. 7.

halberds in Britain reveals similar (but much fewer) foci of commercial activity, and, as is well known, these weapons also were widely spread in Europe.[1]

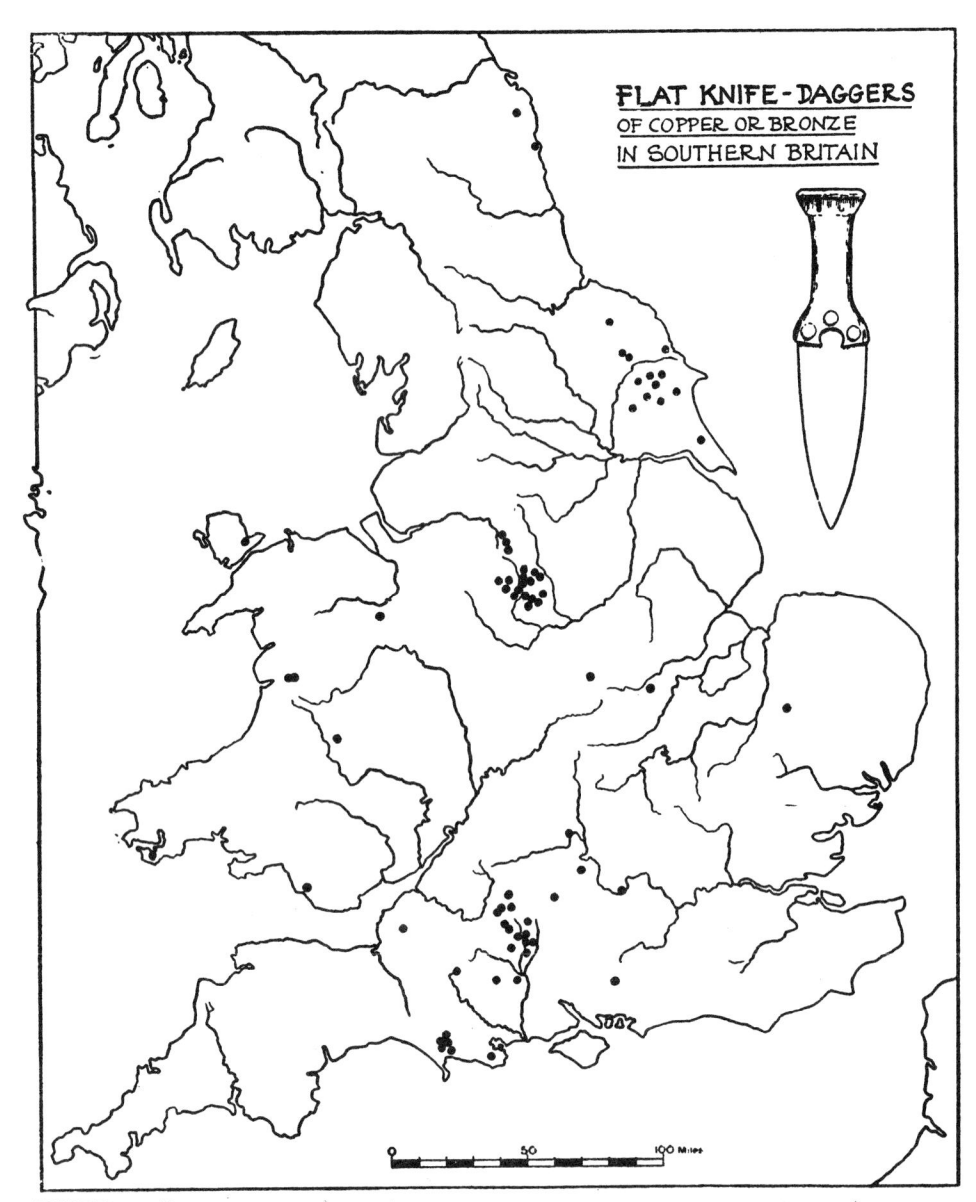

FIGURE 20.—DISTRIBUTION OF FLAT RIVETED COPPER OR BRONZE KNIFE-DAGGERS ATTRIBUTED TO THE EARLY BRONZE AGE IN SOUTHERN BRITAIN. (Page 45. Illustrated also in Fig. 39, 2.)

By Cyril Fox (1943). Based on Fox and Grimes, *Arch. Camb.*, 1928, Fig. 7, p. 150, and register, pp. 161–74; also on Piggott, *Proc. Prehist. Soc.*, 1938, p. 59, Fig. 2, and pp. 59–60, 97–8.

Knife-daggers with ribs, grooves and incised ornament are omitted, as are late (Middle Bronze Age "A") examples associated with burials of the "Wessex" culture. Nine additions have been supplied by Lily F. Chitty.

[1] S. P. O'Riordain, The Halberd in Bronze Age Europe, *Archaeologia*, 86, p. 195 ff., *esp.* maps, Figs. 54 and 58.

This intense Irish activity in the manufacture of bronze tools for export appears to have ended as far as Lowland Britain is concerned about 1600 B.C. Mention was made in the Introduction of the establishment in central Europe of a flourishing bronze industry (based on the earlier copper culture), the type-station of which is Aunjetitz (Map A). Here was produced a beautifully formed axe, broad-bladed with cast flanges, more effective as a tool

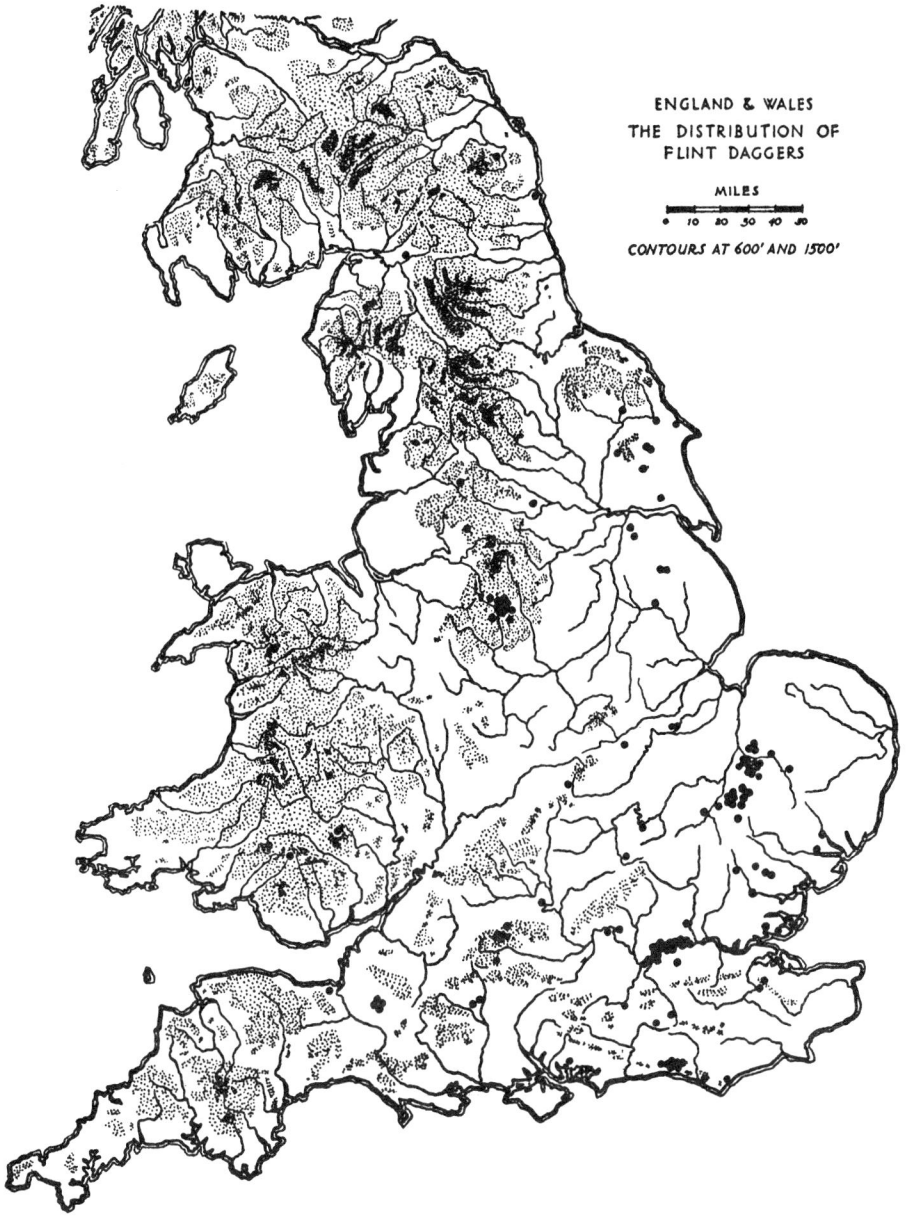

FIGURE 21.—DISTRIBUTION OF FLINT DAGGERS OF THE EARLY BRONZE AGE IN SOUTHERN BRITAIN.
(Page 45. Illustration in Fig. 39, 3.)

After W. F. Grimes, " The Bronze Age Flint Dagger in England and Wales," *Proc. Prehist. Soc. East Anglia*, 1931, Vol. VI, p. 343.

than the early Irish types. Britain's entrepôt trade familiarized our merchants with the new pattern, and by this time we had learnt the art of bronze-founding; cast-flanged axes then were produced widely in Lowland Britain and even exported to Ireland, as the map, Plate VII, also by Miss Chitty, shows.[1]

From about 1600–1000 B.C. the influence of Ireland on British techniques was mainly confined to the Highland Zone, the British Isles as a whole being in the forefront of western European cultural development. It may be that the finest craftsmanship in bronze was centred in Ireland throughout the period—witness the 3-foot rapier found at Lissane, Co. Derry[2]; and I hold that Late Bronze Age masterpieces in hammered bronze plate—the British shields—were exported thence. (This was certainly the case with the cauldrons and buckets, involving similar technical skill, produced in Ireland under Hallstatt influence about 600 B.C.)[3]

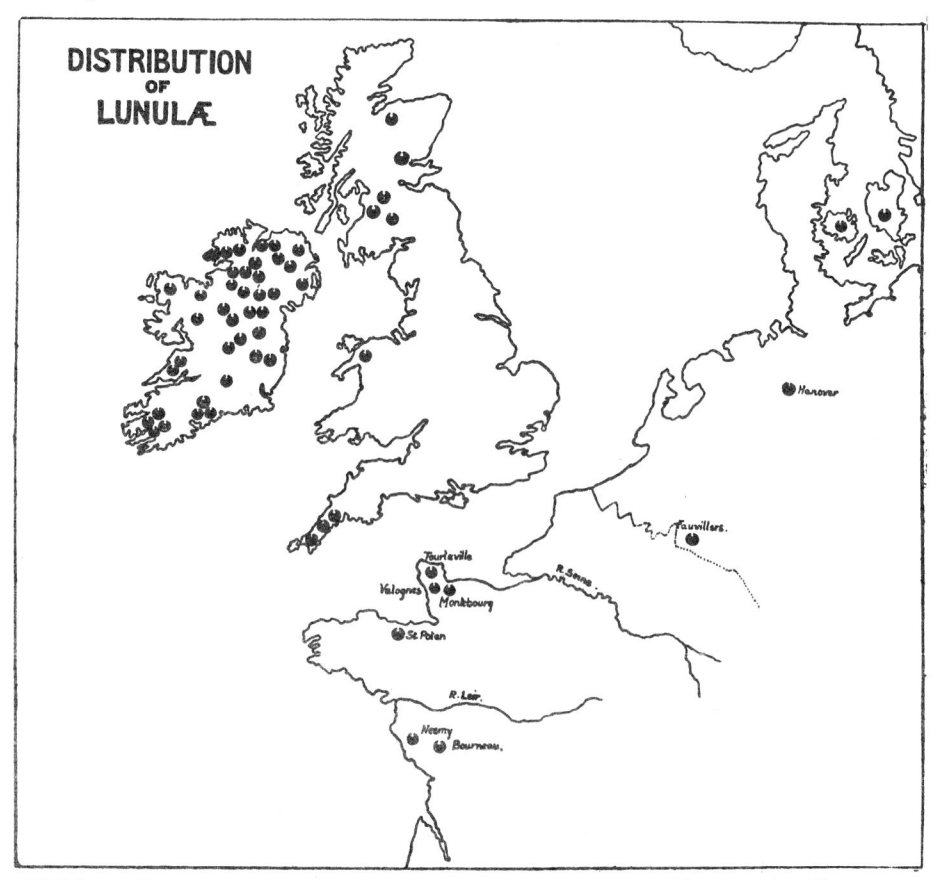

FIGURE 22.—DISTRIBUTION OF GOLD LUNULAE OF THE EARLY BRONZE AGE. (Pages 49, 69. Illustration in Fig. 39, 1.)
Based on G. Coffey, *The Bronze Age in Ireland* (1913), p. 55, Fig. 54, by permission of the Controller of the Stationery Office, Irish Free State. [Several additions have been made (in 1932) to the map.]

[1] The cast-flanged axe represents the first hint in Britain of the change in European trade that limited the use of western sea-ways. It was exported to Ireland probably by the same routes as the flat axe trade used! from north Britain to northern Ireland and from north Wales to Meath. The two maps have much in common, despite their contrasts.

[2] Evans, *Ancient Bronze Implements*, Fig. 318.

[3] For the distribution map of these latter, see Fox, *Antiq. Journ.*, 1939, Pl. lxxviii, and p. 382. For Irish influence on the development of a British technique see a paper on the bronze socketed sickle, Fox, *Proc. Prehist. Soc.*, 1939 (distribution map, Fig. 11, and p. 238).

In its later phases the Irish trade to Lowland Britain, deflected apparently by the commercial importance of the Bristol Channel coasts, followed a southerly route, by sea up that Channel, instead of across Wales. Evidence of this will be found in the above papers.

The history of the Irish gold trade follows a somewhat different but not less interesting course. A well-known distribution map, that of the gold lunulae (Figure 22, after Coffey) of the Early Bronze Age illustrates this Irish trade radiating N.E. and S.E. across Britain to the continent, the channels of absorption or transmission being Scotland, Wales, and Cornwall. No lunula has been recorded from the Lowlands of Britain, and gold objects of this phase are relatively uncommon here. In the next phase, the Middle Bronze Age, much of the Irish gold was intercepted by the Lowland civilization now launched on its path of independent development (Figure 23). At first sheet gold seems to have been imported, and "made up" by Wessex smiths.[1] Later, when bar gold-work in the form of "Tara" torcs was fashionable, Lowland Britain, principally Wessex and East Anglia, absorbed much of the available Irish export, the route thereto being that across North Wales, which had then been in use for some 600 years. As O. G. S. Crawford showed,[2] the continental market for these torcs was northern France; Towednack (Penwith) hoard, which includes two such, suggests that the gold traffic in them may have followed in part the sea-road of the lunulae to Brittany.[3] In the third phase, the Late Bronze Age, the gold trade increased enormously in the Highlands; in the Lowlands the greatest concentration is no longer in Wessex, but in south-east England (Figure 24).[4] The evidence we possess as to the conditions of the time is, I now think, insufficient to explain these changes in distribution.[5]

Tin: The problem of the tin required by the bronze industry in these islands, first in Ireland, then also in Britain, must now be considered. Cornwall is on all grounds the most likely source; and while direct evidence for the exploitation in the second millennium of the tin-stream region from Lands End to Bodmin is lacking, the rich association of this comparatively barren peninsula with the cultural development of the period in on other grounds so inexplicable, that we need not doubt the early discovery here, and by Irish metal-workers, of the essential alloy. To the Early Bronze Age belong no less than four of the gold lunulae, together with several flat or hammer-flanged axes of Irish manufacture. Equally significant is the presence in Cornwall of distinctive elements of the "Wessex" culture of Middle Bronze "A": the superb Rillaton gold cup with its Mycenaean parallels, many grooved daggers, and faience beads. These latter finds suggest that Cornwall became an industrial province of the bronze-dagger folk, playing an essential part in the development of the British bronze industry under the control of the Wessex overlords, who thus lessened the economic dependence of southern Britain on Ireland. In the Late Bronze Age the St. Just hoard, including tin and bronzes with a heavy tin content, provides direct evidence of the industry; the Morvah gold treasure reveals the persistence of Irish activities, while finds of axes from Wales, France and Spain indicate widespread trade for which the industry was the obvious magnet. Deverel-Rimbury wares tell the same tale; it was not the lure of farming land which brought their makers to the far west.

Cornish tin became known to literate Mediterranean (Greek) trading communities not later than the fourth century B.C., and references thereto of varying value by Greek and Latin writers survive. The Iron Age "B" concentration in Penwith (Lands End) shown on

---

[1] On this subject Piggott's study of the Wessex *entrepreneurs* is illuminating: *Proc. Prehist. Soc.*, 1938, pp. 77–80. *Cf.* C. F. C. Hawkes, *Foundations*, pp. 323–4, 377.

[2] In *Proc. Soc. Antiq.*, 1911–12, p. 41, with map.

[3] Hencken, *Cornwall and Scilly*, p. 287; Hawkes, *Man*, 1932, 222; Maryon, *Proc. Roy. Irish Acad.*, 44, p. 206.

[4] The late date of ribbon torcs (included in Fig. 24) has recently been questioned, e.g., by Childe, *Prehist. Comm.*, p. 125 (with references); but the evidence for earlier date is not convincing.

[5] For the cause of the shift northwards, the disturbed condition of the Lowlands in the Late Bronze Age was suggested in previous editions of this Essay; but insufficient weight was attached to the fact that the chief aggregation in the Lowlands was then in S.E. England, the area most liable to oversea raids and intrusions.

Figure 11 is probably mainly due to Celts from the Atlantic seaboard of the Continent attracted by the tin trade,[1] and archaeological evidence for the period, in tin streams and in the workshops of hillforts, is adequate. Native control seems to have persisted for a long time after the Roman conquest of Britain; but finds dateable in the late third and fourth centuries A.D. suggest that the exploitation of Cornish tin then became of more direct importance to the Roman government.[2]

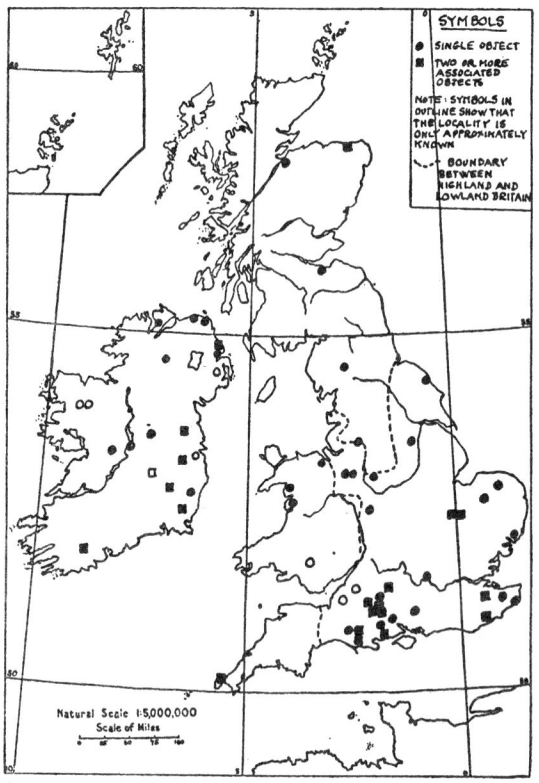

FIGURE 23.—DISTRIBUTION OF GOLD OBJECTS OF THE MIDDLE BRONZE AGE IN THE BRITISH ISLES. (Page 49.)
By L. F. Chitty and C. Fox (1932), using (*inter alia*) O. G. S. Crawford in *Proc. Soc. Antiq.*, Vol. XXIV, 1911–12, p. 41, Fig. 2 (for Tara torcs); and E. C. R. Armstrong, *Catalogue of Irish Gold Ornaments*, Dublin, 1920.

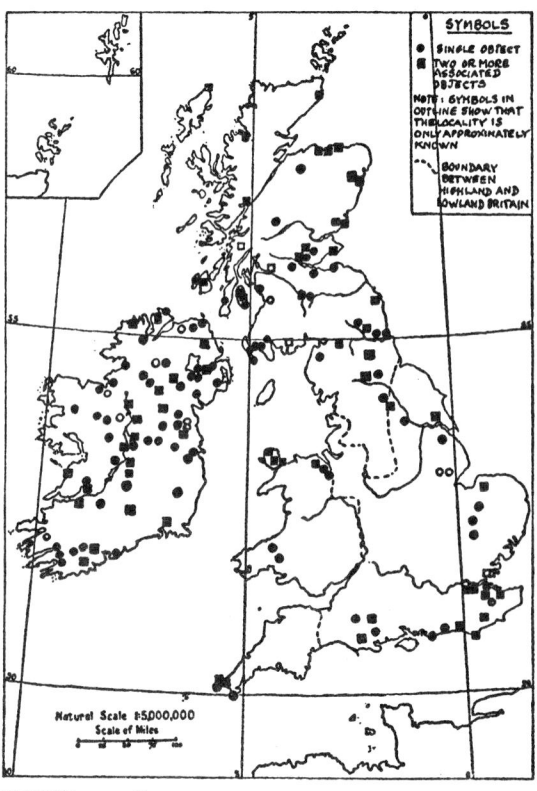

FIGURE 24.—DISTRIBUTION OF GOLD OBJECTS OF THE LATE BRONZE AGE IN THE BRITISH ISLES. (Page 49.)
By L. F. Chitty and C. Fox (1932), using for Wales, Wheeler, *Prehistoric and Roman Wales* (1925), pp. 166–79; for Scotland J. G. Callander, *Proc. Soc. Antiq. Scot.*, LVII, pp. 162–6; for Ireland, Armstrong, *op. cit.*

The only continental source of tin reasonably close to these islands is Brittany. While there is no evidence that any of the metal used here came thence, the existence of tin streams (as well as copper deposits) in the peninsula accounts for the presence therein of the bronze dagger folk and for the rich culture which they brought to Britain and developed.[3] It also accounts for the very large Breton output of bronzes in the Late Bronze Age. (Cf. Plate X and p. 23.)

[1] E. T. Leeds suggests from N.W. Spain (*Archaeologia*, 76, p. 235).
[2] Hencken, *Cornwall and Scilly*, Chap. V, and maps, provides the basis for this summary account. For various aspects of the subject see also *Antiq. Journ.*, 1936, p. 321; J. M. de Navarro in *Camb. Anc. Hist.*, VII, p. 50 ff., also Hawkes, and Piggott, *supra*.
[3] Piggott, *loc. cit.*, p. 94; Hawkes, *Foundations*, pp. 311–14, and in *Annual of British School at Athens*, XXXVII, 1939, p. 141 ff.

The Climate, Flora and Fauna of Britain

(A) THE CLIMATE OF BRITAIN:

The climate of Britain is essentially damp and comparatively sunless. The wet winds being south-westerly strike the mountains of the Highland Zone first, and this zone gets a large amount of (orographic) rainfall; the total fall ranging from 30 to well over 100 inches a year. On the other hand, the Eastern Plain receives from 18 to 30 inches a year (see Figure 25, from *British Rainfall*, 1930).

It is an important factor in the early use of the western sea route by mariners from the Atlantic coasts of the continent that the prevailing wind in the neighbourhood of these islands is the south-west, permitting during the greater part of a voyage the use of the early form of sail, the square sail, in place of the laborious oar. Conversely, the period of the year when invaders could be sure of getting to Britain from the North Sea coast of the continent is the spring, when east winds prevail.

Climatic Changes: The climate has not been constant throughout our period, but has been alternately of continental and of oceanic type described respectively as " Boreal " and " Atlantic." The sequence, character and dating are based mainly on the researches of Scandinavian scholars. There is evidence that, following the moist conditions which prevailed from the sixth to the third millennia, the climate (*circa* 2000 B.C.) became drier

Approximate Duration.	Continental climatic phases subsequent to last glaciation.	Forest history in Britain. †	Earth movements in southern Britain.	Cultural periods.
B.C. *c.* 7000–5500	" Boreal " phase, dry, warm.	Zone V: pine.	Subsidence begins.	Mesolithic.
	NOTE.—The Boreal-Atlantic transition is the "climatic optimum" of the post-glacial.	Zone VI: pine, hazel.		
B.C. *c.* 5500–2000	"Atlantic" phase, moist, warm.	Zone VII: alder, oak, elm, lime.	Land connection with continent severed, *c.* 5000 B.C.	Neolithic.
B.C. *c.* 2000–700	" Sub-Boreal " phase, drier, warm summers.		Subsidence ends: (*c.* 1800 B.C.).	Bronze.
B.C. *c.* 700– A.D. 200	" Sub-Atlantic " phase, wet, cool summers.	Zone VII–VIII Transition: Herein the *Grenzhorizont* occurs.	Period of unchanging sea-level (*).	Early Iron. Roman.
		Zone VIII: alder, oak, elm, birch (beech).		
A.D. 200 onwards	Present conditions; amelioration of " Sub-Atlantic " phase.			

† For this Zonation see H. Godwin, in *New Phytologist*, 39 (1940), pp. 370-400, esp. pp. 391, 392; and cf. A. G. Tansley, *op. cit.*, 1939, Fig. 38.
* But see footnote, p. 27.

than it is to-day, with warmer summers (" sub-Boreal " phase) and so remained until about 700 B.C., i.e. the closing period of the Bronze Age. The wet cool blustery " sub-Atlantic " phase which supervened is held to have lasted until historic times—and, with ameliorations, to the present day. These changes, presented in tabular form above, seem to have been substantially the same over the north-western European mainland. In the British Isles, however, with its exposed westerly position, close correlation with the mainland in vegetation cycles has not proved possible. This is because the drier phases were never dry enough here seriously to restrict forest growth, and in the wetter phases, favourable to forest on the continent, upland forests were ousted by peat in our Highland Zone. The forest succession in the Table is part of that worked out for southern Britain on the basis of pollen analysis; it masks a regional (Highland and Lowland) differentiation.[1] The Zonation scheme, proposed by H. Godwin, has been correlated by him with archaeological finds of prehistoric objects in peat deposits.

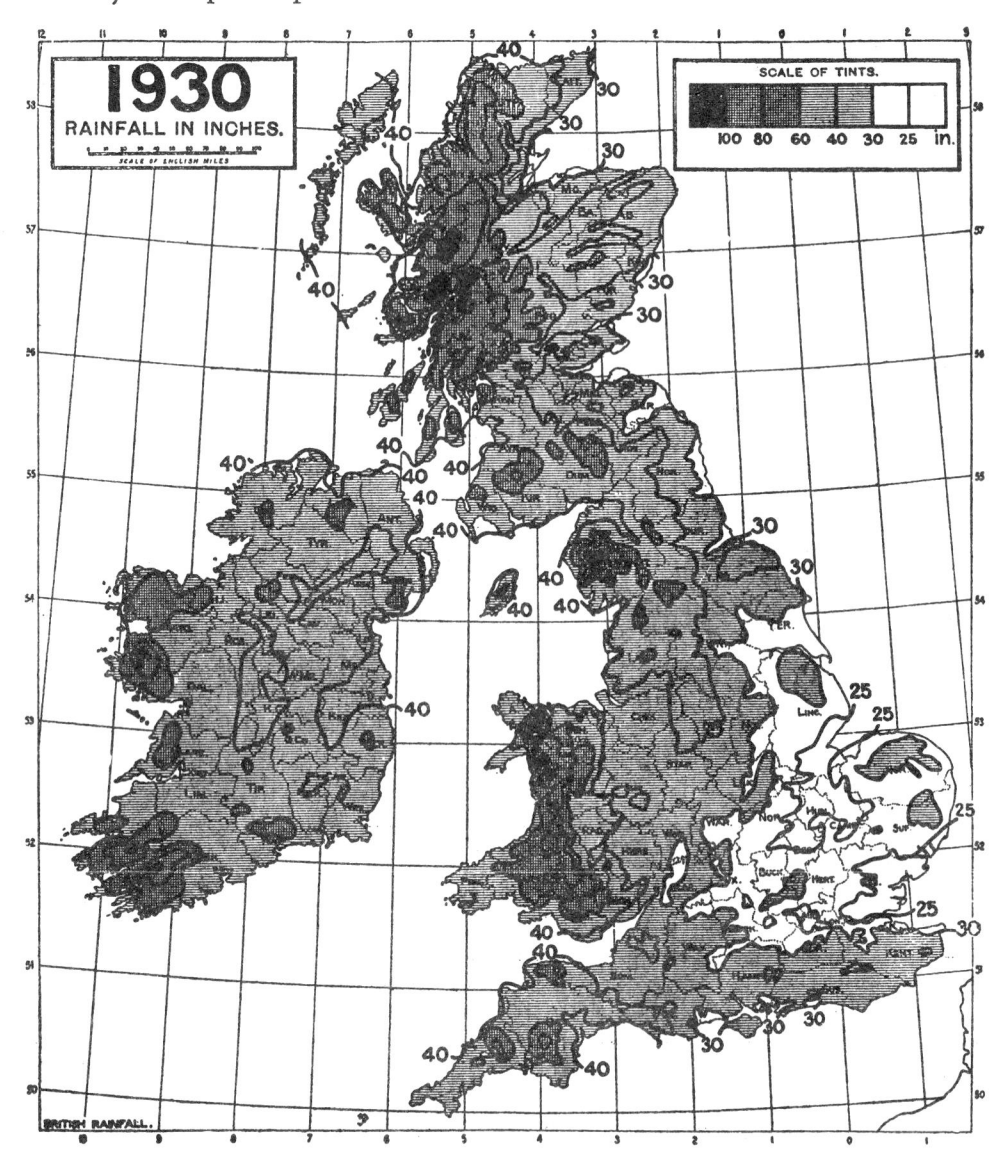

FIGURE 25.—DISTRIBUTION OF RAIN IN THE BRITISH ISLES DURING 1930. (Page 51.)
From *British Rainfall*, 1930, by permission of H.M. Stationery Office.

[1] For the British evidence, see C. E. P. Brooks, *The Evolution of Climate*, 1925; *Climate through the Ages*, 1926; and " The Climate of Prehistoric Britain," *Antiquity*, 1927, p. 412 ff.; Burkitt and Childe, Chronological Table, *Antiquity*, June, 1932; L. Dudley Stamp, *op. cit.*, pp. 158–163; see also H. Godwin in *The New Phytologist*, 1934, p. 39, for S. Baltic correlations; in the same Journal, 1940, p. 396, for difficulties attending recognition of the Sub-Boreal of Blytt and Sernander in Britain, and p. 388 for regional differentiation in connexion with the " forest succession."

The influence of the British Climate: The surface conditions in a highland area tend in any case to limit arable farming and to encourage pastoral farming, but the great contrasts between the rainfall in the Highland and Lowland Zones of Britain respectively render the economic life of the two areas unusually distinct. This has the effect of enforcing the physical barrier between the two zones; invaders from the lowlands have not only to conquer the hill area, but must change their mode of life.

The dampness of the climate generally has an important effect on the distribution of population; it renders suitable for arable cultivation in the lowlands a whole range of light soils—sandy soils and chalk hills where the humus is very thin; crops on such soils in a drier climate would suffer severely from drought.

(B) THE FLORA OF BRITAIN[1]:

Three factors—climatic, edaphic (soil), and biotic (animal activity, man and grazing animals in particular)—determine the vegetation in a given region. Of these, the first two are primary, determining the " climatic climax " type of vegetation—the highest, that is, which a given region is capable of supporting. The activities involved in the third factor may prevent vegetation in a particular area from reaching its climatic climax, stabilizing it at some lower stage of development; or, if it has reached the climax, reducing it to a lower stage.

Luxuriant vegetation has always been a marked feature of a southern British landscape, the climatic climax of the Lowland Zone being the deciduous summer forest association (oak or ash or beech) of Western and Central Europe.[2] The climatic climax vegetation of the Highland Zone is complex. On the lower hill slopes and the valleys of southern Scotland and Wales this same deciduous forest association is dominant; in northern Scotland the forest consists of pine-birch associations—for the area belongs to the region of North European coniferous forests. Again, in the highland region the climatic factors involved in altitude, and (on the coast) exposure to sea winds, fix limits above or beyond which woodland does not extend, the climatic climax vegetation in such areas being moorland or heath-land, or maritime or mountain grass associations; the moorland areas of Britain are very extensive.[3] Such are the broad contrasts.

Turning to the edaphic—soil—factor, this is seen to be of especial importance, from our point of view, in the Lowland Zone. The natural vegetation of the better-drained soils (sands, gravels, chalk, limestones) appears to have covered a wide range of plant communities: heaths, dominated by *Calluna vulgaris* often interspersed with birch; grassland; ashwoods; woods of beech and yew with little or no undergrowth; " dry " oakwoods (Durmast Oak, *Quercus petraea*) associated with birch or holly and with thick but patchy undergrowth. The natural vegetation of the ill-drained clay soils is " damp " oakwood (Common Oak, *Quercus Robur*) associated with hazel, blackthorn, hawthorn, briars and brambles, the undergrowth being very dense. An intermediate soil-type, loam, is of

---

[1] This section is based on Tansley, *Types of British Vegetation*, 1911, and his *Practical Plant Ecology*, 1923, Chap. V; and owes much to my friend Mr. H. A. Hyde, M.A. The following have also been consulted: Clement Reid, *Origin of the British Flora*; Dunn, *Alien Flora of Britain*; Hilda A. Wilcox, "A Map of the Prehistoric Woodlands . . . of England," in *Studies in Regional Consciousness and Environment*, Oxford, 1930; E. Price Evans, Cader Idris, *Journ. Ecol.*, 1932; A. S. Watt, " Ecology of British Beechwoods," *Journ. Ecol.*, 1923–24–25; T. W. Woodhead, " History of the Vegetation of the S. Pennines," *Journ. Ecol.*, 17, 1929, pp. 1–34; *Map of Roman Britain*, 2nd ed. Ordnance Survey; and Fleure and Whitehouse, *Arch. Camb.*, 1916, p. 108 ff. Tansley's monumental work, *The British Islands and their Vegetation*, 1939, has been consulted for this (1943) revision.

[2] Tansley, *op. cit.*, 1939, pp. 162–164.

[3] And, indeed, on the Atlantic fringe extend down to sea level to the total elimination of the woodland zone (H.A.H.).

importance; it naturally carries oakwood (p. 79). Wet lands other than claylands are fens—the East Anglian Fen covers 1,300 square miles—which carry shrubby woodland with sedge, bordered by reedswamp; marshlands, rush-encumbered, in places dense with alder and sallow, and lowland moors (wet heath) as in the New Forest, where bog moss is dominant, with alder scrub.

The shales and sandstones so common in the Highland Zone carry the durmast oakwoods; the peat and peaty soil above the tree line (1,000–1,500 feet) in this zone varies from a few inches to 30 feet in depth, and carries cotton grass or deerhair sedge, less frequently bog-moss, as dominants. Drier and ocean-facing portions of these extensive and often dreary wastes show the heath community (*Calluna*). Man cannot support himself on such peaty soils. Dry ridges and summits are frequently dominated by bilberry (*Vaccinium Myrtillus*).

The question as to how far grassland or heathland are " climatic climax " associations introduces the biotic factor. Our pasture lands for the most part are areas, it is held, where trees could and would grow were their seedlings not eaten off as soon as they appear. The prevailing opinion appears to be that, prior to the appearance of Neolithic man and his domestic animals, there was very little if any open country (country free from forest trees) in Lowland Britain.

Modifications resulting from Climatic Changes: The changes in climate already referred to, in addition to producing the " forest succession," caused modifications in the vegetation of considerable areas, especially in the Highland Zone. Generally speaking, the sub-Boreal phase down to 700 B.C. favoured heathland rather than moorland, and encouraged forests at a higher level than in the sub-Atlantic Time which followed. Pine forests were very extensive in the north during the sub-Boreal period, which is accordingly known as the Upper Forestian. Godwin considers that the " blanket peat of the Pennines, the Welsh mountains, Dartmoor and Bodmin Moor was very largely the result of the sub-Atlantic climate, whilst the tree layers " (pine and birch and yew) " so constantly at the base of this peat are somewhat older "; and H. A. Hyde's researches at Ffos ton Cenglau had previously indicated that upland woods in Glamorgan had disappeared at the close of Godwin's Zone VII. During the latter part of the period covered by our survey, then, the high plateaux and mountains were mainly treeless.[1]

The Relation between Vegetation and Human Distribution: We may now consider the relation between vegetation and human distribution as shown on our maps. The Beaker map, Plate III, is a convenient one for this purpose, since it represents an early phase of culture in which we may suppose man was more at the mercy of his environment than in later times. We observe that four of the eight important segregations—on the Wolds of Yorkshire, in the Peak district, in the Salisbury Plain-Dorset region, and in Sussex—are on the chalk or the carboniferous limestone. The finds in the Cambridge region are also partly on the chalk.

Why did Man choose these uplands? To-day the chalk downs (where not covered by clay) and the limestone hills are nearly always bare of trees; wide expanses of short springy turf, perfect pasturage for sheep. Can we suppose they were always treeless and it was open country that Man preferred?

The chalk downlands, in Wessex and in Sussex, have yielded to air photography and field observation ample evidence that they were extensively cultivated in the Early Iron Age (as well as later). The hill-forts of this Age, moreover, whether on chalk or limestone, are sited so as to command wide views, and almost certainly were surrounded by open country. To carry the evidence further back, the careful siting of Bronze Age barrows in every part of

---

[1] Godwin, *New Phytologist*, 39 (1940), p. 395; H. A. Hyde, *New Phytologist*, 39 (1940), p. 232.

the downland, so frequently on " false crests " which appear as skylines from adjacent viewpoints,[1] is such as to warrant the belief that when they were built the downs were clear of timber, or were at least parkland; certainly not forest.

But the ecological botanists, as we have seen, hold that very little, if any, of the downland was originally free from forest. The beech, which, if introduced, is very ancient in S.E. Britain,[2] is the dominant tree of the chalk, clothing the steep slopes of the valleys and escarpments; it typically forms pure high forest in close canopy. Ash woods, yew woods, and box woods occur, and the juniper is abundant in places, forming an open scrub.[3] Ash woods, with wych-elm, hawthorn and hazel, are characteristic of the limestone hills such as the Mendips and the Derbyshire dales, and Tansley has suggested that " the whole of the limestone areas below about 1,000 feet were covered by a primeval ash forest." The open character which the downland had in the Bronze Age and later, then, was mainly artificial —" a biotically determined sub-climax association "—the result of Man's activity and that of his grazing animals.

If the chalk and limestone hills were originally forested, why were they chosen by Man? The answer may more readily be found if the enquiry be extended. The beaker map shows aggregations of finds indicating settlement in low-lying areas such as the upper Thames valley, the Orwell estuary in east Suffolk, the edge of the Fens in west Norfolk and west Suffolk. Now whenever the geology relating to such an area of prehistoric settlement is studied, it is seen that the soil is gravelly or sandy.[4]

Though unlike the chalk or limestone of the uplands, these soils have characteristics in common; they are light and pervious; they are not rich. The plant ecology of sandy or gravelly soils is interesting. Heath is the characteristic feature; ling (*Calluna vulgaris*) is widespread, and gorse is locally abundant. On some of these soils, e.g. the East Anglian district known as Breckland, it is possible that woodland never flourished.[5] On others, such as the plateau or valley gravels, " dry " oakwood is encountered, with birch or bracken. The beech also occurs.

Thus it would appear that Man had no difficulty in accommodating himself to such forest as he met with on pervious soils (chalk, limestone, sands, gravels); these were thus suitable for his occupation.

Significance of the " damp " oakwood: The " damp " oakwood is a different matter. This type of forest was definitely shunned by Man (prior to the closing phases of the Early Iron Age, and again to some extent in the Dark Ages), as is well shown in certain limited areas which have been studied in detail.[6] The Cambridge region may be selected for illustration.

---

[1] Neolithic cairns and barrows conform to no such rules: they were probably placed near to the homes of the living. See, e.g., The megalithic monuments of Gower, *Arch. Camb.*, 1937, p. 159-161.

[2] Mr. H. A. Hyde, who has been working on the identification of charcoals for some years, informs me that all the recent evidence is in favour of the nativity of this species in Britain. See his paper in *Cardiff Nat. Soc. Proceedings*, 68, pp. 46-54, and *cf.* Elsie M. Clifford in *Proc. Prehist. Soc.*, 1938, p. 206 (4).

[3] Mr. Hyde notes (March, 1938): Primeval ash woods may have covered the chalk before the arrival of beech. It has been shown that ash woods to-day are only a developmental stage in the succession of vegetation on chalk. The general succession is: grassland—scrub—ash—oak-wood—beech-wood. Watt, A. S., *Journ. Ecol.*, 12, 1924, p. 145 ff.

[4] For an interesting study of the occupation of lowland gravels, see Leeds, " Early Settlement in the Upper Thames basin," *Geography*, 1928, pp. 527-535. See also Hilda A. Wilcox, *loc. cit.*

[5] For the opposite view, see E. Pickworth Farrow, " On the Ecology of the Vegetation of Breckland," *Journ. Ecol.*, 13, 1925, esp. pp. 126-135.

[6] For example, L. V. Grinsell has examined and plotted over a thousand barrows in Hampshire. He concludes that, so far as is known, there are no barrows on the clay soils. *Hants. Field Club and Arch. Soc.*, XIV, p. 23 and Map iv. A later study by this writer of 2,130 barrows in Wiltshire (*Proc. Prehist. Soc.*, 1941, p. 81 (map) and p. 74), gives similar results.

Figure 26 shows the distribution of finds and constructions of the Bronze Age in a region 40 miles by 40. The belt of country marked as " open " consists of chalk downs and, in the north, sandy heaths. The settlements are on the heaths (Breckland) and on the chalk slopes ; the burials in barrows mainly on the chalk hills. The finds in the Fens are in gravel patches on islands, or represent tools and weapons lost in meres or streams.[1] The barren areas (dotted

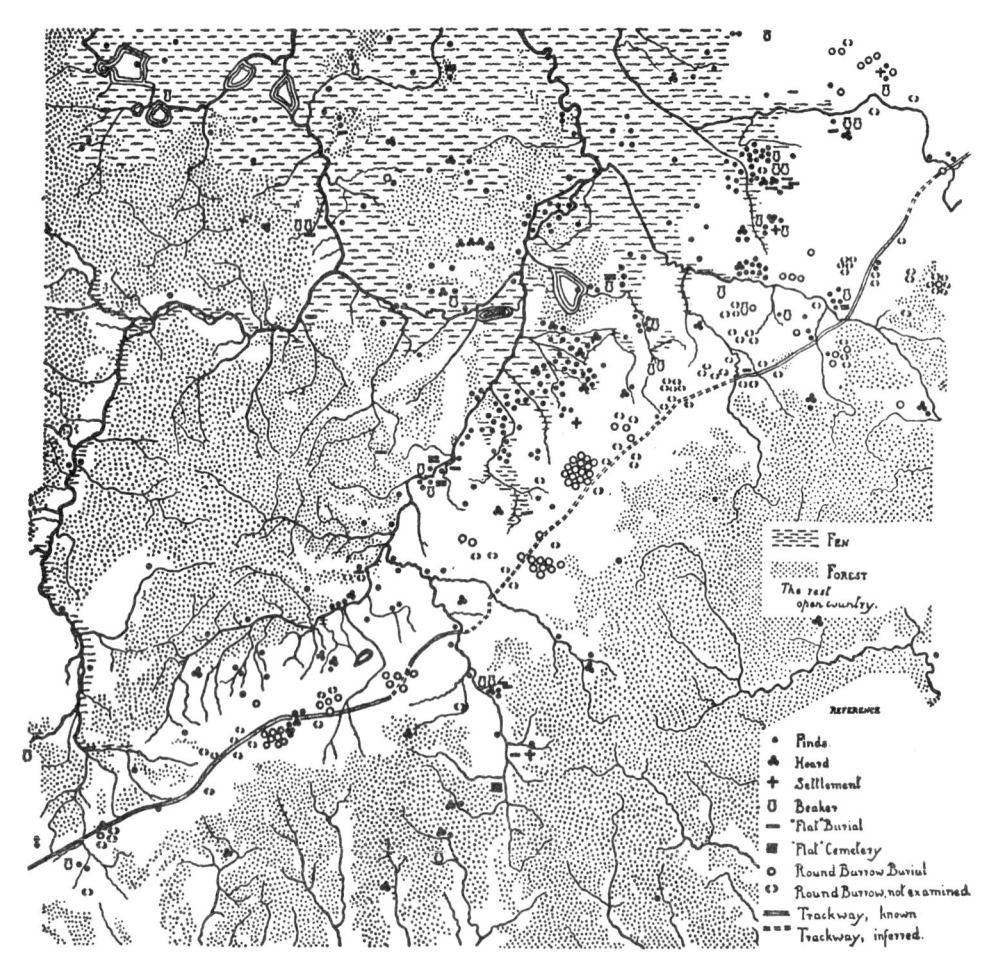

FIGURE 26.—DISTRIBUTION OF FINDS AND REMAINS ATTRIBUTED TO THE BRONZE AGE IN THE CAMBRIDGE REGION. (Pages 55, 66, 79.)
Based on Fox, *Archaeology of the Cambridge Region* (Cambridge University Press), 1923, Map II.
Scale : 1 inch = 8 miles.

on the map) consist of gault or chalky boulder clay, heavy soils unbelievably sticky in winter, caking into ironhard clods in the summer, very retentive of water. On such lands the forest, as we have seen, would be " damp " oakwood—an unending tree canopy of oak with interlacing undergrowth of hazel, thorn, holly and bramble. Apart from occasional settlement on

---

[1] Research by the Fenland Research Committee has shown that prior to subsidence (p. 26) Bronze Age occupation extended over areas of the Fens subsequently waterlogged and overgrown with peat. See (e.g.) *Antiq. Journ.*, 1935, p. 284 ff. For a soil map of the uplands see Tansley, *op. cit.*, 1939, Fig. 32.

gravel terraces beside streams penetrating these claylands, occupation of the great forest belts was limited to a few bronze-workers who required charcoal for their smelting furnaces (these were late in the period).

It was the combination, then, of unsuitable soil (waterholding, muddy) and dense forest that early Man objected to.[1]

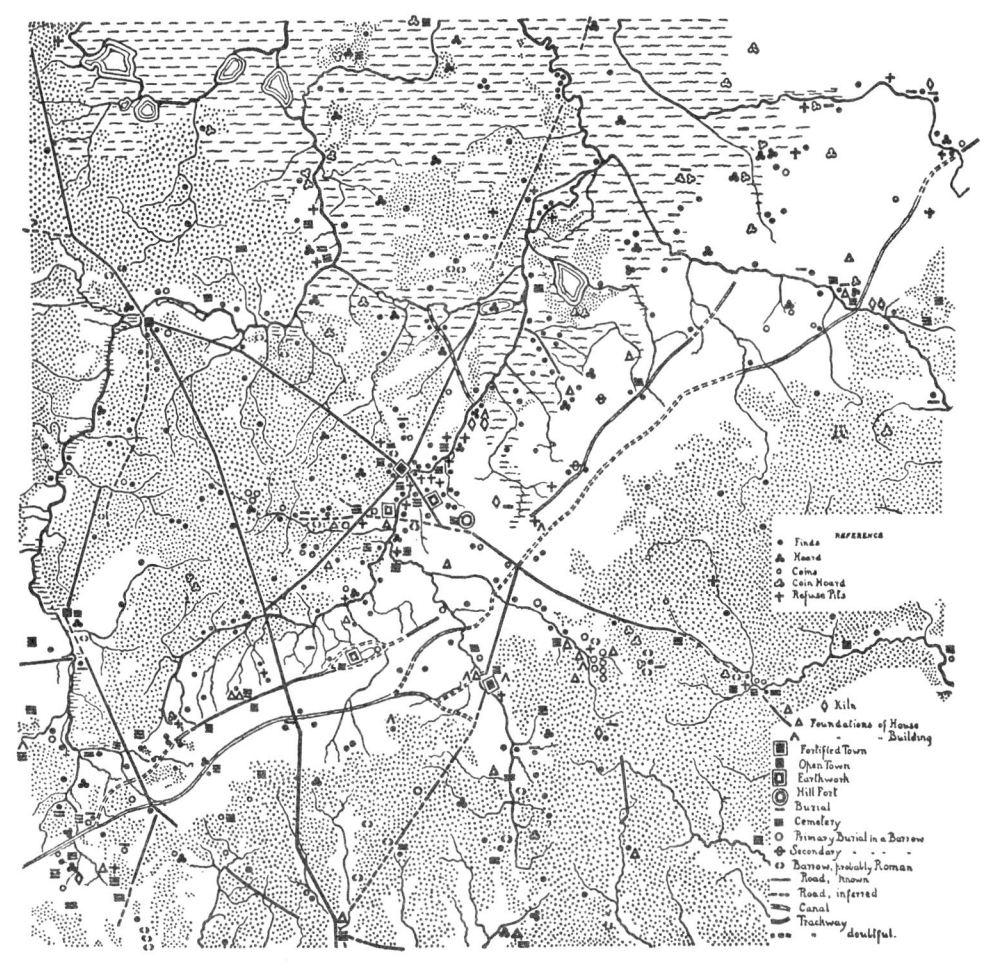

FIGURE 27.—DISTRIBUTION OF FINDS AND REMAINS ATTRIBUTED TO THE ROMAN AGE IN THE CAMBRIDGE REGION. (Page 79.)
Based on Fox, *Archaeology of the Cambridge Region* (Cambridge University Press), Map IV.
Scale: 1 inch = 8 miles.

[1] It is perhaps necessary to emphasize that the presence of Early Man in forest country is not here in question. The megalith builders must have made clearings in thick ash forest on limestone, in the Cotteswolds and the Vale of Glamorgan, for example, before they could practise agriculture; moreover, they must have had plenty of opportunity for dealing with the problem of tree growth, since practically the whole country below the 1,000-foot level, the windswept coastal cliff-lands apart, was forested. The polished stone axe, again, Man's first effective tool, seems to have been developed to meet forest conditions. It is not forest *per se* that inhibits man's occupation, but a deep clayey waterholding soil on which a particular type of forest, "damp" oakwood, is the natural flora. Numerous distributional studies other than our own illustrate this point: the Ordnance Survey Map of Neolithic Wessex, with the clay forest shown, is a good example. An intensive

Such soils as these Cambridge clays, such forests as they carried, were very extensive, particularly in the Midlands and the south-east. Of solid rocks yielding such soil, the most important are the Oxford and Kimmeridge clays of the Jurassic system, which extend diagonally across Britain from Lyme Regis to Lincoln; the Wealden of Sussex; the Gault clays which form a narrow outcrop at the base of the chalk; and the London Clay of the lower Thames valley. Clay-with-flints is found in patches on certain of the chalk uplands, especially on the North Downs. Of superficial deposits the Glacial Drift, covering large areas of East Anglia (and of the above-mentioned Cambridge region), Lincolnshire, Yorkshire, the Midlands, and the lowlands of Lancashire and Cheshire, is the most important.[1]

The greater Dyke systems which seem with few exceptions to belong to the Dark Ages in Britain[2] emphasize the impenetrability of woodlands clothing the heavier soils. All the East Anglian dykes which, starting from fen or riverside, cross the chalk belt, terminate on the edge of the clay-lands (Figure 28). Offa's Dyke, the western frontier of Mercia in the eighth century, forms a continuous barrier both in forest and open country on the comparatively light soils of the Highlands; but when, in Herefordshire, a belt of rich lowland country is crossed, it becomes intermittent, being constructed only in the Saxon clearings. It is a fair inference that the intervening forest here was then considered an impassable obstacle (Figure 30; see also Figure 29). The absence of Bronze Age finds in this part of Herefordshire is in this connection suggestive, but the forts on the foothills hereabouts point to Iron Age clearances (Figure 11).

The distribution of the "damp" oak woodland and Man's dislike for it explains many curious features in the prehistoric maps: the barrenness of the clay belts of the Weald of Sussex for example; and the scantiness of occupation, until the beginning of the Christian era, in the great Midland triangle fronting Wales. It also explains the neglect by successive

study of a Midland region, the Coventry district, is important in this connection: F. W. Shotton, in *Proc. Coventry Nat. Hist. Soc.*, 1938, p. 184 ff. All human communities, of course, throw off groups and families below the poverty line of their particular culture, who scratch a miserable living how they can in the less desirable areas. Evidences of such will certainly be found from time to time on the clays of the Lowlands; but they are negligible. See Fox, *Proc. Prehist. Soc. E.A.*, Vol. VII, p. 162.

That the avoidance of the clay is a rule as near as may be absolute—until the Early Iron Age—in the Lowland Zone seems certain. That it is as fully valid in the Highland Zone is doubtful. Its general application offers no difficulty; Childe, for instance, in his *Prehistory of Scotland*, remarks that "the correlation between the earlier prehistoric monuments and recent alluvial gravels is surprizingly accurate" (p. 7). Replacing "gravel" by "limestone," the same result is noted by a writer in the Anglesey Volume (p. xxxix) of the Royal Commission on Ancient Monuments (Wales).

The general pattern of prehistoric distributions in the Highland Zone again, is, as will be seen (p. 69 ff.), amenable to the same explanations as in the Lowland. But certain recent studies reveal exceptions in detail. W. F. Grimes points out that the long cairn builders in the Black Mountains of Brecknockshire occupied an area "the conditions of which at their worst must have approximated to those of damp oak-wood" (*Arch. Camb.*, 1936, p. 267). I can parallel this, from recent experience in the excavation of an Early Bronze Age barrow on glacial drift at Talbenny, Pembrokeshire (*Arch. Journ.*, 1943, pp.1-32). In another Highland area, the Pennines, W. J. Varley has shown (*Antiq. Journ.*, 1938, p. 154 ff.) that the Bleasdale Circle, a work of the Middle Bronze Age, was constructed on a boulder-clay site.

It is much to be hoped that further research in various parts of the Zone may enable us to learn more about the occupation of the claylands, and the reason therefor.

[1] The references to outcrops of Chalk and other important rocks in this paper will not be found to coincide with the record of the ordinary "solid" geological map of Britain. This is because this map necessarily ignores the superficial deposits, in particular the Glacial Drift; and it is a disadvantage that no general "Drift" map of Great Britain has yet been prepared which shows its distribution and extent.

[2] Certain large scale dykes near St. Albans and Wheathampstead are of the Early Iron Age. See R. E. M. and T. V. Wheeler, *Verulamium*, 1936, Soc. Antiq. Lond., esp. pp. 14-22. These and other loose-knit defences of Belgic towns, as at *Camulodunum*, Chichester, and probably at Minchinhampton, Glos.—see Elsie M. Clifford, *Trans. Bristol and Glos. Arch. Soc.*, 1938, p. 300—simulate "running earthworks" proper, which are frontier delimitations, or which protect districts.

vigorous lowland cultures of the Midland Gap, between the Pennine and Cambrian barriers, which leads to the estuaries of the Dee and Mersey, and the Irish Sea. By a remarkable chance this tongue of lowland is composed of Triassic and Glacial clays, and was consequently dense forest; it lies in front of the south Lancashire and Cheshire drift-plain, originally a morass of water-filled pans resting on boulder-clay.[1] Such trickle of traffic as passed through the Midland Gap seems to have followed the Malpas and Peckforton Hills to the Mersey estuary.[2]

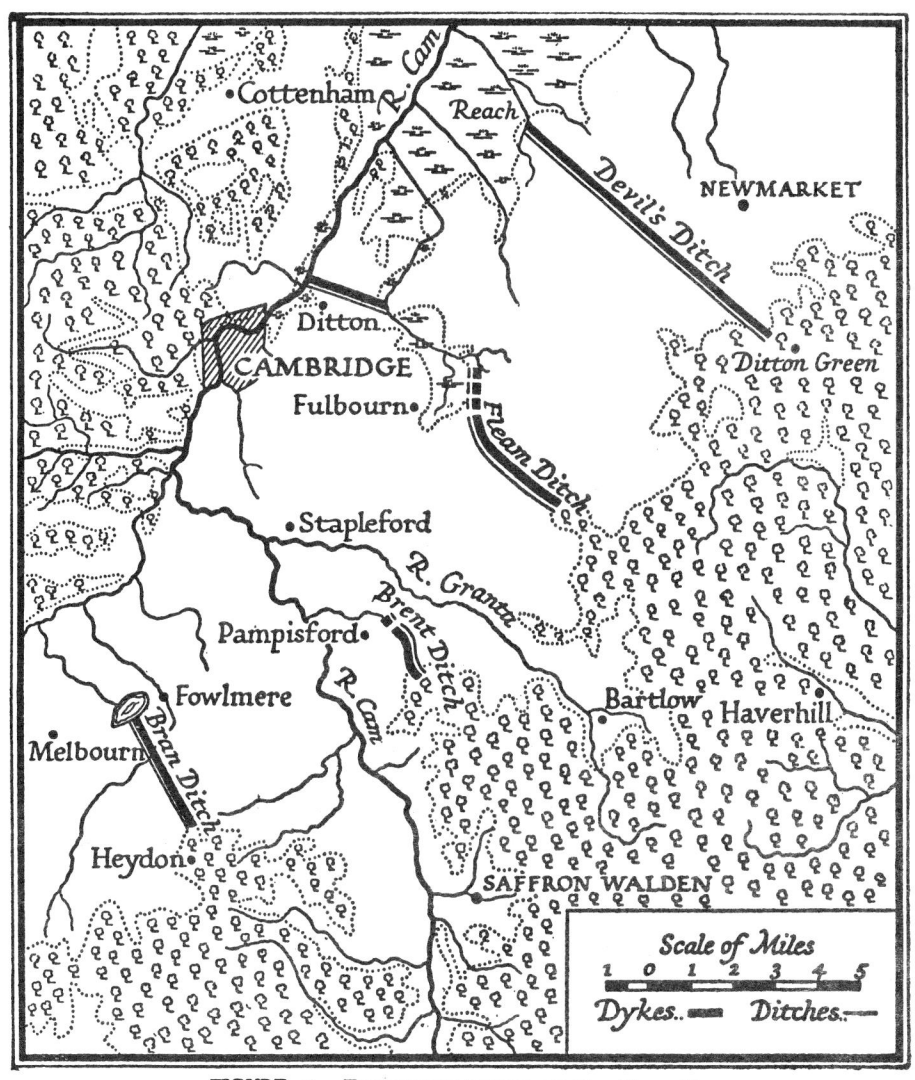

FIGURE 28.—THE CAMBRIDGESHIRE DYKES. (Page 58.)
After Fox, *Antiquity*, 1929, p. 137, Fig. 1.

To this belt of forest Ireland owes her comparative immunity from cultural intrusion or military conquest as from Britain in early times; it blocked the only easy route for the lowlander to the shores of the Irish Sea.

[1] Information from Dr. F. J. North, F.G.S.
[2] See p. 70 and W. J. Varley, *Prehistoric Cheshire* (1940), pp. 11–12, and map by L. F. Chitty, Fig. 24 (*b*).

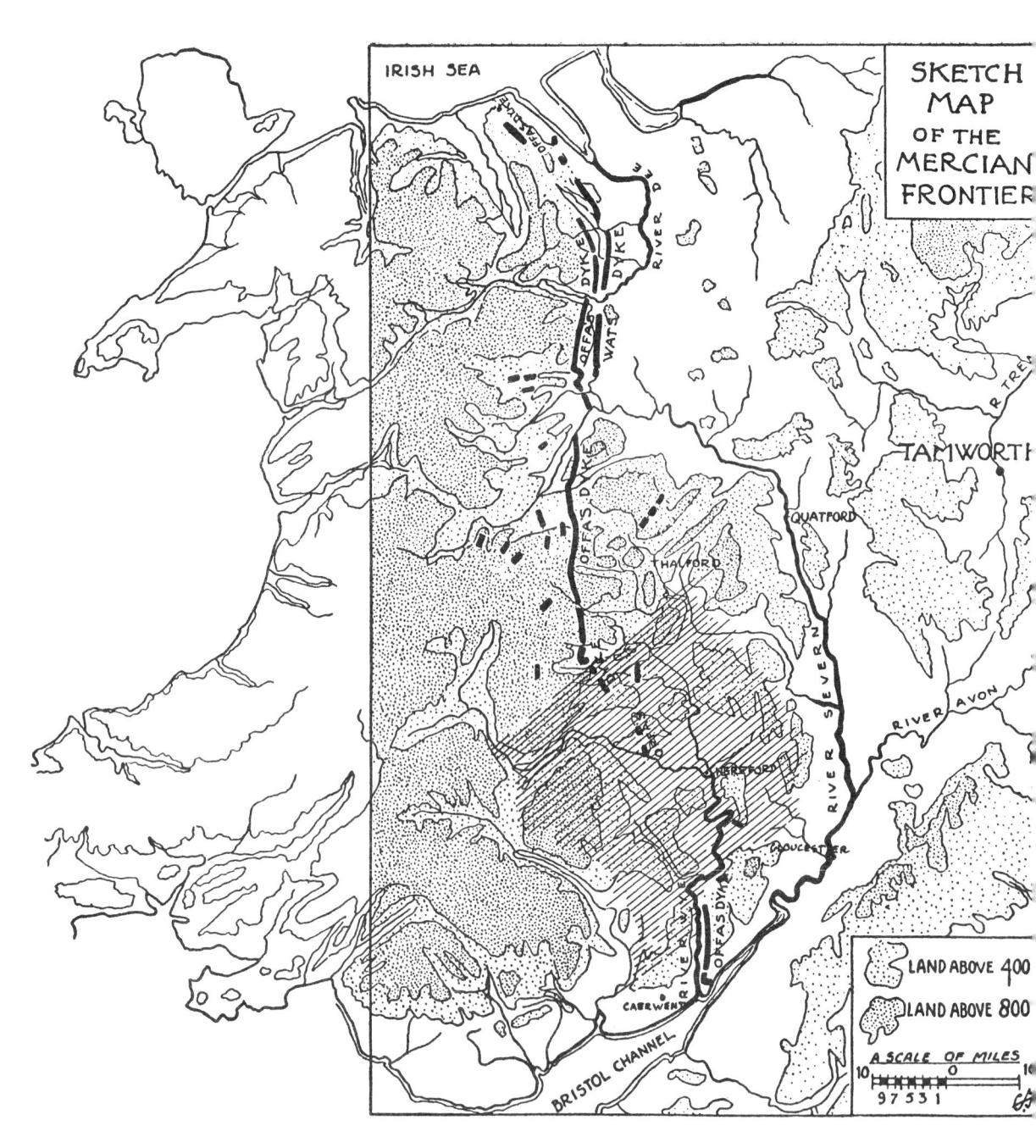

FIGURE 29.—THE FRONTIER DYKES OF WALES IN THE EIGHTH CENTURY A.D. (Pages 33, 58.)
Offa's Dyke, Wat's Dyke, and the cross-ridge and cross-valley Dykes of central Wales are shown. The shaded area represents the outcrop of Old Red Sandstone.

Based on Fox and Phillips, *Arch. Camb.*, 1930, Fig. 27, and embodying a later survey of Wat's Dyke, Fox, *Arch. Camb.*, 1934, p. 205 ff.

The character of central Britain, moreover, militated against such a thrust to the north-westward. The N.E.–S.W. trend of the outcrops means that successive belts of forest have to be crossed by those moving from eastern Britain in this direction; and so powerful was the influence of geological structure, reinforced by the consequent phyto-topographical conditions (see Map B), that such movements are hardly perceptible in any map of culture distributions.[1]

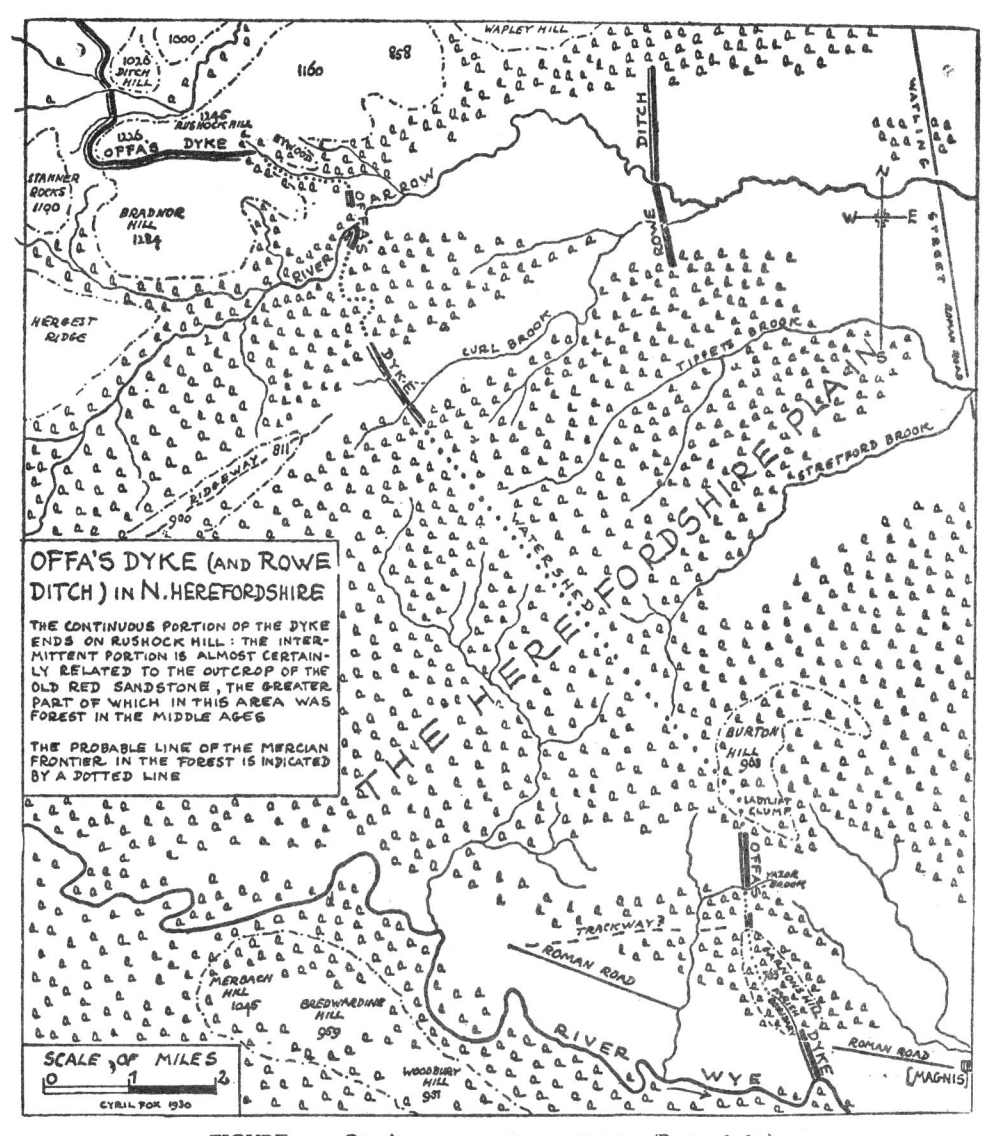

FIGURE 30.—OFFA'S DYKE IN HEREFORDSHIRE. (Pages 58, 81.)
After Fox and Phillips, "Offa's Dyke, Sixth Report," *Arch. Camb.*, 1931, p. 49, Fig. 22.

The only place where readily accessible lowland touched the western sea was near Bristol on the Severn estuary. Hence this was the first point at which the Anglo-Saxons reached it

---

[1] See *An Historical Geography of England*, Fig. 14, p. 95. The chapter by S. W. Wooldridge, in which this figure occurs, is relevant to the subject of this Essay.

(Figure 13). Hence we get evidence of settlers from the Lowland Zone on the other side of this estuary—the Welsh sea-plain—*earlier* than in most places in the Highland Zone. Early Bronze Age beakers of the "A" group from this area, for example, are less debased than those found in other parts of Wales, and closely resemble in decoration examples in Gloucestershire and Somerset; Middle Bronze Age intrusions have recently been demonstrated and there is evidence of peaceful settlement here in the Early Iron Age.[1] This being so, it is not surprising to find a large Romano-British courtyard villa, covering two acres of ground, with good mosaics, on the Glamorgan coast at Llantwit Major.[2]

(C) The Fauna of Britain:[3]

The fauna of Britain, as an important part of Man's environment, bearing directly on his mode of life as hunter or herdsman or in other ways, requires a brief survey. Many formidable animals existed in these islands in the Palaeolithic Age, and in Neolithic times the number was still considerable. The following list, which ignores all the smaller types, probably includes all those of importance from the human standpoint.

Carnivores: Brown Bear, Wolf, Lynx, Wild Cat, Fox, Otter, Badger. The Brown Bear probably survived until the post-Roman period in parts of Britain. It was a valuable food animal, and has played a part in man's religious life from the earliest times in northern Europe and Asia.[4] The representations of the bear on tenth-century "hog-back" stones in Durham and Yorkshire—"the queer fancy that made the muzzled bear climb on the roofs of these houses of the dead," to quote W. G. Collingwood,[5] may have been inspired by such motives. The Wolf appears to have lingered in England and Wales until the fifteenth or sixteenth century, and in Scotland until the close of the seventeenth. Of all British carnivores, it was the most dangerous to man and his livestock; and in some districts there is evidence that extensive woodlands were burned down to exterminate it. We have no evidence when the Lynx became extinct, but it is considered possible that it may have lived until early historic times; it was not extinct in France until the nineteenth century. The Wild Cat is still found in parts of Scotland, and lingered in the wilder districts of Wales and northern England until towards the end of the nineteenth century or even later. The other animals mentioned still survive.

Ungulates: Giant Irish Deer? Reindeer, Elk or Moose, Wild Ox (Urus or Aurochs), Wild Boar, Red Deer, Roe Deer.

The Giant Irish Deer ("Irish Elk") may have survived in places into early Neolithic times. Remains of Reindeer have been obtained from many parts of the country, and it is considered by some that the species may have survived in the north of Scotland until the twelfth century. Remains of Elk (Moose) also have been obtained from various localities,

---

[1] A fine series of well-potted and decorated "A" beakers from Glamorgan can be seen in the National Museum of Wales. For the Middle Bronze Age evidence, see Fox, Two Bronze Age Cairns in South Wales, *Archaeologia*, 87 (1938), pp. 158–164; also W. F. Grimes, A Barrow on Breach Farm, *Proc. Prehist. Soc.*, 1938, pp. 117–120. For the Early Iron Age evidence, see Fox in *Arch. Camb.*, 1927, pp. 44–66. There are, it is true, a few early Celtic bronzes from north Wales, such as the Cerrig y Drudion bowl; but their presence is probably to be accounted for by trade following Atlantic seaways, not settlement.

[2] Wheeler, *Prehist. and Rom. Wales*, Fig. 105.

[3] This section is based on Sir H. Johnston, *British Mammals*; Harting, *Extinct British Animals*; Barrett Hamilton and Hinton, *History of British Mammals*; and owes much to my friend Mr. Colin Matheson, M.A., B.Sc. See this author's *Changes in the Fauna of Wales within Historic Times*, and a paper in *Antiquity*, 1943, pp. 11–18. For the beaver, see also Bulleid and Gray, *Glastonbury* II, p. 646. For domestic animals, see Ridgeway, *The Origin and Influence of the Thoroughbred Horse*, p. 352; J. Cossar Ewart in *Trans. Highland Agric. Soc., Scot.*, 1904, p. 230 ff.; Reid, *Submerged Forests*, p. 63; Rastall, *Agricultural Geology*, p. 302 ff.

[4] O. Abel in *Proc. Linnean Soc., Lond.*, 1935, p. 58 ff.

[5] *Northumbrian Crosses of the Pre-Norman Age*, 1927, pp. 167–169.

and this deer survived in some parts until at least the time of the Roman occupation. The Aurochs, which was certainly familiar to Neolithic Man, is thought to have survived in the north of Scotland till within the historic period. The Wild Boar is frequently figured in La Tène art. It is often mentioned in early records and survived until the seventeenth century in England. Red and Roe Deer still survive in some parts of Britain (the Fallow Deer appears to be a re-introduction of the historic period).

Rodents : Two rodents of some importance are the Hare and the Beaver.

Caesar mentions the Hare as occurring in Britain, and it figures in brooches of the Roman period.[1] Its smaller relative, the Rabbit, which has had a profound effect on the woodlands of Britain, is probably an introduction of the Norman period. There is ample evidence of the presence of the Beaver in this country in prehistoric times, but it appears to have become scarce early in the historic period; in Scotland and in Wales it probably lingered until the thirteenth or fourteenth century. The periodic outbursts of rapid multiplication which characterize *Microtus agrestis* and some other small rodents may have had a considerable effect at times on primitive pastoral and agricultural communities, as they still have to-day.

Birds : In addition to these mammals, various birds now extinct or rare in Britain were probably common and widely distributed. The Golden Eagle, and in coastal districts the White-tailed Sea Eagle, were probably familiar sights to prehistoric Man. Remains from the Glastonbury lake village indicate that Pelicans were found in that district almost down to Roman times, and there are earlier remains of the bird from other districts. Such types as the Great Bustard, the Spoonbill, and the Crane may have contributed to the food supply of early Man, as we know they contributed to the food and the sport of his medieval successors.

Domestic Animals : The chief domestic animals were undoubtedly present not later than the close of the Neolithic phase. The horse, though it flourished in Palaeolithic times in Britain, may have become extinct and so have been reintroduced. Ridgeway holds that until the Iron Age was well advanced the only horse in Britain was the Celtic pony, which still lingers in the Hebrides, Connemara (Ireland), the Shetlands, etc. Whether wild sheep inhabited Britain is uncertain; some authorities think that they did, but the general trend of recent opinion is to the contrary. The goat is one of the most destructive of mammals to young vegetation; within 300 years of its introduction to St. Helena in 1513, it had been so effective in preventing new growth to replace that cut by man, that what was once an island of luxuriant vegetation had become a barren waste. In this country Leland about 1540 commented on the bareness of once wooded hills round Strata Florida, stating that after the woods were cut down the goats so bit down the young growth that it never grew " but lyke shrubbes." The breed of dog known as the Irish Wolfhound, a fine Romano-British representation of which, in bronze, was found at Lydney, Gloucestershire, is doubtless the British hunting dog described by Strabo, as being in demand for export.[2]

Biotic Influences on Man's Distribution : It is probable that wild animals and epizootic disease intensified early man's distaste of the wet forest lands, which we have seen that he avoided. He learnt by experience that if his sheep strayed for any length of time into such lands, they sickened and died of liver-rot,[3] a disease known to-day to be most prevalent in low wet grounds. He himself, doubtless, under similar conditions, suffered from ague

---

[1] We cannot be certain whether Caesar's reference (*De B.G.*, V, § 12) is to the Mountain Hare (*Lepus variabilis*) or to the Brown Hare (*L. Europaeus*). Some consider the latter to have been introduced by man, possibly as late as Roman times (C.M.).

[2] Strabo, IV, ch. V, 2 : Lydney Report, *Soc. Antiq., Lond.*, 1932, p. 88.

[3] See Appendix by Mr. Colin Matheson, p. 94.

(malaria, due to the *Anopheles* mosquito, an inhabitant of stagnant pools)[1] and from rheumatism, a disease of wet lands. In the " damp " oakwood his natural enemies, wolf, boar and bear were most at home, and attacked him more easily, and the charge of the Urus was difficult to escape. Thus, though Man the hunter may have ventured in search of food into the bad lands, the less he had to do with them the better pleased he was.

The General Distribution of Population in Britain

We have now marshalled a considerable body of evidence likely to help us to a correct estimate of the importance of the various factors governing the distribution of population in Britain generally in early times.

For the completion of this task something more is required than is provided by the maps showing the distributions of megaliths and of beakers, complementary though they be; we need to know the distribution of population throughout at least one culture period in the greater part, if not the whole, of Britain. The Bronze Age is the most suitable culture period for our purpose.

Such a corpus of evidence as is here envisaged was not available (in 1932) in any published form: but it had been collected during the five years 1927–32 for southern Britain (as part of wider schemes) by L. F. Chitty and the writer in collaboration.[2] On Map C then, Miss Chitty's data are set out, necessarily in a very condensed form, the endeavour being to indicate the sites of all structures proved to be of the Bronze Age (*c.* 1900–500 B.C.) and of all portable antiquities of that period.[3]

We may first consider the distribution in the Lowlands.

(*a*) *In the Lowland Zone*: The importance to Man of the chalk and limestone hills of the Lowland, indicated in the beaker map, is in this massed map fully established. Of those

---

[1] Malaria was prevalent in parts of England until the mid-nineteenth century. The worst districts were the fens of East Anglia, the marshes about Sedgmoor and Huntspill, and Kent along the estuary of the Thames. See Nuttall, Cobbett and Graham-Smith, " Distribution of Anopheles," *Journ. of Hygiene*, 1901, I, p. 4, esp. p. 26 ff., also Ministry of Health Memo. 230/MED (Revised October, 1942). Mr. Matheson informs me that there is contemporary evidence for the prevalence of malaria in a Perthshire district in the late 18th century.

[2] The circumstances of the writer prevented these schemes from materializing, and the distributional work carried out by Miss Chitty since 1933 has been done independently. Discoveries subsequent to 1932 are not shown on map C. They do not alter the general picture provided by it, save in the Cotteswolds— for this, see comment on p. 68, and Fig. 2.

[3] A uniform blue dot is the symbol used to represent either a single find, a group of associated objects, or a monument of the Bronze Age with its contents.
   The Map includes:—
   (*a*) *Monuments*,
      e.g. Barrows proved by their contents to date from the Bronze Age;
      Circles of stone or earth found to contain urns of that period.
   (*b*) *Settlements* dated by potsherds or other remains of definite Bronze Age character.
   (*c*) *Bronze Age Pottery*, viz., Beakers, Food Vessels, Cinerary Urns, Pigmy Vessels, including the Deverel-Rimbury series and certain Irish urns which probably belong to the Transition to the Early Iron Age.
   (*d*) *Bronze Implements*, i.e.,
      a single bronze or copper implement, weapon or ornament characteristic of the Bronze Age;
      a hoard, viz., 2 or more found together in direct association; and moulds for casting bronze implements and weapons.
   (*e*) *Gold Objects* of the Bronze Age, single and collective finds.
   (*f*) Certain *Stone and Flint Implements* of types proved to have been used in the Bronze Age, viz.:—
      Perforated *Stone Axe-Hammers*, *Mace-heads* and related forms, although some few of these may possibly have persisted into later times (large axe-hammers characteristic of N.W. England and Wales);
      Flint Arrow-heads, Barbed-and-Tanged only, either isolated finds or areas where such forms are plentiful;
      Flint Daggers of Early Bronze type (Beaker series).
   The collaborators have utilized, *inter alia*, the Catalogue of Bronze Implements prepared by Harold Peake, F.S.A., for the British Association, by kind permission of Mr. Peake. This invaluable corpus is now housed in the British Museum, where it may be consulted.

areas described on p. 29 f., the most fully occupied are Salisbury Plain and its extensions to north and south—the White Horse Hills and the Western Downs; the downs of east Sussex; the Yorkshire Wolds. The chalk downs of Cambridgeshire carry a large population which extends northward and eastward on to the light sandy Breckland of East Anglia and the Suffolk heathlands, and westward into the Fens, where finds are mainly on gravel patches in the islands, or in the meres. Settlement becomes more widespread on areas occupied by the beaker folk, and there are extensions to similar areas. The southern slopes of the North Yorkshire Moors and the eastern slopes of the Cleveland Hills are fully exploited.

These aggregations suggest that the choice of country among the great variety of pervious soils available to Man in lowland Britain was largely determined by *extent*.[1] Man, as pastoralist and agriculturist, flourished most where there was a hinterland for his flocks and herds— ample space for him to marshal his defence against the attacks of wolf and lynx—a wide area available for changing the patches of land on which he practised a " scratch " agriculture. The chalk and limestone (together with certain sandy heathlands) gave these unbroken extents: once occupied, Man's domestic animals prevented regeneration of the forests thereon, which decayed and died; woodland thus thinned to parkland, parkland to open country, without the process being realized or appreciated by any one generation.[2] As this change took place the advantages of these areas as grazing grounds became more and more apparent.

The scarcity of finds on those chalk hills which are largely capped with clay, and on which open ground is therefore limited—the Chilterns, the North Downs, the western part of the South Downs—tends to confirm this view. The only area which yields little evidence in support of it is the Cotteswolds, a wide expanse of limestone plateau, fully occupied in neolithic times, but only locally in the Bronze Age (p. 68).

Let us turn to the other important aggregations which the map shows in the Lowland Zone. We may conveniently start at the northern part of the Zone. Crossing the Humber and leaving behind us that thickly populated area, eastern Yorkshire, we notice a string of finds from Wintringham to Brigg on Lincoln Edge close to the Weir Dyke, with a lateral (easterly) extension across the flats to Caistor. Returning to Lincoln Edge we find settlements at Lincoln on the River Witham, near Ancaster where the Edge is gapped by streams, at Grantham where we cross the Witham again, at Peterborough on the Nene, and on the eastern-facing slopes of the Northampton uplands, which are dissected by numerous tributaries of the Nene. Such are the chief groups on the line between the Humber and the upper Thames. Two points strike us about them. The first is that the majority lie on the Jurassic strata and are related to the high ground—mostly oolitic limestone—which is the chief physical feature of this formation hereabouts. This high ground is bordered by claylands (Oxford Clay and Lower Lias) and, therefore, by dense forest. Again, the extension to Caistor leads to the chalk ridge of the Lincoln Wolds.

So far, the distribution seems normal; we appear to be studying settlements necessarily small on small patches of country of the familiar types. But there is a curious feature which needs emphasis. These settlements are on those portions of the open or lightly forested country which lie nearest to rivers or streams. The central, widest, part of the Lincoln Wolds is barren; so is the Lincoln Edge between the streams which gap it; settlement is on the lower slope of the limestone outcrop in Northamptonshire. We perceive a paradox: the greater aggregations, such as that on Salisbury Plain, appear to be on the hills; the smaller are situated at the lowest levels where a suitably open environment can be found.

[1] In the second millennium the influence of accessible supplies of fine flint, in Norfolk, Sussex and Wiltshire, on the concentrations of population must not be overlooked. Mining in the chalk was probably introduced by Neolithic "A" folk, but it continued into Bronze Age times, and the product was widely distributed in Britain. See a useful summary with distribution map, by Clark and Piggott, *Antiquity*, 1933, p. 166 ff.
[2] Cf. Fleure and Whitehouse, *Arch. Camb.*, 1916, p. 128 ff.

It will help us to solve the difficulty if we turn for a moment to an area of chalk downland which was intensively occupied by Bronze Age man and has been studied in detail—the Cambridge region (Figure 26). This map shows that the majority of surface finds of bronze implements, and other objects attributable to the age are located by rivers, or where the chalk downland meets the Fens or by the spring line at the base of the chalk. The Cambridgeshire downs are, however, covered on this map with symbols indicative of Bronze Age activity; these are nearly all burials. Here, I am convinced, lies the explanation. Bronze Age man, whether on Salisbury Plain or any other large extent of upland, or on a small upland like Lincoln Edge, lived as near to a supply of fresh water as he could; he drove his flocks on to the hills, which were essential to him; but most of the finds far from water on the plateaux of the Plain will, I think, prove to be from burials. There is indeed evidence suggesting that this tendency to live near a water supply may be generally true in lowland Britain. For example, the finds on the line of the North Downs in Kent are not on the plateau but on the Lower Greensand which forms the spring line at the foot of the slope.[1]

We have seen that it was possible to travel along the Jurassic outcrop from the Humber to the upper Thames, Gloucestershire, and Salisbury Plain. There is, however, no *continuous* string of finds along the Jurassic outcrop on the massed Bronze Age map or any other; it looks as if only in areas where *settlement* is more or less continuous can we expect to find such continuity in find sites. Where narrow ribbons (ridges) of open country unsuitable for settlement but convenient for traffic occur, finds will turn up only near or at the obstacles provided by rivers, streams, or marshes which have to be crossed;[2] these are the places where in the Bronze Age, as to-day, hamlets or villages were likely to grow up.

If the map be studied from this point of view, it will be seen that there is no continuous find-spot evidence for the great series of ridgeways which converge on Salisbury Plain along the fingers of downland described on p. 31; these ridgeways are certainly of high antiquity (Dark Ages), and almost certainly prehistoric. The Icknield Way, a trackway extending along sandy ridges or chalk downlands skirting forest, from Norfolk by way of the Cambridge uplands and the Chilterns to Berkshire and Salisbury Plain, is a famous example, and yields the best evidence of use in the Bronze Age; but every one of the belts of downland has one. (It is to its *accessibility*, as well as its extent of pastoral land, that the undoubted primacy of Salisbury Plain in early times as a religious centre, in wealth, and in culture must be referred.)[3]

We may now turn to the region of the Thames, which we have reached in our enquiry. The beaker map showed aggregations on the upper Thames and a few sites above London; but the massed map shows that the great river, practically from end to end, from Oxford to Shoeburyness, is marked by a string of finds, the most extended and continuous in the country. The river is bordered by terrace gravels forming dry well-drained occupation sites, but has not, except in certain limited areas, much effective "hinterland." It is thus a type of country favoured by Bronze Age man which we have not yet studied in detail.

The occupation of fishing, which has not hitherto been considered in this paper as an economic factor in settlement, no doubt enabled a fairly numerous Thames-side population to gain a livelihood. Moreover, the Thames-side terraces provide good agricultural land, highly cultivated in the Iron Age, and probably before. But a large number of the finds are from the river-bed itself, and their character renders it probable that the river was a highway, and a very important one; it was a route up which came, in the Late Bronze Age (if not earlier), and thereafter in increasing numbers, goods traded from overseas. It was the natural

---

[1] See an instructive map on p. 124 of R. F. Jessup's *Kent* (County Archaeologies), and D. P. Dobson's *Somerset* in the same series (p. 67). The Late Bronze Age occupation of the uplands of N.E. Yorkshire is to be regarded as the result of invasion-pressure; Elgee, *Early Man in N.E. Yorkshire*, pp. 88-89.
[2] Crawford, *Man and his Past*, p. 144.
[3] Crawford, *op. cit.*, pp. 158-159.

highway from the south-east of England to Salisbury Plain.[1] The density of the finds, moreover, suggests that the river was a traffic way for the everyday comings and goings of the inhabitants.[2]

This possibility is worth further study. The slow-moving rivers centred in the four zones of lowlying lands referred to on an earlier page may represent not merely convenient means of entry for invaders, but important factors in prehistoric life; lowland landways and waterways are taking shape as an accidental but effective network of prehistoric communications. When the natural excellence of both in Britain for transport is considered, it is no wonder the Lowlands tended to unity of culture in prehistoric times! The Humber and the Wash group do not, it is true, show evidences of settlement in their lower reaches, because the last 25 miles or more of their courses are through marsh or fen, but settlements are frequent beside the middle or upper reaches.[3] Moreover, the largest dug-out boats found in Britain come from these rivers, and indicate long-distance river traffic, as I pointed out in 1926.[4]

Thus we see that Bronze Age man occupied sites with the requisite pervious soil, even though the area for pasture or agriculture was limited, if there was fishing and fowling available; and that a further economic stimulus to the occupation of such sites was probably provided by river trade, local and general.

There is striking evidence that the development of human occupation at the high-water mark of a tidal estuary or at the lowest point where hard ground touches the river on either side, a feature of medieval town-siting, started in the second millennium B.C. In the Middle Ages such sites became populous because they provided both a convenient fording place for land-traffic, and a market for the coasting trade carried on in shallow-draught boats. Whether both these reasons operated in our period I am not prepared to say; but it is certainly remarkable to see the aggregations at sites which fall into this category—such as Norwich on the Yare, Peterborough on the Nene,[5] Canterbury on the Stour, Maidstone and Rochester on the Medway, and Bristol on the Gloucestershire Avon.

A recent study has shown that the intensity of coastal settlement in the Ipswich area—the Orwell, Deben, and Stour estuaries—which is a feature of the massed map, has a definite connection with the concentration of population in the hinterland—the Cambridge Region.[6] These estuaries were the main portals of entry for traders and settlers in early times. We may then suggest that the extension of the Yorkshire settlements in the Late Bronze Age down to the sea-shore at good landing places such as Bridlington, Scarborough, and Whitby is largely the result of coastal and other sea trade.

This is problematical; but there are of course coastal sites which we can with some certainty describe as ports, owing their existence to their functions as entrepôts for oversea trade. Among these are Weymouth (Radipole) and Hengistbury Head (Christchurch), the nearest harbours for traders exploiting the Salisbury Plain market.

An interesting little river which, though short, yields evidence suggesting that its mouth was a harbour and its valley a highway is the Itchen, near the head of Southampton Water, leading to the chalk downs at Winchester. In Southampton Water, moreover, we can

---

[1] The traveller would leave the river for the Berkshire ridgeway at Goring gap.

[2] Crawford, *op. cit.*, pp. 145–146.

[3] E.g. on the Humber group of rivers, settlements occur in the York, Ripon, Sessay, Leeds, Wakefield, Doncaster, Haxey and Nottingham areas.

[4] Brigg   (Humber rivers)   48 ft. long.
    Deeping Fen } (East Anglian Fen rivers) { 46 ft. long.
    Warboys   }   { 37 ft. long.

The date of these boats is unknown, but the use of the dugout goes back to Neolithic times in Britain. *Antiq. Journ.*, 1926, pp. 122–151.

[5] Fox, *Archaeology of the Cambridge Region*, p. 85.

[6] Fox, *Proc. Prehist. Soc. East Anglia*, VII, p. 149 ff., esp. p. 161; cf. Crawford, *Geog. Rev.*, 1922, p. 260.

appreciate the limitations of Bronze Age traffic and its dependence on phyto-geographical factors; though land-locked and sheltered, it is mainly bordered by the poorest soils and lowland moors, and hence its shores are largely barren.

The connection shown on our map to exist between intensive human settlement and geological structure was anticipated; but it was hardly expected that the relationship would be so intimate. Two examples may be given. In East Anglia the pattern of the massed find-spots coincides, from Royston to Kings Lynn, with the pattern formed by the outcrop of chalk and of the Tertiary sands of Breckland. In Wessex the indented western boundary of the massed finds coincides with the junction of the chalk or greensand with the Kimmeridge clays.

Interesting as are the occupied areas of our map, the unoccupied are equally important; they confirm the evidence of the beaker map (Plate III) as to the dependence of early man on a suitable environment—his dislike of clay soils and of wet lands generally. If Map C be compared with Map B, it will be seen, for example, that the western margin of the basin of the Humber which is shown as alluvium on the geological maps, is exactly defined by the Bronze Age distributions; the oak forests of Essex, East Anglia, and Kent, and the great triangle of forest lands which forms the Midlands, are virtually barren. No wonder Wales, doubly defended by her own mountains and by this forest barrier, was, save in certain areas, little affected in this period by direct influences from the Lowlands!

It is true that occasional finds do occur in such forest regions as these; but scattered dots mean little on such a small-scale map as ours, where hundreds of finds in the thickly occupied areas fail to be recorded for lack of space. Once an area is completely dotted over, no more finds can be shown.[1] Moreover, it must be remembered that, partly owing to the exceptional diversity of the geological structure of Britain, narrow belts or small patches of well-drained soil are present here and there in wet-soil areas, and detailed analysis far beyond the scope of this paper, and indeed far beyond the geological evidence of soil conditions at present available, is needed if we are to account on physiographical grounds for all evidences of primitive Man's occupation.[2] There are, again, many economic factors which we have only lightly touched on, such as the use of forest by bronze founders in the Late Bronze Age (p. 57). Also, Man has here and there in this Age taken advantage of the inaccessibility of fens and marshes by occupying islets and patches of dry ground, as in the East Anglian Fens.

On the other hand, the map shows that there are areas apparently geologically suitable for early Man's occupation which show scanty traces thereof. The Cotteswolds is the outstanding example. There was, of course, some occupation, for round barrows, probably but not certainly of the Age, are fairly common; but implements are scanty. During Bronze Age times the area was undoubtedly a backwater, but I am inclined, in view of recent discoveries,[3] to regard the barrenness as due in some measure to the imperfection of the archaeological record. In other cases, such as the Forest and Ragstone Ridges (sand) in the

---

[1] Recent developments in technique—the use of very small dots on a finely-drawn base-map, have greatly extended the accuracy, from this point of view, of such records. Cf. in this country, L. V. Grinsell's map in *Proc. Prehist. Soc.*, 1941, p. 81, and on the continent, the maps in *Danmarks Oldtid, II, Bronzealderen,* by Johannes Bröndsted, Copenhagen, 1939. But such delicately drawn patterns are not readily impressed on the mind, and preclude record of sites approximately known.

[2] Rastall, *Agricultural Geology*, p. 165, remarks that the county of York "seems to contain soils of every conceivable kind." Generalization such as is here attempted necessarily involves neglect of minor variations. Cf. Shotton, *Proc. Coventry Nat. Hist. Soc.*, 1938, p. 184 ff.

[3] By Elsie M. Clifford, H. E. Donovan, and G. C. Dunning. See *Antiq. Journ.*, 1932, p. 279 ff., and *Proc. Prehist. Soc.*, 1937, map on p. 160. The fresh evidence gives definition to lines of Bronze Age traffic across the Cotteswolds, linking the Evesham and Oxford Basins, which can only be suggested by our (1932) map.

Weald of Sussex, it is probable that, islanded in forest, they were isolated from traffic routes. Thus they were less desirable than other intrinsically similar but more accessible regions.

(*b*) *In the Highland Zone* : The most striking aggregation in the Highland Zone is in the north. The flanks of the narrow valley of the Tyne and the broad shale and sandstone plateaux and foothills on the south and east of the Cheviots (Northumbria) carried a large population. Occupation extended up the Tweed valley and beyond (p. 71).

The next large settlement area is on the flanks of the Eden valley; at one point this nearly joins up with the north-eastern concentration. A third group of settlements, more diffuse, occupies the area of upland, deeply dissected by rivers, which divides the North Pennine Moors from the South Pennine Moors, and which has throughout historic times provided, in the Aire Gap (500 feet, see Map B), a convenient crossing place in this extended mountain barrier. To the south, on the southern spurs of the Pennines, and at the head-waters of the Derwent and the Dove, is the concentration familiar to us from study of the beaker map. This concentration, as marked on Map C, almost exactly conforms to the outcrop of the carboniferous limestone in this area.[1]

Turning to Wales, it may first be noted that the finds of objects of Irish origin or of Irish type in Pembrokeshire and on the coasts of Merioneth, Caernarvon, and Anglesey justify us in attributing much of the evidences of Bronze Age activity in these areas to the stimulus of overseas trade. The mass of finds at Dublin shown on the margin of the map are of interest in this connection. Finds in or adjacent to the Taff estuary in Glamorgan also suggest continental and Irish trade.[2]

Crawford in 1912 explained the finds of lunulae in Cornwall on the assumption that there was an "isthmus" road from St. Ives Bay to Mounts Bay, the dangers of the sea passage round the cliffs and skerries of Land's End more than counterbalancing the inconveniences of transhipment.[3] Various arguments point to the exploitation of tin deposits as the correct explanation here, but it is probable that transhipment accounts for some of the finds at other places in Cornwall mentioned by him, e.g. Fowey–Padstow. The massed map also affords evidence of this practice on both the Welsh peninsulas, the chance finds and burial mounds on the Lleyn[4] in the north and in Pembrokeshire in the south forming trans-peninsular patterns. The terminals of the Lleyn pattern rest on the mouth of the Llyfni in the north and Traeth Mawr by Portmadoc in the south;[5] those of the Pembrokeshire pattern, less apparent, on Newport Bay in the north and Carmarthen Bay in the south. The routes are indicated, but not defined, on Map B.

Certain finds in the Mersey estuary suggest that this may have been an entrepôt for east-and-west (Irish) trade; and, having regard to the well-established cultural connections between south-western Scotland and Ulster across the narrow North Channel, the close settlement on the shores of the Irish Sea in Galloway was doubtless in part due to the geographical advantages of Luce and Wigtown Bays in relation to this east-and-west trade. So, doubtless, is the concentration on the opposite coast, round Belfast Lough, shown for this reason on the map. (The find-sites here, it may be noted, have been plotted as carefully as in Britain.) Moreover, the mass of finds between Loch Ryan and Luce Bay hints at the use of this neck of land as a trans-peninsular crossing by the north-and-south trade, which thus avoided the Mull of Galloway.

---

[1] Crawford pointed this out in 1912: *Geog. Journ.*, XL, 184.
[2] *Antiq. Journ.*, 1939, p. 389.
[3] *Geog. Journ.*, XL, 1912, p. 196. See the Middle and Late Bronze Age Gold maps (Figs. 23, 24) and p. 49 of the Essay.
[4] See W. J. Hemp, *Proc. Soc. Antiq.*, XXX, p. 167 ff., and Fig. 8.
[5] The only gold lunula found in Wales comes from this route—Ty'r Dewin Farm (Fig. 22).

These coastal settlements can hardly all have been maintained by overseas trade, which at its most flourishing time must have been intermittent. It may well be (on the analogy of Norway, and bearing in mind the sea-going activities of the Celtic saints in the sixth century A.D.)[1] that *local* traffic in the Highland Zone in prehistoric times tended to take to the seaways, and that some of these sites—for example, on the Cumberland coast—are thus to be accounted for. Land communications between the several parts of the Zone are difficult; its upland trackways are exposed, lonely, and dangerous, its lower (coastal) ways difficult and devious. Moreover, if Bronze Age man were in the habit of getting about by sailing or rowing along the coast from bay to bay, occasionally making longer voyages, as for example from Anglesey to Luce Bay by way of the Isle of Man, the community of culture so often apparent between sundered elements of the Highland Zone, and so well marked in the case of the encrusted urns (Plate V), would be explained. It is not unlikely that " curraghs " were then in use.[2]

Taking the most favourable view, we must then regard these settlements as only *partly* accounted for by trade, local or general. There are other reasons for their existence. The structure of western Britain is such that much of the habitable country it affords is on the coast (Anglesey has always been famous for its corn crops), or at all events not far from the sea. Such coastal sites thus have, in addition to the value represented by their geographical situation, an intrinsic (economic) value to farmers and herdsmen and, of course, fishermen.[3]

A striking feature of the find pattern of the Bronze Age in the Welsh mountain area is the greater intensity of inland occupation in the north than the south. This occupation—the Flintshire hills apart—is densest in Snowdonia, on the lower slopes of the Berwyns, on the northern side of the Plynlimon complex, and among the south Shropshire hills. How far it is related to the Irish trade which persisted in one form or another for some thirteen hundred years (and certainly, in so far as it affected lowland Britain, passed through north rather than south Wales), how far to a problematic Bronze Age exploitation of copper in this area, and how far to the undoubted higher fertility of the habitable flanks of intermont valleys in the northern mountains than in the southern, is at present uncertain. The clue to this complex pattern, as far as Early Bronze Age trade is concerned, is afforded by Plate VI (the flat axe distribution), which enables us to distinguish two main streams. From bays and estuaries in north-west Wales traffic crossed the Berwyns to the Oswestry region and descended to the Severn in the neighbourhood of Montford Bridge. From the Dyfi estuary it reached the Severn at Bewdley.[4] It should be noted that, on the massed map, a clearly defined line of finds to the Wrekin district leads from another port where Irish bronzes have been found, the Mersey estuary.[5]

This invites consideration of other similar diffusions. One cannot but be struck by the

---

[1] See an instructive map illustrating the travels of St. Samson of Dol in *Aberystwyth Studies*, XIII, 1934, p. 61 ff., by E. G. Bowen; and O. G. S. Crawford in *Custom is King*, 1936, pp. 195-198.

[2] For the type, see James Hornell, *British coracles and Irish curraghs*, 1938.

[3] Analyses of Bronze Age find-sites in east Glamorganshire illustrate the range of inductions which a topographical survey of a coastal and upland area permits, and the use of traffic routes. C. Fox in *Antiq. Journ.*, 1939, pp. 379-382; Aileen Fox. in *Arch. Camb.*, 1936, pp. 100-117.

[4] Miss Chitty points out that the course of this trade along the ridgeway over the Kerry, Clun and Clee Hills is clearly marked by finds on or near the route.

[5] Knowledge of the traffic from north Wales to southern England has been amplified by recent work by T. A. Glenn, Alex. Keiller and others on the trade in hard-stone axes. A large number of those found in the Salisbury Plain region come from north Wales. See, e.g., T. A. Glenn in *Arch. Camb.*, 1935, p. 189 ff., esp. map, p. 206. A recent authoritative survey, *The Petrological Identification of Stone Axes*, by Messrs. Keiller, Piggott and Wallis may be consulted with advantage: *Proc. Prehist. Soc.*, 1941, pp. 60-63. Cf. W. J. Varley, *Prehistoric Cheshire*, Fig. 26 (L. F. Chitty).

masses of find-spots leading to the Aire Gap in the Pennines[1] to which reference has already been made. Just as the Jurassic outcrop, known to have been a line of cultural diffusion linking east Yorkshire with the south-west, is marked by successive segregations of finds, so this series of objects may indicate not only settlement, but also trade; a route by which the same folk maintained touch with the west. The connections appear to be mainly with the head of the estuary of the Ribble at Preston, where many finds occur. There is evidence also of a route adjacent to this, from the head-waters of the Calder to those of the Roch (Halifax to Rochdale), which seems to have led to the estuary of the Mersey at Warrington. The latter was the harbour by which the inhabitants of the Peak district of Derbyshire maintained contact with the west.

One of the most interesting features of the prehistory of Britain is the way in which eastern Yorkshire, the northern outpost of the Lowland Zone, fluctuated in its allegiance; at times it is culturally part of the adjacent Highland Zone, at other times part of the uniform lowland culture area. I think that this trans-Pennine activity provides us with information as to one source of the highland (and Irish) influences on the Wolds.

In the same way there are indications, in an east-and-west string of finds along the Irthing and the lower reaches of the Eden, that the tribes of "Northumbria" established contact with the west (the Solway estuary) by the low col known as the Tyne Gap. Again, the sinuous ribbon of finds north-west of the Northumbrian segregation suggests that the line of contact with Clydeside, a very important Bronze Age area for the people of this region and an entrepôt for the Irish trade, was up Lauderdale, round the north of the Moorfoot hills, by Eddleston and Biggar Waters to the upper Clyde at Culter [the Clyde-Forth lowland was probably forest]. That there should be gaps in these chains of finds is what, on the analogy of such series in the Lowlands, we ought to expect; the absence of any finds at the highest point of the Tyne Gap, for example, or across the valley of the Derwent on the way from the Irish Sea to the Yorkshire Wolds, tends to confirm the reliability of the map as an accurate record, despite its small scale, and in no way puts these series out of court as indicative of long-distance contact.

Since we have found chains of finds linking the great aggregations of Northumbria, the Eden valley, the Wolds and the Peak to estuaries on the west—the Clyde, the Solway, the Ribble, and the Mersey—we may conclude that Crawford was justified in writing in 1922[2] that the main factor which determined the selection of ports in prehistoric times (we might add as in modern) was "the presence of a populous hinterland of effective buyers." Still, I think we can make too much of this trade hypothesis. Such alignments of human occupation as we have been considering, whether they carried a trickle of goods for barter or no, are mainly important in that they represent the lines of diffusion of culture, routes by which ideas, new techniques, art motives, etc., travelled in a primitive country. Most of such movement is involuntary; it depends on human contacts from point to point in a long line; where such a chain of settlements exists there will be culture-creep, whether any "trade" follows the route or not. Much work remains to be done on these routes by the study of the distribution of types in such things as socketed bronze axes; I suspect that the cultural connections (east and west, and north and south) of every extensive aggregation of population in the North could be worked out in this way. Consider, for example, the distributional pattern shown in Plate X (*b*) which represents the focus, and spread, of a Late Bronze Age tool. The east Yorkshire folk who created the type had contacts with Lincolnshire people and East Anglians; with the inhabitants of the west Yorkshire dales and (probably by the

---

[1] E. Kitson Clark, *Proc. Soc. Antiq.*, XXIII, 1911, pp. 309–325; A. Raistrick, *Yorks. Arch. Journ.*, XXIX, 1929, pp. 354–365.
[2] Prehistoric Geography, *The Geographical Review*, 1922, p. 260.

Aire Gap) with tribes on the west of the Pennines. The axe reached also the pastoral people of the Cheviots. The " strays " on the map also are suggestive of lines of diffusion.[1]

We may now enquire into the use of rivers as highways in the Highland Zone. The map reveals little evidence that the greater rivers were utilized for traffic or riparian settlement. One might expect that the Severn, a medieval highway, would in these respects provide a parallel with the Thames. It is, however, more like the Trent; it shows an important aggregation of finds above Worcester 30 miles from the head of the estuary at Gloucester, just as the Bronze Age settlement near Nottingham is 50 miles from the head of the Trent estuary near Althorpe. The lower reaches of both rivers were bordered by broad marshes or " damp " oakwood, which inhibited occupation.

FIGURE 31.—DISTRIBUTION OF CHAMBERED CAIRNS IN CAITHNESS AND SUTHERLAND.
(Pages 22, 32, 73.)
After V. G. Childe, " The Early Colonization of N.E. Scotland," *Proc. Roy. Soc. Edin.*, Vol. 50, 1930, Map IV, p. 63.

The Severn does not lead to any dense area of occupation to which trade would naturally be drawn, but the concentration of lines of settlement (or traffic?) on the Shrewsbury bend of the river, and on Bewdley, to which reference has just been made, does suggest the possibility that its middle and lower reaches may have carried some of the Irish and north Wales trade to south Britain. Two other rivers require a note. The river Dee, bordered by marsh and " damp " oakwood forest throughout its lower reaches, with a stony or rocky bed in places shallow in its upper reaches, is not likely to have been much used by Bronze Age Man. The Wye certainly was not.

We may now turn to another interesting problem; that of the physical relation between human settlement and the mountain masses of the Highlands. The northern region shows this relation to be both definite and explicable. The find-sites are on the lower plateaux, the foothills, the flanks of intermont valleys; or if higher, adjacent to cols which permit a mountain range to be crossed. In short, the pattern formed by the find-sites conforms

---

[1] For the distribution-picture of a south Wales axe-type, see *Antiq. Journ.*, 1939, p. 390, Pl. LXXXI.

to the major physical features of the country. The only apparent exception is the Peak district; and here the wealth of finds in upland barrows obscures, if it does not entirely misrepresent, the actual distribution of Man's settlements. I suspect these to have been on the flanks of the Derwent and the Dove, not on the high plateau.

In south and central Wales the conclusion reached in respect of the northern Highlands also applies; in north Wales some find-spots certainly occur high up the mountains. Again, in the south-west, over a great part of Dartmoor there is evidence of permanent Bronze Age occupation. Either, then, our generalization is of limited application or special circumstances in these regions mask its operation.

The Relation between Elevation and Human Settlement: The extent to which elevation affected occupation in prehistoric Britain has been but little studied. Of the available evidence, that from Scotland may first be examined.

Figure 31 (after V. G. Childe) shows that the megalithic folk of Caithness lived entirely in the coastal area and mostly between the 200 and 400 foot contours; in no case on the high moorlands above 800 feet. Figure 33 (also after Childe) shows the distribution of the Pictish culture in Scotland in the Early Christian period; this culture was concentrated on the eastern sea-plain to which reference has already been made.[1]

Figure 32 (also from Professor Childe's valuable paper on northern distributions) is especially interesting. It shows on a larger scale than Plate VI the find-sites of objects of the Early Bronze Age which must have been in demand everywhere where man congregated in the north. Marking as it does the 600 and 1,200 foot contours, the map illustrates clearly the intermont and coastal character of the finds. Everywhere in the north, then, in the second millennium B.C. and in the first millennium A.D. alike, the high moorland and mountains seem to be barren of recorded finds.

A new distribution map of the Welsh area by Miss L. F. Chitty gives equally significant results. Plate IX records the find-sites of portable antiquities (bronze and gold) of the Late Bronze Age, 180 in number, plotted on a contoured map. Of these, only 16 are above the 1,000 foot contour, four of them being above 2,000 feet. This suggests that few people who had anything to lose lived above that height.[2] Again, Figure 34 (based on Willoughby Gardner) shows the distribution of hill-forts in north Wales, many of uncertain date, but probably all to be included in the thousand years from 300 B.C. to 700 A.D. Though elevation was an important factor in the selection of such defensible sites, and though forts are occasionally met with up to 1,500 feet (Tre'r Ceiri), this distribution map shows that they are on the sides of intermont valleys or on the margins of the mountain complex, not in its heart. A recent study of hill-forts in Carmarthenshire gives similar results.[3]

These detailed studies confirm the general picture of hill-fort distribution in Wales in Figure 11. Essentially, then, Wales conforms to type; the high-level finds are of secondary importance in the Bronze Age, and localized in the Iron Age. They are, however, interesting

---

[1] Cf. a distribution map by Cecil L. Curle: *Proc. Soc. Antiq. Scot.*, Vol. 74, p. 61.

[2] The scattered observations on the distribution of Bronze Age finds in Wales, and the cultural significance of the pattern, may thus be summarized: the influences which unite to form the culture of north Wales are mainly derived from northern England—more particularly east Yorkshire and the Peak district—on the one hand, and northern and eastern Ireland on the other; the best defined connection with the Lowland Zone is the trade route to Wessex via the middle Severn valley. The influences which form the culture of south Wales are derived directly from southern, and to a less extent from eastern England, also from southern and eastern Ireland. Unifying influences as between the two halves of Wales were probably mainly provided by traffic along the western coasts, in part by land traffic which seems to have crossed the central plateau near Rhayader; tenuous contacts at the best. Thus, there were strong forces tending to make north and south Wales separate entities. Students of the archaeology of Wales will find much to support these views in distribution maps in this Essay.

[3] *History of Carmarthenshire*, Vol. I, map V, and pp. 86–88.

and cannot be summarily dismissed. *Intermittent* occupation, in all periods, may account for a certain amount of human life at high levels in the Highland Zone. An early type of economic organization involving seasonal migration from hills to valleys survived in Wales until a late date; it is in evidence in northern Scotland, and may thus be assumed for the Highlands generally. The herdsmen " migrated to the moorlands in summer, and down to shelter in the upper ends of the valleys in winter. Here occur the names ' Pentre,' ' Hendre,' and so on, indicating probably the chief settlement where, as time passed, goods accumulated

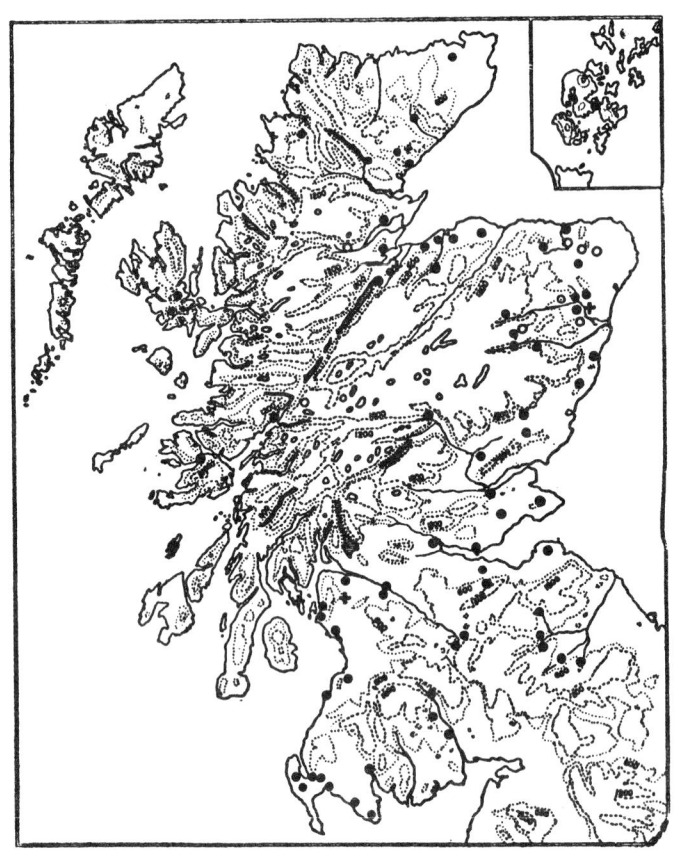

FIGURE 32.—DISTRIBUTION OF FLAT AXES, MOULDS, AND HALBERDS OF THE EARLY BRONZE AGE. (Pages 45*n*., 73. Illustrations in Figs. 39, 4; 40, 1 and 3.)
After V. G. Childe, " The Early Colonization of N.E. Scotland," *Proc. Roy. Soc. Edin.*, Vol. 50, 1930, Map II, p. 54.
● Flat axe.   O Mould.   + Halberd.

and organization developed, leaving at the upper centre (' Hafod ') less and less share of the people's life and possessions."[1] Such habits of life may account for many pre- or proto-historic moorland enclosures seen on the Welsh uplands, and for the scantiness of finds associated therewith. R. E. M. Wheeler, examining, in 1921, hut circles and other enclosures on the 1,500 foot contour line 1¼ miles north of Blaenrhondda, Glamorgan, came to the conclusion that the site was probably the summer " hafod " of a small pastoral community. The finds were scanty.

[1] Fleure and Whitehouse, *Arch. Camb.*, 1916, p. 127.

The struggle for survival, moreover, may account for a certain amount of human life on the high moorlands. The areas in the Highland Zone mostly desired for occupation clearly were the coastal belts, the lower plateaux and, in the mountains, the thinly-forested zone lying between the densely-forested valley bottoms and the open moors.[1] In these areas lived the well-to-do; here the bearers of new cultures established their aristocracies.[2] The moorlands received the dispossessed; on them some of the poorer members of the communities whose goods were scanty no doubt won their livelihood. In a word, the struggle

FIGURE 33.—THE DISTRIBUTION OF PICTISH SYMBOLS, SIXTH-SEVENTH CENTURY A.D. (Pages 41, 73. Illustration, p. 94, tailpiece.)
After V. G. Childe, "The Early Colonization of N.E. Scotland," *Proc. Roy. Soc. Edin.*, Vol. 50, 1930, Map VI, p. 74.

---

[1] In this originally thinly-forested zone house-sites of a distinctive type are widely distributed in Glamorgan, and have since been found in central Wales. Five, on Gelligaer Common, Glamorgan, have been excavated by Aileen Fox: finds in one indicated a fourteenth century A.D. date, but the type is held to be of Dark Age rather than medieval origin. *Arch. Camb.*, 1937, pp. 247–265, and 1939, pp. 163–193. See also Cyril Fox, *Arch. Camb.*, 1939, pp. 220–223 (site in Radnorshire).

[2] My attention has been directed to an interesting note by William Rees in *South Wales and the March*, 1924, p. 29: "The old Welsh villages still line the hillsides at heights ranging from 500 to 900 feet, a fact which bears out the statement of Giraldus that the Welsh were a hill people. Hence the importance in early Wales of rivers as boundaries between the upland units. The occupation of the valleys would result in hill boundaries."

for survival tended to drive the weaker elements of the population to the highest limit compatible with continued existence.[1]

We have, then, reason to suppose that human settlement above the 1,000-foot level did exist fairly widely in the Highland Zone; it was poor, and to some extent seasonal. The rest of it, in the Iron Age, was due primarily to the preoccupation of the Celts with warfare. But why is the most extensive evidence of it to be found in the southern part of the Zone? The reason is probably climatic. The upper limit of *permanent* occupation tends to fall as one proceeds north; one could live all the year round more easily on Dartmoor at 1,500 feet than on the Cheviots at 900 feet.

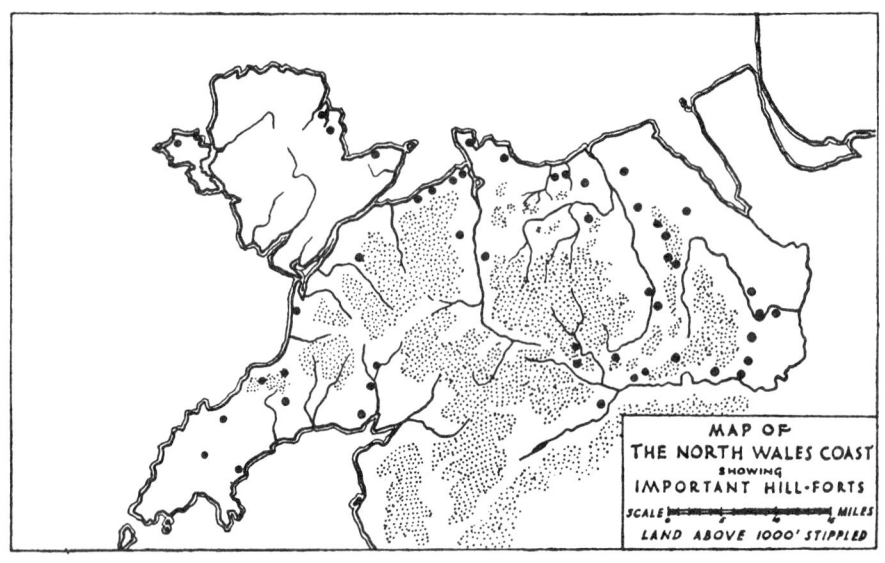

FIGURE 34.—DISTRIBUTION OF HILL-FORTS IN NORTH WALES (C. 300 B.C.–700 A.D.) IN RELATION TO THE MOUNTAIN MASS, WHICH IS STIPPLED. (Page 73.)
Based on Willoughby Gardner, *Arch. Camb.*, 1926, p. 226, Fig. I.

One more comment perhaps is necessary. Permanent habitation and seasonal occupation apart, there is considerable evidence in Wales, at all events, of man's presence on the high moorlands. There were numberless burials on them in cairns and barrows,[2] and the routes from one settlement area to another crossed them. The situation of the former was dictated by custom, that of the latter by convenience; Man moved along the watersheds, in open country, the major landmarks all in sight. Game, too, must have attracted hunters then as to-day.[3] Lastly, many and many a time in all parts of the Highland Zone, loot must have been taken by robbers to the mountains for safety, and hoards may thus be from time to time discovered at any level in Britain, however high.[4]

---

[1] Similar causes produced the same effects in the less desirable areas of the Lowlands: speaking of the migration to the moors of north-eastern Yorkshire in the Late Bronze Age, Elgee says: "Necessity only could have compelled the urn people to face and to endure the sterility and the climatic conditions of Blackamore." *Op. cit.*, pp. 88–89.

[2] The cairns and barrows in such an area—the Glamorgan plateau—have recently been surveyed and plotted: see Aileen Fox, The Dual Colonization of East Glamorgan, Map II, in *Arch. Camb.*, 1936, p. 109. The problems of the levels at which the builders of these burial mounds lived is not yet solved; no prehistoric settlements are known and finds in the area are scanty.

[3] The numerous flint arrowheads which can be picked up on some moorlands (e.g. Bugeilyn, Montgomeryshire) suggest this.

[4] The famous Llynfawr Hoard, found in a lake 1,200 feet above O.D. in Glamorgan, is held to be an example of this: Fox and Hyde, *Antiq. Journ.*, 1939, pp. 369–404, esp. pp. 379–381.

Long-term Changes in the Distribution of Population and their Causes

The Effect of Climatic Changes.

(*a*) *In the Lowland Zone.*—Extensive as was the use made of the chalk downland area in the Bronze Age which we have just studied, it was probably more widespread in the Early Iron and Roman Ages which followed, and was certainly different in kind. The evidence which is available (for Sussex) from the Late Bronze Age, and for the whole of south England from the beginning of the Iron Age onwards, consists of extensive series of rectangular ("Celtic") fields; the stony banks defining these, the associated lynchets, the farmstead sites and roadways, indicate intensive arable cultivation and the *occupation* rather than the *use* of the plateaux. The large number of hill-forts ("camps") on the downs which are known to have been in permanent occupation in the Early Iron Age, is a phenomenon equally and similarly significant.[1] That is to say that in the Bronze Age down to the eighth century B.C. Man tended to live at the springline below the downs, driving his flocks and herds on to the plateaux and hill tops for pasture; thereafter he moved his actual dwelling sites on to the uplands, using them both for arable and for pasture, and driving his flocks down to the springline for watering. It has been suggested that this change is to be associated with the climatic variation to which reference has been made. The Bronze Age falls almost entirely within the dry sub-Boreal phase,[2] the Early Iron Age in the sub-Atlantic phase; the dryness of the former period may well have made large areas of downs unsuitable for tillage or occupation, while the wetness of the latter provided just the right conditions for corn growing on the uplands. Furthermore, it is possible that a more extended cycle of change may in the future be demonstrated; namely, that in the wet Atlantic phase the downs were inhabited as in the sub-Atlantic phase. The wide range of implements of the Neolithic Age discovered thereon points to this, as does the fact that certain upland sites appear to have been occupied in the Neolithic and Early Iron Ages, deserted in the intervening Bronze Age.[3] On the whole, however, one is inclined to give the credit to Man's ingenuity rather than to Nature's bounty, since the earliest evidence for the change is associated with invaders.[4]

---

[1] "In Romano-British times practically the whole of Salisbury Plain, Cranborne Chase, and the Dorset uplands were under plough" (*Wessex from the Air*, Crawford and Keiller, p. 9). The evidence carefully analyzed by O. G. S. Crawford in "Air Survey and Archaeology," *Geog. Journ.*, 1923, p. 342 ff., goes to show that the intensive cultivation and occupation of the downlands of Wilts and Dorset date from the beginning of the Iron Age. See also the Ordnance Survey map, "Celtic Earthworks of Salisbury Plain," Part I. Recent research in Sussex shows that there the Celtic field system was initiated in Late Bronze Age times. See G. A. Holleyman in *Antiquity*, 1935, p. 443 ff.

[2] That conditions dry enough to enforce this change were present in Britain in sub-Boreal times has been denied. But the evidence does not as yet appear to justify a revision of the text.

[3] Good examples are The Trundle, Sussex, and Hembury, Devon. At each of these sites excavation (by Dr. E. C. Curwen and the late Miss D. Liddell respectively) has revealed a causewayed "camp" of the Neolithic Age underlying a large Iron Age fortress.

[4] On Plumpton Plain, Sussex. One of the discoverers, E. Cecil Curwen, well sums up the significance of this development: "This (system) marks a major turning-point in the history of agriculture in Britain, for henceforth corn-growing, instead of being an adjunct to cattle-rearing, takes pride of place—with the following implications: (1) the two-ox plough, upon which this field-system seems to have been based, must have been introduced by this time, presumably by the same people; (2) some kind of rotation of crops must have been practised, with manuring, to maintain the fertility of the soil, for there is evidence that some areas were cultivated continuously for many centuries; and (3) the flocks and herds must have been pastured, as in later times, on the waste land beyond the limits of the arable, and probably also on fields lying fallow." *Proc. Prehist. Soc.*, 1938, pp. 38-39.

(*b*) *In the Highland Zone*.—There is some evidence which suggests that in the Bronze Age there was an extension of occupation upwards from the coastal foothills at several points in the Highland Zone. For example, the evidences of human activity on the higher plateaux in Wales are more frequently referable to the Bronze than to the Neolithic Age.[1]

In so far as this phenomenon is related to climatic change—the progressively drier conditions of the sub-Boreal phase—such change appears to have had the opposite effect in the Highlands to that in the Lowlands. And this is what might on *a priori* grounds be expected. For the moorlands of the west, having in "Atlantic" phases an excessive (orographic) rainfall, should be at their best in the sub-Boreal period.

The Effect of Increasing Population in Early Britain : There are considerable differences in the distribution of Man in Britain as shown on the one hand on the megalithic and beaker maps, and on the other hand on the massed map of the Bronze Age. Some of these changes may be due to climatic variation; but after allowance is made for this, the greater range of occupation sites shown on the latter map can hardly be explained on any grounds other than an increase of population. This may happen in times of peace; or it may be due to invaders seizing the better lands, and driving their owners to the worse. It appears probable that the available areas of pervious soil in Britain, open or thinly-forested, were very far from being taken up by the close of the beaker period (*circa* 1600 B.C.) and that there was a tendency during the thousand years which followed towards exploitation of the less desirable patches of such country. "Less desirable" in any given case either by reason of isolation, restricted area, poorness of soil, or (in the case of the Highland Zone) situation near the upper limit of settlement—which we may describe as the "poverty level."

How far did this expansion go? A long way, judging from the evidences of settlement which took place in the latter part of the Bronze Age on what appears to us to be very undesirable country, such as Blackamore in N.E. Yorkshire.[2] But the scanty evidences of settlement on such a light-soil area as the Forest Ridge in Sussex[3] even at the end of the Bronze Age suggests that the population never fully occupied or utilized the whole of the pervious thinly-forested soils of Britain. Why not? Probably because before the process of expansion—under the limitations imposed by Man's scanty equipment in early times—was complete, his increasing control over his environment enabled him to switch over to a new and wholly different line of economic development—the exploitation of the richer soils.

Areas of Easy and of Difficult Settlement : The conditions governing such a change are interesting. The argument can briefly be set out as follows: Though preference by Early Man for certain light soils over others can be established, all these pervious soils—limestones, chalks, sands, gravels—can conveniently be lumped together as *areas of easy settlement*. Though variations in detail can, as we have seen, be demonstrated, evidence of continuity of Man's occupation or utilization of such pervious soils in Britain throughout the pre- and proto-historic periods is abundant. *The areas of difficult settlement* are the deep clay soils,[4] impervious, on which human occupation is intermittent. Settlement in this type of country

---

[1] This movement was in part the result of Early Bronze Age intrusion from the Lowland Zone. Cf. Aileen Fox, *Arch. Camb.*, 1936, p. 100 ff.

[2] The problem is complex. Depopulation may have taken place from time to time in certain areas. It is remarkable, for example, that small groups of intruders bringing in Late Bronze or Early Iron Age "A" culture, apparently peaceful peasants, seem to have been able to establish themselves in undefended settlements in the most desirable and accessible areas of southern Britain. This countryside must surely have been underpopulated at the time.

[3] One can hardly predicate a survival of the Mesolithic occupants so late as this. J. G. D. Clark, *The Mesolithic Age in Britain*, Map II and pp. 90–91.

[4] Carrying "damp" oakwood; see p. 55.

is normally dependent on a certain standard of civilization being attained by an agricultural community. Development in such forest districts involves a certain amount of labour (tree felling, root stubbing) for which no immediate return is possible; and also hard work on the heavy land thus cleared (with suitable and efficient implements and draught animals). Such development therefore depends, in addition, on a sense of security, a reasonable amount of political stability, and " capital." When these conditions are present the effort is worth while, for the heavier lands yield the heaviest crops to tillage. The notable increase in the population which political stability tends to bring about is probably the immediate stimulus. To a limited extent, the clearing of the " damp " oakwood in such an intensive culture phase is involuntary. The development of pig-breeding with its use of the forest for pannage, for example, prevents its regeneration; and the demand for timber for firing and house building involves constant tree-felling.

S. W. Wooldridge and D. L. Linton[1] rightly emphasized the importance of the soil-type intermediate between the pervious and impervious—the loams. Loams with a high clay content are, I think, best classed with the impervious soils, those with a high sand content with the pervious; the remainder are certainly individually important. They are best regarded, in work on prehistoric periods, as a link between the two main groups rather than as an independent group. For it was probably on the Hertfordshire–Bedfordshire borders, where there is much soil of this intermediate type, that agricultural exploitation on an effective scale of a countryside definitely not an area of " easy " settlement first occurred.[2] This was in the Early Iron Age; the distribution pattern of the culture involved, mainly Iron Age " C " (Belgic), is shown on Plate XI. In the Ivel-Hiz district on the left centre of this map the British agriculturist seems to have worked out his technique, possibly with the aid of the heavy wheel plough with mould-board.[3] Here he reached forward to attack the " damp " oakwoods—areas of " difficult " settlement properly so called. That real progress was made in this adventure is certain; there are sites in the Belgic map already referred to that are definitely on clay. Convincing evidence is provided in the Roman period which followed on, and which is agriculturally and economically an extension of, Iron Age " C " in eastern Britain; the distribution pattern in the Cambridge region in Roman times, represented on Figure 27, shows activity on the heavy clay lands flanking the Chalk belt. A comparison with the Bronze Age map of the same Region on the opposite page (Figure 26) emphasizes the change.

The Anglo-Saxon conquest is of great interest from the point of view of " difficult " settlement, and attention may be directed to a map referred to in the opening paragraphs of this essay—Figure 14, which shows the sites of the pagan cemeteries of the fifth to seventh centuries. Leeds rightly says of this Anglo-Saxon pattern: " Hardly too great stress can be laid on the importance of the river systems as the key by means of which the whole distribution of the settlements can be solved."[4] The pattern is indeed intimately related to these. The numerous cemeteries in the valley of the Warwickshire Avon, a region of limited occupation in Bronze Age times, suggest that the Low German farmers were not deterred by forest; while the scarcity of such evidences of settlement on the downlands of Berkshire and Wiltshire presents the other side of the picture.

[1] The Loam-terrains of S.E. England, *Antiquity*, 1933, pp. 297–310. For the author's rejoinder, elaborating the argument in the text, see *Antiquity*, 1933, pp. 473–475.

[2] There is evidence suggesting localized exploitation of areas of " difficult settlement " in the Highland Zone in earlier periods (see p. 58 f.).

[3] This type of plough was certainly present in Britain, in East Anglia in particular, in Roman times, and there is some evidence for it in Iron Age " C " contexts. See Hawkes, *Antiquity*, 1935, p. 339, and E. C. Curwen, *Proc. Prehist. Soc.*, 1938, p. 45 ff.

[4] *Archaeology of the Anglo-Saxon Settlements*, p. 18. But the Trent may have been an exception. See K. D. M. Dauncey, and J. N. L. Myres, in *Antiquity*, 1942, pp. 60 and 333.

For it is a fact that the Anglo-Saxons were seldom interested agriculturally in the lighter soils which, right up to the end of the Roman period (in spite of local developments such as those recorded above) formed the chief arable areas in Lowland Britain. As Crawford, Curwen and others have shown, it is because the Saxons, having destroyed the Romano-Celtic agricultural system, left the downland fields untilled, that we have such a wonderfully complete record (village plans and field boundaries) of that peasant civilization. The Saxons settled beside the rivers and streams and cultivated nearby land, the upland ("waste of the

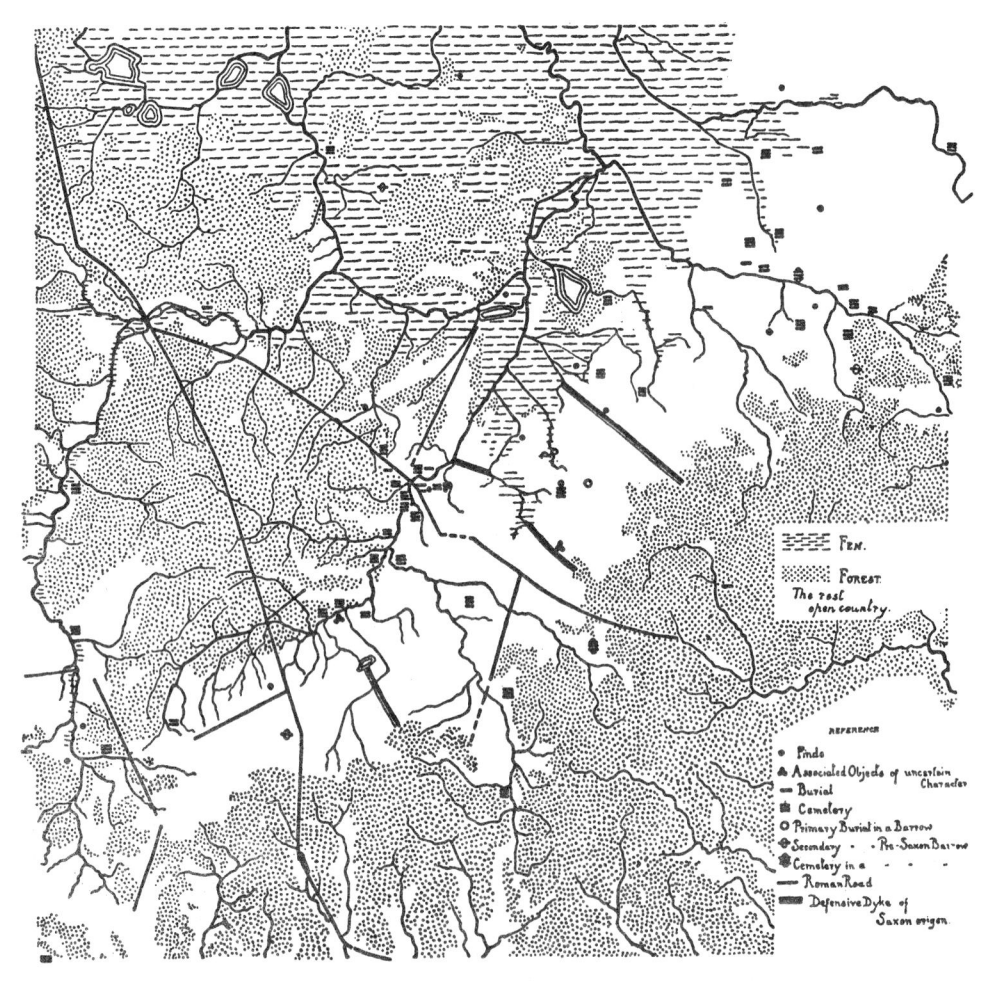

FIGURE 35.—DISTRIBUTION OF FINDS AND REMAINS ATTRIBUTED TO THE ANGLO-SAXON PAGAN PERIOD IN THE CAMBRIDGE REGION. (Page 81.)
Based on Fox, *Archaeology of the Cambridge Region* (Cambridge University Press), 1923, Map V.
Scale: 1 inch = 8 miles.

manor" in later days) being but slowly brought under control. They preferred the deep meadow to the hill-pasture; and were probably the first people in Britain to bring order into the marshy alder-choked alluvium of our lowland valley floors.

It is archaeologically possible to see the Saxon farmer at work, turning the valley bottoms into water meadows, the forest margins into arable and pasture. Offa's Dyke is intermittent in the rich and well-wooded lowlands of Herefordshire; the only places where it was constructed are in the valleys. These must have been as densely forested as the hills before man commenced to occupy the region; the existing sections of the Dyke thus accurately show the extent of his occupation, and the lines on which his attack on natural obstacles developed (Figure 30).

This was in the eighth century; the extent to which the Saxons cleared the forested claylands (the " damp " oakwood) in the pagan times with which Figure 14 deals, is unknown.

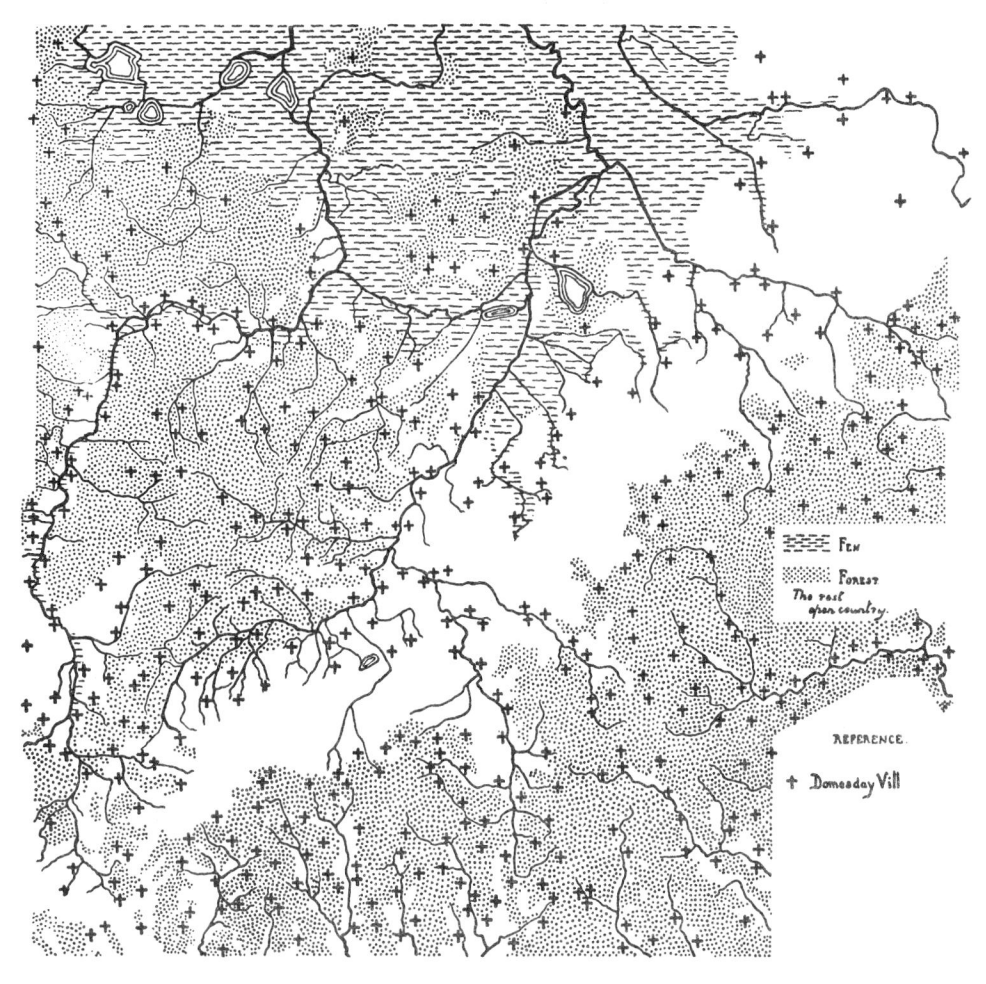

FIGURE 36.—DISTRIBUTION OF SETTLEMENTS IN THE CAMBRIDGE REGION AT THE CLOSE OF THE ANGLO-SAXON PERIOD AS EVIDENCED BY DOMESDAY BOOK. (Page 82.)

Based on Fox, *Archaeology of the Cambridge Region* (Cambridge University Press), Map V.
Scale : 1 inch = 8 miles.

Probably very little, despite the Worcestershire distribution; there are no cemeteries in well-known stretches of such forest (e.g. the Weald and the Essex uplands). This negative view receives support from the Cambridge evidence; Figure 35 shows the distribution of pagan cemeteries in the area; they are wholly concentrated in the areas of " easy " settlement. But the tendencies to which we have referred, as inherent in the Anglo-Saxon culture from the earliest times, lead us to expect developments. And a very different picture is presented by Figure 36 which illustrates the distribution of settlements (Domesday vills) at the close of the Dark Ages in the Cambridge region. Villages are present, of course, adjacent to all the pagan cemeteries; but the interesting feature is that occupation is now widely extended in the forest belts. Settlements are indeed as thickly placed on the boulder-clay as on the sands, gravel or chalk. This remarkable change then was wrought between 650 and 1050 A.D.

The Chronology of the Exploitation of Richer Soils: The history of this economic revolution, the importance of which justifies the phrase, "the change from the dominance of the environment to the dominance of Man," can tentatively be summed up as follows:

The exploitation of areas of "difficult" settlement, the richer soils, started in late La Tène times and in eastern Britain.[1] It continued in Roman times; for in one area at least which has been closely studied the claylands were definitely attacked. The process was, moreover, politically stimulated in this period; cantonal capitals were built on lowland sites, and hillforts deserted. Such action must in many cases have resulted in extensive forest clearing.

There followed a period (400–650 A.D.) of political disturbance, of invasion and conquest. This period is marked by the shrinkage of occupation to sites which, though they represent a change in agricultural outlook and treatment of the valley floors, are within the area of "easy" settlement. The beginning of this period is also marked by the refortification of deserted hillforts; Lydney (Gloucestershire) and Cissbury (Sussex) are examples.[2]

But by the end of the pagan phase the Anglo-Saxons had settled down. Their economic and political order had become to a large extent stabilized, and the population was doubtless increasing; the attack on the claylands was started again. This time the achievement was permanent, and there was no recession. The agricultural policy initiated in the seventh century or thereabouts[3] has had a clear run of a thousand years, forming the firm economic basis on which our industrial civilization has been founded. The change had, of course, the negative effect of inducing an ebb of human life from the least desirable areas of "easy" settlement into which, as we have seen, that life had been forced.

It should be added that, while the process under review tended to operate in Highland and Lowland Zones alike, it is more in evidence in the culturally advanced areas (the lowland), and did not in all probability effectively reach the highlands until the Saxon (or Norman) infiltration or conquest.[4] It must, of course, be remembered that until the period of continuous record-keeping such changes in the distribution of population in the Highland Zone as may have occurred are not always easy to detect, for movement from one type of country to another in mountainous areas tends to be limited to descent from the flanks and lower plateaux bordering a valley to the floor thereof, a change which may be undistinguishable in the records of provenance of finds.

But in many parts of Wales at least we have evidence that occupation of the uplands by well-to-do folk continued well into the Dark Ages, for contemporary memorials of sixth-

---

[1] The hillfort development along the Welsh Marches, a region thickly forested for the most part and thinly occupied in Bronze Age times (see L. F. Chitty, *Arch. Camb.*, 1937, pp. 129 ff., and Fig. 11 of this essay), suggests that similar exploitation was carried on in this area also during the last century or so of independence; but detailed information of soil types in relation to individual structures in this district is at present lacking.

[2] In the Highland Zone it is probable that hillforts were occupied until late in the Dark Ages.

[3] There are fairly early place-name forms on the claylands in the Cambridge Region. See *P.N. of Cambridgeshire*, English Place-name Society, map in pocket.

[4] Save possibly on the Welsh Marches. The early economic history of this area has still to be worked out. For its condition in the Dark Ages some archaeological evidence has been provided: Fox, Survey of Offa's Dyke and Wats' Dyke, *Arch. Camb.*, 1926–31 and 1934, esp. 1929, Fig. 26, p. 58; 1930, Fig. 26, p. 69; 1934, Fig. 25, opp. p. 233.

century chieftains are to be seen on what are now uninhabited sheepwalks. In such localities in south Wales, for example, lived Dervacus the son of Justus (Ystradfellte), Bodvoc the son of Catotigirnus (Margam Mountain), and several others.[1]

The "Valleyward Movement" : In many cases, then, the change we are discussing, whether due to conquest or cultural progress, or increased security of life and property, resulted in the desertion of hillforts and plateau villages, and the clearing and occupation of valley floors. This aspect of the change was described by Professor Fleure as the " valleyward movement."[2] The phrase, useful as it is, is in some respects misleading, especially when applied to lowland Britain. It suggests that early man did not dwell in valleys, and that his successors did, whereas throughout the prehistoric period he has dwelt at valley level, on gravel terraces by rivers, for example, where the conditions were suitable. The value of the phrase lies in the fact that conditions, for him, were more often suitable on the hills and plateaux and valley flanks than on the valley floors ; for valley bottoms, which tend to have a deeper, richer soil than the uplands, were usually marshy and densely forested. The " valleyward movement," however, should clearly be taken to imply not merely (or even necessarily) a moving downhill, but a moving from poor soil to rich soil, from open or lightly-forested land to densely-forested land; it is essentially a change in economic outlook, rather than a change in the level at which man lived.[3]

The Change in the Economic Centre of Lowland Britain : The exploitation of the richer soils of the Lowland Zone in late La Tène times had repercussions of great importance. The establishment of the dynasty of Tasciovanus and Cunobelinus at Verulamium and Camulodunum by Belgic agriculturists[4] represents a shift of the economic centre of Britain from the chalk plateaux—the Salisbury Plain region—to the richer lowlands of East Anglia. From the first century B.C. onwards, Salisbury Plain declined in importance. No longer as in Bronze Age times did it gather to itself gold, the symbol of wealth and power ; in Roman times it was still thickly-inhabited, but by peasants alone.[5] East Anglia gained what Wiltshire lost ; its gold coinage,[6] its luxuries of imported wine and silver goblets, mark its supremacy.

Changes in the " Southern Trade " : On pp. 44-6 the early history of the import traffic in goods under the stimulus of Mediterranean contacts has been summarized, and the fact that the great majority of these came to Britain from the west into western harbours emphasized. In the 17th century B.C. the spread of Aunjetitz culture and the development of European land-routes brought trade goods of the class we are considering, from the east into the ports of south-east Britain. Trade contacts were indeed established by the Wessex overlords with far-distant Mycenae, and even with Crete and Egypt, probably by the Rhine, the Danube corridor, and the Vardar-Morava pass (Map A).[7] A trickle of import trade from Spain into southern ports is also on record.

---

[1] On this point, see Aileen Fox: " The siting of some inscribed stones . . . in Glamorgan and Breconshire," *Arch. Camb.*, 1939, pp. 30–41, with distribution map. The same author's papers on Gelligaer house sites also are relevant (p. 75 f.), as is " The Re-erection of Maen Madoc, Ystradfellte, Brec.," by Cyril Fox, *Arch. Camb.*, 1940, p. 210.

[2] *Arch. Camb.*, 1916, pp. 101–140, esp. p. 124 ff.

[3] R. E. M. Wheeler in *Antiquity*, 1932, p. 92.

[4] Recent writers have ascribed to the German elements in the Belgic, as in the Anglo-Saxon culture, the readiness of this people to exploit the loams and clays of East Anglia. Be this as it may, it was the comparatively high level of their agricultural technique which made such activities profitable.

[5] " The native villages . . . are most thickly concentrated on Salisbury Plain, where villas " (i.e. country houses of the landed gentry, C.F.) " are almost wholly absent." Introduction to *O.S. Map of Roman Britain*, 2nd ed., p. 3.

[6] The earliest in Britain, *c.* 75 B.C. G. C. Brooke, in *Antiquity*, 1933, pp. 271–272. For a map of wine-jar and other imports, see *Proc. Prehist. Soc. E. A.*, VII, p. 156, Fig. 6c.

[7] Piggott, *loc. cit.*, p. 95 ; Hawkes, *Foundations*, p. 377–378.

In the Late Bronze Age commercial links between the secondary centres of European civilization north of the Alps—which now extended to include northern France—and eastern Britain became much stronger, and as we have seen played an important part in the " industrial revolution " which initiated this phase of our cultural history. The sea trade from Spain to Britain did not, however, die out, and was revivified when the Celts occupied the north-west of the peninsula.[1] Very important in its cultural effects was the demand for Cornish tin by Greek merchants operating in the western Mediterranean. The trade route from " *Ictis* " was mainly to Corbilo, an *emporium* on the Loire, and thence to Massilia; the estuary of the Garonne, and Narbo, were also important (Map A).[2] Brittany is again a mart for the import trade into our southern harbours, and was herself a producing centre; but though south-west Britain thus developed an individual and vigorous culture the drift of economic power south-eastward was very pronounced, and in the first century B.C. the ports of Kent were actively in use for continental trade.[3] The tendency thus was to concentrate not only the derivative " southern " trade, but the true southern trade, now centred in the western Mediterranean, on the shortest sea crossing; to make the Straits of Dover the main traffic route between Italy and Britain. Barbarian pressure on northern Gaul hindered this development, but after 51 B.C., when Caesar's conquest of the country was complete, Roman traders were able to use more northerly landways than the Corbilo route, and direct imports from the Mediterranean, probably by Alpine passes as well as by the Rhône corridor, transformed the court culture of eastern Britain. This tendency was naturally confirmed when both Britain and Gaul were Roman provinces, and it is probable that then most of the oversea trade into Britain came by way of *Gesoriacum* (Boulogne) and the Rhine estuary into Kentish or Essex harbours, and to Thames-side wharves.

It should be noted that the Straits of Dover and the Rhine–Thames crossing represent the effective limit of the north-eastward movement of the " southern trade "; and that so firmly entrenched was it on this alignment that it survived the withdrawal of Roman power and played its part in the development and maintenance of the pre-Christian Jutish culture in Kent, and of the East Anglian court culture in Suffolk, in the sixth and early seventh centuries A.D.

Summary

The principal facts, deductions and inferences set out or arrived at in the course of this Essay are in this section summarized in twenty-five propositions. A brief survey of the chronological sequence of events from the geographic and cultural points of view, and with particular reference to southern Britain, precedes this summary; the Table on p. 9 should be used in connection with it.

I. *Chronological Outline.*

Elements of the new mode of living achieved in the East first reached Britain from northern France. A stock-breeding folk, makers of bag-like pottery and of stone axes, flint miners, practising an elementary agriculture, builders of earthworks (probably cattle kraals), crossed a narrower Channel to southern Britain about 2400 B.C.

Shortly after this event adventurers and pioneers more closely in touch with the eastern Mediterranean sources of civilization, equipped with a magical religion expressed in a ritual

---

[1] See E. T. Leeds' important study: *Archaeologia*, 76, p. 223 ff.
[2] See p. 49 of this Essay.
[3] Up to the middle of the first century B.C. the trade with Britain in general was in the hands of the Veneti of Brittany. Strabo, *Geog.* IV, 4. 1. The statement in the text is based on Caesar's locally-obtained evidence: *Cantium, quo fere omnes ex Gallia naves appelluntur. De B.G.* V, 13.

of collective burial in stone tombs, acquainted with (but probably not possessing) metal tools, were colonizing western Britain from Land's End to Caithness, and Ireland; they came from Iberia by sea about 2300 B.C. Other folk with the same group of ideas crossed France and joined in the colonization of the Atlantic coast from Loire-mouth to Finistère; some of the Breton colonists passed into western and southern Britain, and Ireland.

Into this powerful and expanding culture the Neolithic herdsmen in Britain became merged. While this fusion and expansion was still in progress groups and tribes from the middle and lower Rhinelands—archers, makers of beakers, holed axe-hammers, and flint knives—crossed (from the Rhine-mouths or further north) to the east coast of Britain: from 1900 to 1800 B.C. This second wave of continental folk had no higher culture than the first. A westerly and more limited movement was in progress about 1900 B.C., of beaker men with similar but slightly more advanced culture; they entered southern Britain from Brittany, their leaders equipped with tanged daggers of copper.

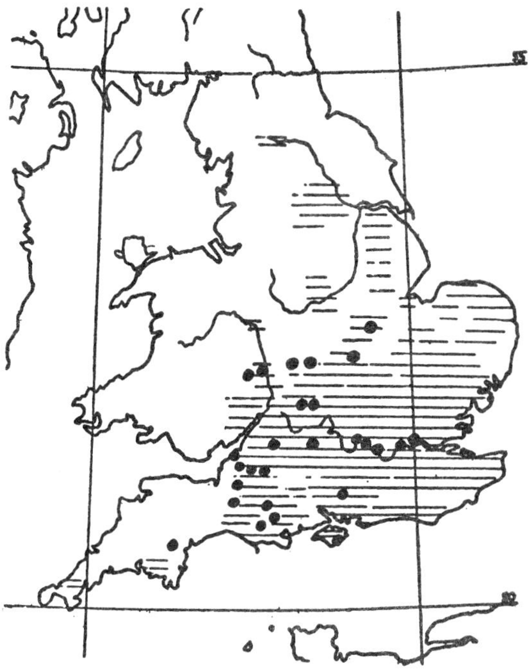

Meanwhile, much was happening in the far west. The Megalithic folk, or those among them who were prospectors, exploited the riches of Ireland in copper and gold; the British Isles found themselves, as it were overnight, in the forefront of the western European advance. Cornish tin deposits were probably discovered, the secret of bronze certainly disseminated, and, through the intermediacy of Britain, western Europe from France to Denmark acquired ornaments of gold, tools and weapons of copper or bronze.

But Ireland—with Scotland, which seems to have shared its prosperity—did not long remain the unchallenged workshop of the western world, save perhaps in the manufacture of gold ornaments. From Brittany, in the 17th century B.C., a dominating breed of men, craftsmen and merchants or with such in their employ, crossed to Britain and seized power in its economic centre, Salisbury Plain. Gold from Ireland, amber from Jutland, trinkets and amulets from central Europe and beads from Egypt are found in their graves; and under the leadership of these aristocratic barbarians Lowland Britain developed her own bronze industry on individual lines, stimulated by the achievement of the Aunjetitz (central European) culture, the patterns of whose bronze tools and weapons were now in advance of those of Ireland. The megalithic west, slowly conforming to a newer outlook on life and death, became a backwater in spite of a trickle of sea-borne trade from Iberia, Atlantic France and Ireland; and Lowland Britain maintained a slowly-diminishing inventive activity undisturbed by invasion, or any notable commercial intrusion, for over half a millennium.

FIGURE 37.—SKETCH MAP SHOWING EFFECTIVE RANGE OF CURRENCY BARS, EARLY IRON AGE "B" (DOTS), AND OF THE NATIVE COINAGE, EARLY IRON AGE "C" (HORIZONTAL LINES), IN BRITAIN.
(Pages 38, 86. Illustrations on pp. 6 and 89.)
Based (1938) on Bulleid and Gray, *Glastonbury*, Fig. 144; R. A. Smith, *Proc. Soc. Antiq.*, XX, 179–95; XXII, 338–43; XXVII, 69–76; and *Arch. Journ.*, LXIX, 423–27. Evans, *Coins of the Ancient Britons*, and *Supplement*, and G. C. Brooke, *Antiquity*, 1933, p. 268 ff. For a revised list of these bars, see Fox, *Antiquity*, 1940, p. 427, and 1941, p. 87.

This phase ended about 1000 B.C., the accepted date for the beginning of the Late Bronze Age. For some 900 years the island, thanks to her position between two worlds, of water and of land, and to the riches of her western neighbour, had attained a standard of culture higher than her actual distance from the power-houses of European civilization justified. The shape and structure of Britain being what it was, however, that standard was not reached everywhere, and in many part of the country metal goods must have been scarce and dear throughout the phase.

In the new phase Britain is seen to be a region on the margin of an expanding central European civilization; the first becomes the last.[1] She received and absorbed, from breeding-grounds of men and cultures such as the middle Rhinelands, the Alpine fringe and northern France and Belgium (Map A), a succession of traders, invaders and intruding groups, the earlier bringing an advanced Bronze culture, the later Iron cultures.

They entered by east and south coast estuaries and ports, the intensity of occupation of the middle and lower Thames valley and Essex foreshadowing a definite shift of the economic centre eastward from Salisbury Plain. This tendency became stronger as bronze gave place to iron and the cultural links with northern France strengthened. Hence we eventually had the most vigorous dynasty in Britain centred in Hertfordshire and Essex, and the cultural superiority of the eastern lowlands to the western is demonstrated by the wealth of exotic objects found in burials in the former area.

That this civilization would normally have become uniform over the whole of the Lowland Zone is probable; but powerful influences were at work which buttressed the declining importance of the West. These influences arose from the intensive exploitation of Cornish tin, which stimulated invasion and trade by the old sea route in so far as south-western Britain was concerned. Hence we have an interesting duality of lowland culture (Figure 37); the western marked by a primitive currency (bar iron), the eastern by a civilized currency (coined money); the Gloucestershire and Somerset region, and the lower Thames region, divide the cultural control of southern Britain.

This duality did not last; the western area was to a large extent overrun by the Belgae (Iron Age "C") and the use of coined money spread westward. Finally, the Straits became, under the Romans, the normal crossing-point to Britain, the Roman commercial centre was quickly established at London[2] and a uniform civilization was imposed on the Lowlands.

II. Propositions.

i. Position, outline, relief and structure are involved in this study of the island of Britain; the climate resulting from position and relief, and the soil related to structure, determine the vegetable life which she nourishes and the animal life which she harbours. The whole represents Man's environment, and Britain's personality.

---

[1] From *circa* 1000 B.C. an economic and cultural gradation downwards, usually from south-east to north-west, is a fairly constant phenomenon, though the geographical incidence of its lowest points varies. The inhabitants of the "black houses" of the Hebrides lived, up to a generation ago, in a Dark Age setting; that is, their material culture was a thousand years behind that of S.E. Britain. (See E. Cecil Curwen, *Antiquity*, 1939, pp. 261–289; Roussell, *Norse Building in the Scottish Isles*, Copenhagen, 1934, p. 47.)

[2] Despite the use of the lower Thames as a waterway and the consequent frequency of finds of all prehistoric periods in the bed of the river, "archaeological evidence does not support the possibility of a prehistoric London" (R. E. M. Wheeler in *London in Roman Times* (London Mus. Catalogue), pp. 14–15). But the economic shift we have studied rendered her creation as a distributing centre inevitable as soon as a civilization should establish itself capable of dealing with the obstacles to land traffic formed by the environing clay-lands of the lower Thames valley. The development of *Verulamium* and *Camulodunum* in succession showed that the Celtic civilization could not do this, but the Roman civilization satisfied the conditions and London arose.

ii. The position of Britain adjacent to Europe renders her very liable to invasion therefrom; her indented outline offers convenient harbourage for invaders, her deep estuaries and slow-moving rivers invite penetration.

iii. Embarkation points for those to whom the sea is a barrier have extended for 500 miles, from Finistère (Brittany) to the Rhine-mouths; from such points settlement along the whole length of the south coast, and the east coast to the Humber and beyond have taken place. Embarkation points for those to whom the sea is a highway have extended from the Spanish peninsula to Brittany on the west, and from the Rhine-mouths to Norwegian fiords on the north; to such the west and north coasts of Britain from Lands End to Caithness, and the east coast from Caithness to the Humber, have also lain open.

iv. In the earliest times under review (*c*. 2400 B.C.) the land of Britain was higher than at present—in S.E. Britain not less than 25 feet. Extensive alluvial and marshy flats fringed much of the coast. The Straits of Dover were narrower, the southern part of the North Sea probably a complex of sandbanks and tidal channels. Little, if any, traffic followed the Channel–North Sea route; by contrast, entry into southern Britain offered little difficulty to landsmen such as the Neolithic "A" and " B2 " beaker peoples. When subsidence and sea erosion had moulded Britain into the now familiar outline, oversea invasion tended to concentrate on the continental angle (Kent) and the Thames estuary.

v. One reservation is, however, necessary. Brittany, a peninsula within easy distance of Britain, with marked physiographic individuality, metalliferous, eminently suitable for early man's occupation, situated at the Atlantic-Channel angle and so stimulated by cultural ideas both seaborne and landborne, has exercised both by invasion and commerce, an influence localized indeed, but disproportionate to its area.

vi. European civilization has its source in the Near East, and Mediterranean societies thereafter are in the van of continental progress. Other things being equal, the nearer the Mediterranean the higher the culture in early times. The further north the homeland of invaders of Britain, then, the greater the likelihood that invasion will lower the level of our insular culture.

vii. Goods reach Britain in the way of trade from both northern and southern Europe. But since traders transmit ideas as well as goods, the products of higher civilizations arriving in this manner are doubly significant for the cultural development of an island in a state of barbarism. In general, then, the further south the port of entry in Britain, the more important culturally was the trade.

viii. The commercial activity of higher civilizations may, under certain circumstances, be almost as powerful an instrument of cultural change in Britain as is invasion.

ix. While the Atlantic sea-way from Spain northwards was in full use in Megalithic and Early Bronze Age times, Britain was in the van of western European progress. But in the Middle Bronze Age land routes (" amber routes ") which had been developing across Europe sapped the European importance of Atlantic commerce. Britain thenceforward tended more and more to occupy a position historically familiar; a country on the edge of the known world, the last to receive and absorb cultures moving from east to west. But the Atlantic routes never fell into complete disuse, and were indeed revivified by an increased demand for Cornish tin.

x. The structure of Britain has exerted a powerful influence on her prehistory. South of the Forth-Clyde isthmus the island consists of two parts, the Highland Zone to the west and the Lowland Zone to the east. A diagonal line drawn from Teesmouth (Durham) to Torquay (Devon) roughly indicates the boundary of the two areas. In the Highland Zone, high plateaux and mountains are characteristic; in the Lowland Zone, such hills as occur are usually of slight elevation. Stone suitable for tombs, for defensive structures, for dry-walled dwellings, occurs everywhere in the Highland; it is localized in the Lowland. The

Lowland provides the largest area of fertile and habitable ground, and hence it nourishes wealthier populations than the Highland.

 xi. The portion of Britain adjacent to the continent being Lowland, it is easily overrun by invaders, and on it new cultures of continental origin brought across the narrow seas tend to be imposed. In the Highland, on the other hand, these tend to be absorbed. Their manifestations are, then, later and less distinctive in the Highland than in the Lowland. There are areas (intermont and coastal) of lowland in the Highland Zone, and in some of these undifferentiated cultures of lowland origin may establish themselves. But no such area in Britain south of the Forth-Clyde isthmus is large enough for such cultures to develop therein an independent character.

 xii. There is greater *unity* of culture in the Lowland Zone, but greater *continuity* of culture in the Highland Zone. A tendency to unity of culture is sometimes seen in the Highland Zone south of the Forth-Clyde isthmus; the Highland north of the Forth-Clyde isthmus, on the other hand, tends, by reason of its remoteness, to develop unique cultures.

 xiii. The ultimate expression of any continental culture in Lowland Britain tends to possess individual characters. The sea barrier inhibits mass movement and encourages independent adventure; Lowland culture at any given period thus tends to represent the mingling of diverse continental elements rather than the extension beyond the Straits of a single continental culture.

 xiv. New cultures of continental origin coming across the "high seas" tend to impinge on the Highland Zone rather than on the Lowland. Again, the heavy (orographic) rainfall of the Highland increases the contrast between it—as an environment for Man—and the Lowland. These factors intensify the cultural differentiation between the two Zones already examined.

 xv. Britain is subjected to influences from a quarter other than those mentioned—Ireland. These influences, though persistent and important, are, owing to the comparative smallness of the exportable surplus of men therein and to the existence of the Highland Zone as a wall protecting the Lowland, not very extensive culturally; the more permanent effects of this Irish contact are usually limited to the Highland Zone. The existence of the Highland Zone tends to isolate the inhabitants of the British coast-lands facing St. George's Channel and the Irish Sea; the lands fronting Channel and Sea thus tend to cultural unity.

 xvi. The influence of Ireland during one of the periods under review (the Bronze Age) was greatly strengthened by her importance as a gold and copper producing centre; Britain, lying between Ireland and the continent, benefited by the trade created by this exportable wealth.

 xvii. Deposits of all the metals important in the Bronze Age, copper, tin, and gold, are present in Britain; only those of tin, in Cornwall, are considered to have been worked throughout that Age. The influence of the tin industry on the cultural history of Britain, then as later, is held to be very great.

 xviii. The distribution of population in Britain in prehistoric times is controlled by physiographical conditions. In the Lowland Zone a pervious subsoil, resulting in open country, parkland, scrub, or forest with not too dense undergrowth, is the chief factor. Low hills of easy contour and plateaux possessing such subsoil (chalk and limestone) form the framework of lowland Britain and thus provide the main field for Man's activities; but gravel terraces by rivers are equally suitable, sandy heaths are sometimes occupied, and harbours offering opportunities for commerce are not neglected.

 xix. The areas shunned by Early Man in the Lowland Zone are the impervious clay-lands, which are very extensive; these tend to be waterlogged and to carry dense forest—"damp" oakwood.

 xx. In the Highland Zone also soils exert a powerful influence on distribution, but this influence is masked by another factor peculiar to the Zone—elevation. Above a certain level, whatever the soil may be, Man cannot comfortably live in our wet and cold winters.

xxi. Hence we may say that *soil character* is the controlling factor in lowland distribution, *elevation* in highland distribution; also that Early Man tends to fit himself *into the mountain pattern* of the Highland Zone, *on to the hill pattern* of the Lowland Zone.

xxii. The type of country which Early Man preferred, open or lightly forested with pervious soil, is comparatively infrequent in Britain. Moreover, a great deal of such country was not available, since the range within which he could live in reasonable comfort was limited to about 1,000 feet—from sea-level upwards. Now the most extensive of the areas fulfilling the required conditions happen to be hills or plateaux from 200 to 700 or 800 feet in height. On these he is accordingly in greater evidence (taking all prehistoric periods, Neolithic, Bronze, and Iron into consideration) than in the equally suitable (intrinsically) but restricted low-lying areas, in the Highland and the Lowland Zones alike; there is little or no difference between the two zones in this respect. But whereas this serviceable upland country *dominates* the pattern of the Lowland Zone, it is for the most part *recessive* in the pattern of the Highland Zone. The psychological effect of this difference in environment can hardly be other than profound.

xxiii. The most complete and full manifestation of any *primitive* culture entering eastern or southern Britain from the continent will come to be in the Lowland Zone. The centre and focus in the Lowland Zone of such culture will tend to be the Salisbury Plain region (" Wessex "), because it has the largest area of habitable country, is close to south-coast seaports conveniently reached by Atlantic and Armorican trade, and is the meeting point of the (natural) traffic routes of the Lowland Zone.

xxiv. As civilization developed, and overseas trade growing more important tended to concentrate at the Thames estuary, an economic change began to make itself felt, a change in the type of country and of soil desired by inhabitants and invaders.

xxv. Pervious soils are more easily worked, but clay-lands are more fertile. Hence the progress from subjection to, to control of, environment, which is that from barbarism to civilization, is expressed physiographically by the utilization of the " damp " oakwoods and their gradual replacement by arable fields. Though this change made but little progress save in Roman and late Anglo-Saxon times, it is probable that the preponderance of heavy soils in south-eastern Britain as contrasted with that of pervious soils in south-western Britain (Salisbury Plain region) influenced the transfer of the chief cultural area to the neighbourhood of the lower Thames in the late La Tène period. The absence hereabouts of any spot combining geographic and economic suitability resulted in varied choice of a centre—St. Albans, Colchester; but these both lay at no great distance from the Thames estuary, the physiographic disadvantages of which for concentrated settlement were overcome when the Roman civilization was established—they recurred when it decayed.

CURRENCY BAR: length 2 feet 5½ inches. ⅛. (See Fig. 37.)

Epilogue: The Personality of Britain

One task remains; it is to present a sketch of the essential Britain, wherein Man ensconced himself so snugly. The picture must be imperfect: on no one canvas can we depict "her infinite variety"; and since her character changed in the course of centuries some one date must be chosen. Let us select the dawn of the Iron Age, 500–400 B.C.

The trader in iron and bronze, and the iron-using invader, coasting along the beaches and the cliffs of southern Britain, found by experience that, though sheltered anchorages, creeks, and landing places were numerous, only those where chalk downs or heaths were visible offered the opportunity they sought for barter or for entry. Where estuary or harbour was fringed with forest, the mudflats and beaches were deserted and no trackways led inland.

To these intruders, as to the native, southern Britain presented an illimitable forest of "damp" oakwood, ash and thorn and bramble, largely untrodden. This forest was in a sense unbroken, for without emerging from its canopy a squirrel could traverse the country from end to end; but in another sense it was limited, for the downs and heaths which here and there touched the sea or navigable rivers, and where the overseas adventurers beached their oaken ships, were the terminals of far-reaching stretches of open and semi-open country, grassland and parkland. These zones it was that nourished much of the human life of the time; here were flocks and herds and patches of corn, groups of thatched huts with trails of smoke, and the palisaded banks of the new and strange fortresses; manifestations which all became scantier as parkland merged into woodland.

This open country was sometimes at valley level, but more often consisted of low hills, plateaux, or ridges of moderate elevation but dominant; so that Man moved on his vocations above the environing forest, and his eye ranged over wide spaces.

Lowland Britain then, to most natives in the dawn of the Iron Age took shape as an environment in which Man's life was canalized, and movement shepherded, along belts of open country which, here expanding into wide acreage, there contracting into a narrow ridge, and occasionally gapped by river valleys, ended either at the sea or in the mountains; the memory of movement along them took the form of a succession of great landscapes—the Weald of Sussex seen from the South Downs; the lower Severn and the hills of Wales from the Cotteswolds; the Fenland from the Icknield Way; the Vale of Trent from Lincoln Edge. The bad lands were crossed only when unavoidable, and by the narrowest gaps. Just as we moderns, reviewing our journeys in Britain along our valley roads, identify our routes by the towns passed through, so they, moving along the now deserted ridgeways, recalled the forms of the higher hills—Chanctonbury, Leith Hill, the Wrekin, their landmarks on long journeys.

The man through whose eyes we see may have witnessed the beginning of encroachment on the "damp" oakwoods, at first shunned and feared. They were haunted by lynx, wolf and boar, bear and fighting ox; and were hostile in themselves to Man, his flocks and herds. The transformation by which these areas became, in historic times, centres of agricultural life, had its small beginnings at this time, for the bronze-founders of the Late Bronze Age were located in such forest near Cambridge, and burnt its oaks for charcoal.

Occasionally our Lowlander might make a long journey to the west. The more mountainous the part visited, the less it is changed to-day from what it was then. Though forest may have clothed the high plateaux originally, he saw in 500 B.C., I think, as we see, country "waste as the sea, red with heather, with the moorfowl and the peewits crying." As he approached the Highland Zone from the lowland, the character thus represented in extreme form slowly became apparent to him. The landscape became wilder, the forest more restricted as the valleys became narrower; moorland replaced grassland, the life of his fellows thinned out along the traffic ways and was to be found, sometimes in strange guise, in the hollows of the hills rather than on the crests. Still, however, the keys to the understanding of this high country, as of the lowlands, were the major landmarks; our traveller steered his way along plateau and spur, past barrow and cairn and stone circle, by the sight of successive mountain tops. So guided he reached his goal, the shore of a now forgotten harbour, and saw against the sunset the black curraghs of the Irish.

FIGURE 38.—BRONZE AGE POTTERY. Scale ¼.
1. "A" Beaker, 2. "C" Beaker, 3. "B2" Beaker (globose type), Figures 2, 6 and Plate III;
4. Food vessel, Yorkshire vase (Abercromby Ia), 5. Food vessel, Irish bowl (Abercromby A),
6. Food vessel (Abercromby 4a), Plate IV; 7. Encrusted urn, northern type, Plate V;
8. Cordoned urn, Plate VIII.

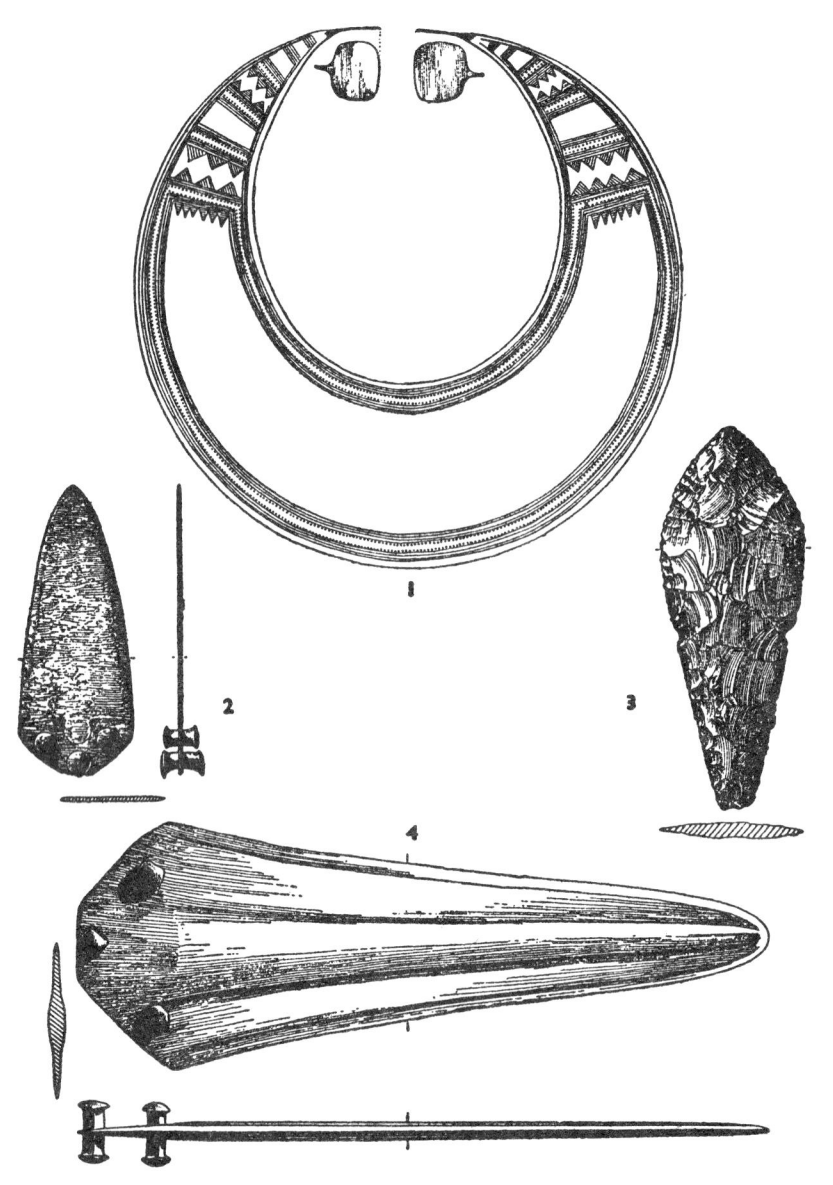

FIGURE 39.—EARLY BRONZE AGE: Ornament, tools, weapon. Scale ⅓.
1. Gold lunula, Figure 22; 2. Flat bronze dagger, Figure 20; 3. Flint dagger, Figure 21; 4. Bronze halberd, Figure 32.

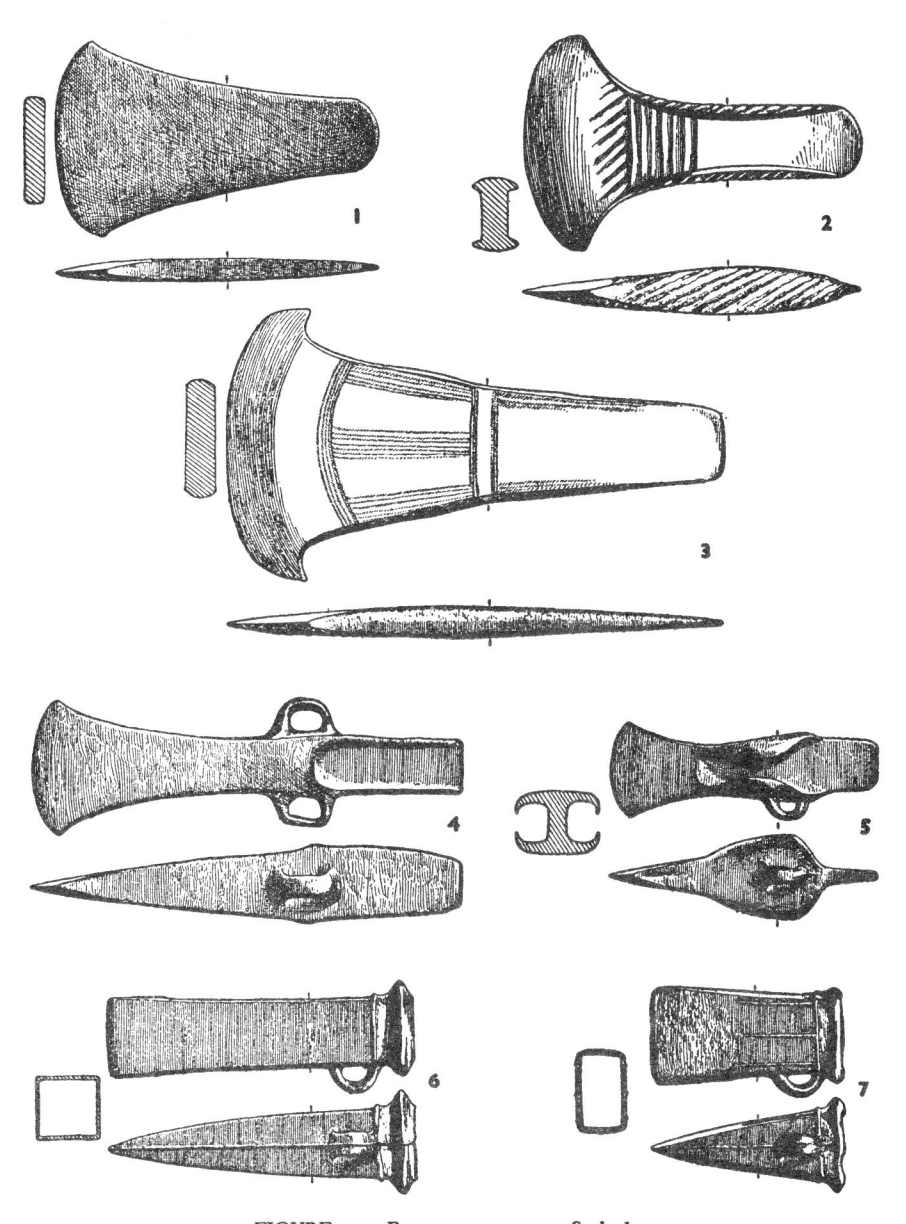

FIGURE 40.—BRONZE AGE AXES. Scale ⅓.

1. Flat axe, 3. Hammer-flanged axe, Plate VI; 2, Cast-flanged axe, Plate VII; 4. Double-looped palstave, Figure 9; 5. Winged axe, continental type, Figure 3; 6. Socketed axe, Breton type, Plate Xa; 7. Socketed axe, Yorkshire type, Plate Xb.

APPENDIX

NOTE ON THE LIVER-FLUKE AS A SUGGESTED FACTOR IN EARLY HUMAN DISTRIBUTION

By Colin Matheson, M.A., B.SC.

The entoparasite, *Fasciola hepatica* Linnaeus, a Flatworm, occurs in the adult stage in the liver and bile-ducts of sheep, and sometimes in cattle, horses, deer, and other domestic and wild animals. The eggs, of which many thousands may be produced by a single fluke, eventually pass out from the body of the sheep to the ground. Unless they fall in or near water they soon perish. Some, however, probably get into water where after a week or two the egg gives rise to a free-swimming larva. This larva, if it does not quickly encounter a particular species of *Lymnaea* or pond-snail, will die; if it does find the snail, it bores its way into the soft tissues of the mollusc. Here it undergoes various developmental changes which result in the production of a number of larvae known as rediae; finally these again give rise to larvae of another type known as cercariae, which finally make their way out of the snail. They swim about for a time and finally moor themselves to blades of damp grass, where they enclose themselves in a capsule. This may be eaten by a sheep, in which case the larva develops to maturity within the sheep and the whole cycle starts over again.

This parasite has caused tremendous losses of stock. In the United Kingdom the annual loss was formerly estimated at a million animals; the loss in 1830 of one-and-a-half million and in 1879–80 of three million sheep was due in considerable measure to liver-rot. In 1882 vast numbers of sheep perished in South America from the same cause.

The importance of water and poorly-drained soil in the life-history of the parasite is obvious. On higher and drier ground the essential conditions for its survival are absent. It seems, then, natural to suggest that the mortality which might result from the grazing of sheep on low marshy areas (although its cause was not understood) would have been a factor in persuading early herdsmen to select other grounds if possible.

Pictish symbol stone (after Anderson). (See Fig. 33.)

Ogham script with transliteration. Voteporix stone, Carmarthenshire, 6th century A.D.
(See Fig. 19.)

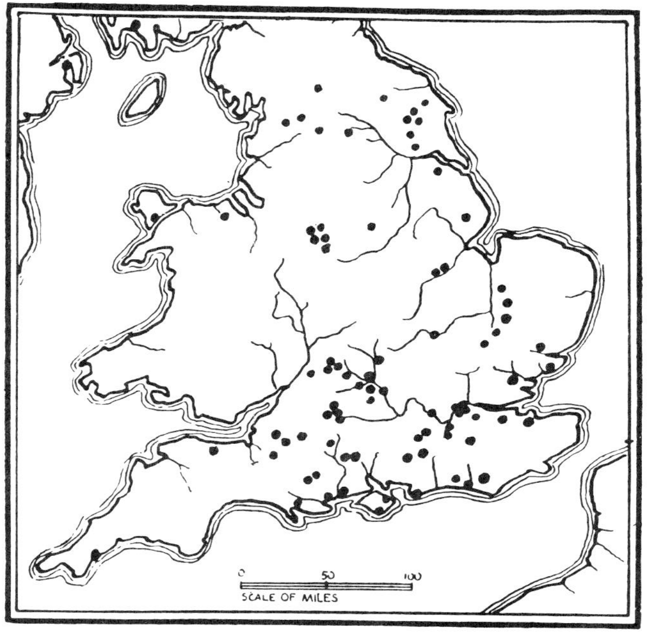

PLATE I.

DISTRIBUTION OF POTTERY OF "WINDMILL HILL" (NEOLITHIC A) TYPES IN SOUTHERN BRITAIN. (Page 15.)

DISTRIBUTION OF POTTERY OF "PETERBOROUGH" (NEOLITHIC B) TYPES IN SOUTHERN BRITAIN. (Page 15.)

These distributions are based on Stuart Piggott, *Archaeological Journal*, Vol. 88 (1931), Figs. 4 and 5; with many additions supplied by Lily F. Chitty, F.S.A. (1943).

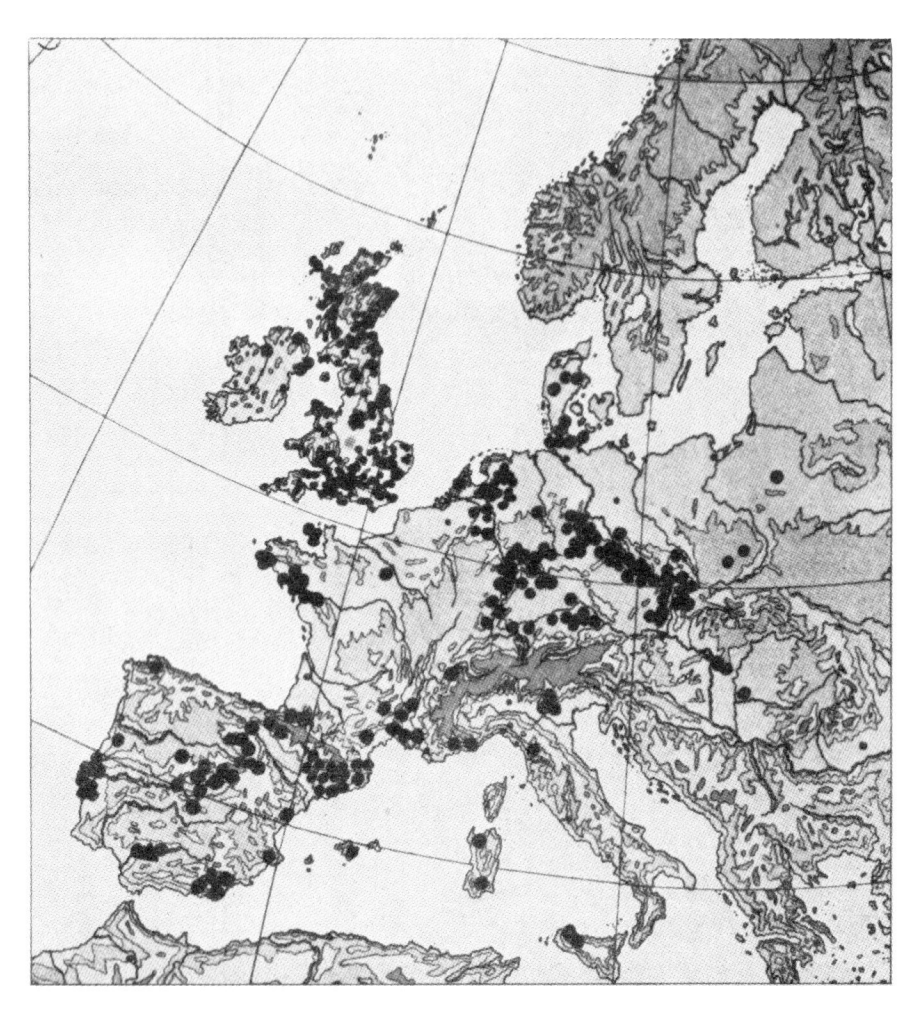

PLATE II.—DISTRIBUTION OF BEAKERS IN EUROPE. (Pages 16, 19–20.)

By L. F. Chitty and C. Fox (1932), using *The Way of the Sea*, by Harold Peake and H. J. Fleure, Fig. 19; V. G. Childe, *Archaeologia*, LXXIV (1925), pp. 159–80, Fig. 1; Abercromby, *Bronze Age Pottery*, I, pp. 9–16, Pls. I–IV.

Note.—Smaller dots have necessarily been used for the British beakers than for those on the Continent.

[Professor V. G. Childe kindly points out that the majority of sites shown in the above map in Denmark are of derivative vessels—"there are only two quite unambiguous Beakers in Denmark." These are from Bigum (Viborg), Jutland, and Kirke Helsinge, Zealand.]

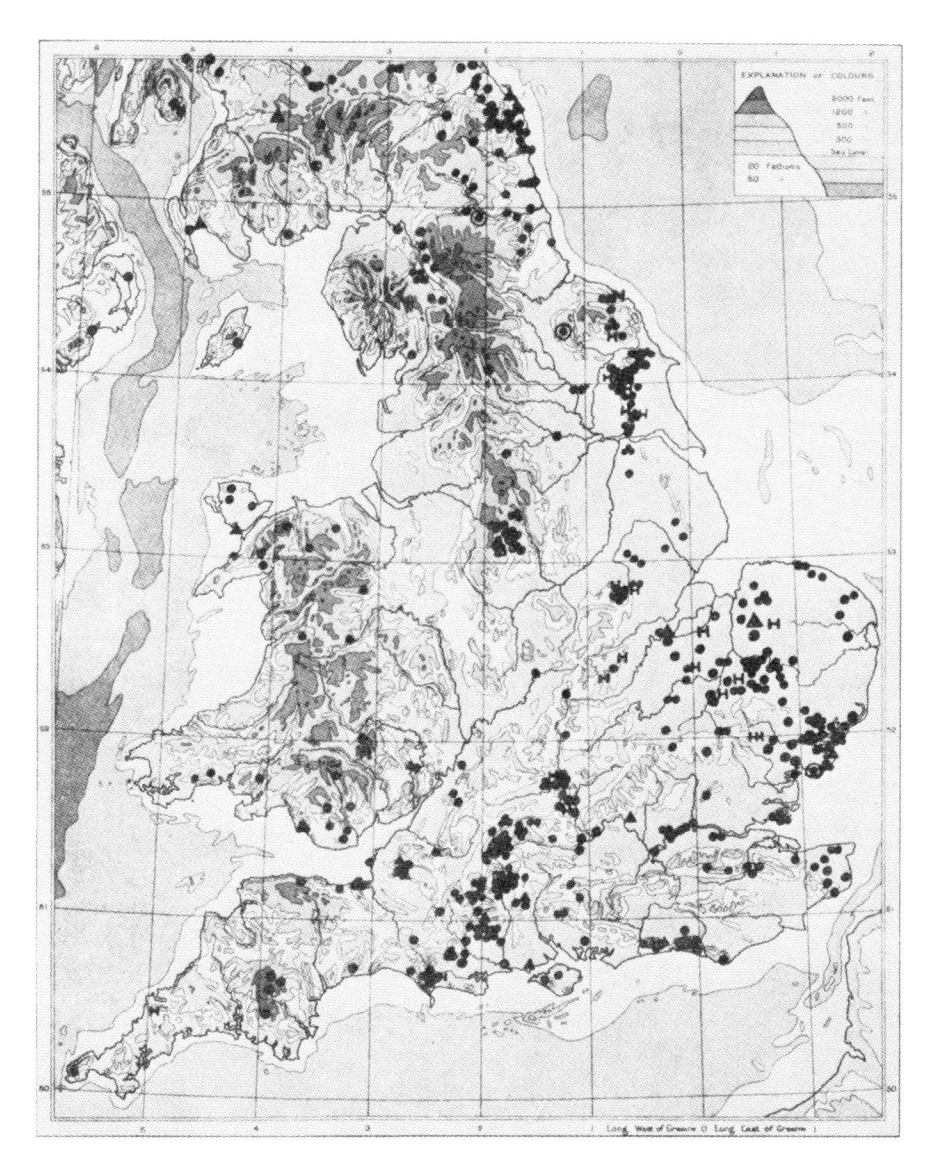

PLATE III.—DISTRIBUTION OF BEAKERS OF THE EARLY BRONZE AGE IN SOUTHERN BRITAIN.
(Pages 32, 54, 68. Illustrations, Fig. 38, 1–3.)
By L. F. Chitty and C. Fox (1932), based on Fox, *Arch. Camb.* (1925), p. 7, with many additions.
● Beaker.   H Handled Beaker.   ⊙ Group of 3 or more associated.   ▲ Settlement.

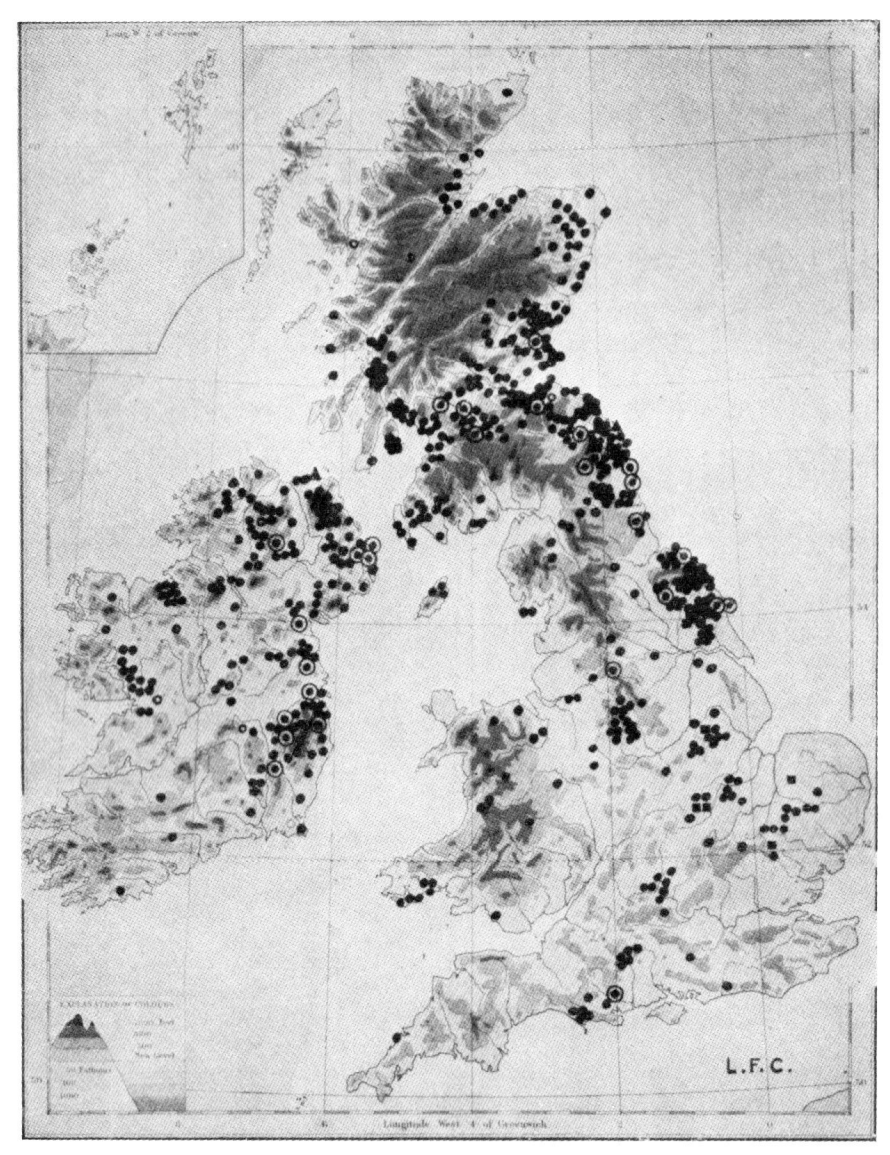

PLATE IV.—DISTRIBUTION IN THE BRITISH ISLES OF FOODVESSELS OF THE EARLY AND MIDDLE BRONZE AGES. (Pages 33, 41, 44. Illustrations, Fig. 38, 4–6.)

By L. F. Chitty and Cyril Fox, revised and with additions by L. F. Chitty (1938), using, *inter alia*, Abercromby, *Bronze Age Pottery*; Greenwell, *British Barrows*; Mortimer, *Forty Years' Researches*; Elgee, *N.E. Yorkshire*; Raistrick, "Bronze Age Settlement of the North of England," *Arch. Ael.*, 4, VIII (1931), 149–65, Pl. XXII; Mary Kitson Clark, *Arch. Journ.*, XCIV (1937), 43–63; Childe, *Prehistory of Scotland* (1935), Map II.

Note that this Map omits miniature collared urns, and L. S. Gogan's "Leinster" series of late Irish foodvessels.

● Foodvessel.   O County only known.   ⊙ Group of 3 or more.   ■ Handled foodvessel.

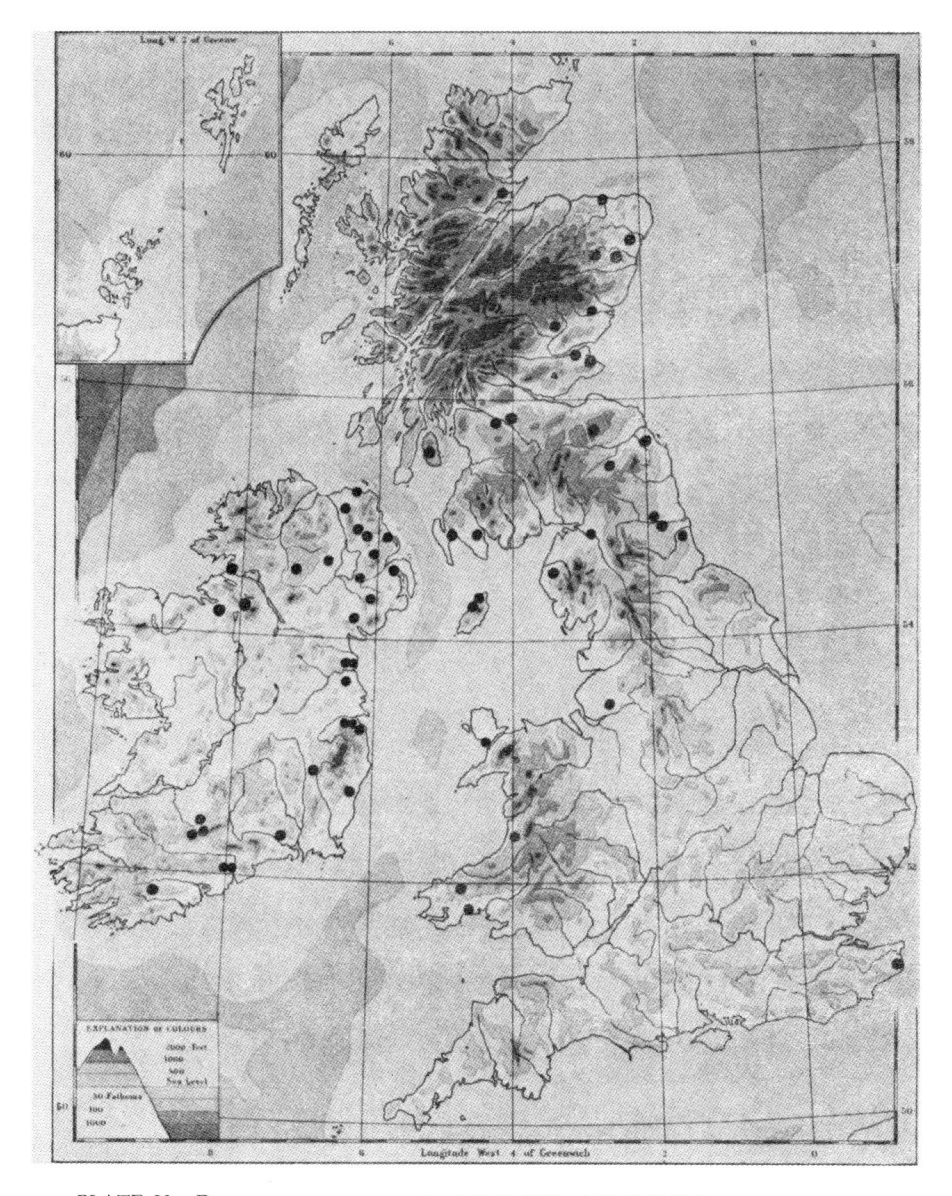

PLATE V.—Distribution in the British Isles of Encrusted Urns of the Late Bronze Age.
(Pages 41, 42, 70. Illustrations, Fig. 38, 7, and tail-piece, p. 8.)

By L. F. Chitty and Cyril Fox (1932), based on Fox, "An Encrusted Urn of the Bronze Age," *Antiq. Journ.*, VII (1927), p. 115. Many fresh discoveries in Ireland do not alter the general distribution pattern. An urn recently found at Holywell, Flintshire, is geographically important.

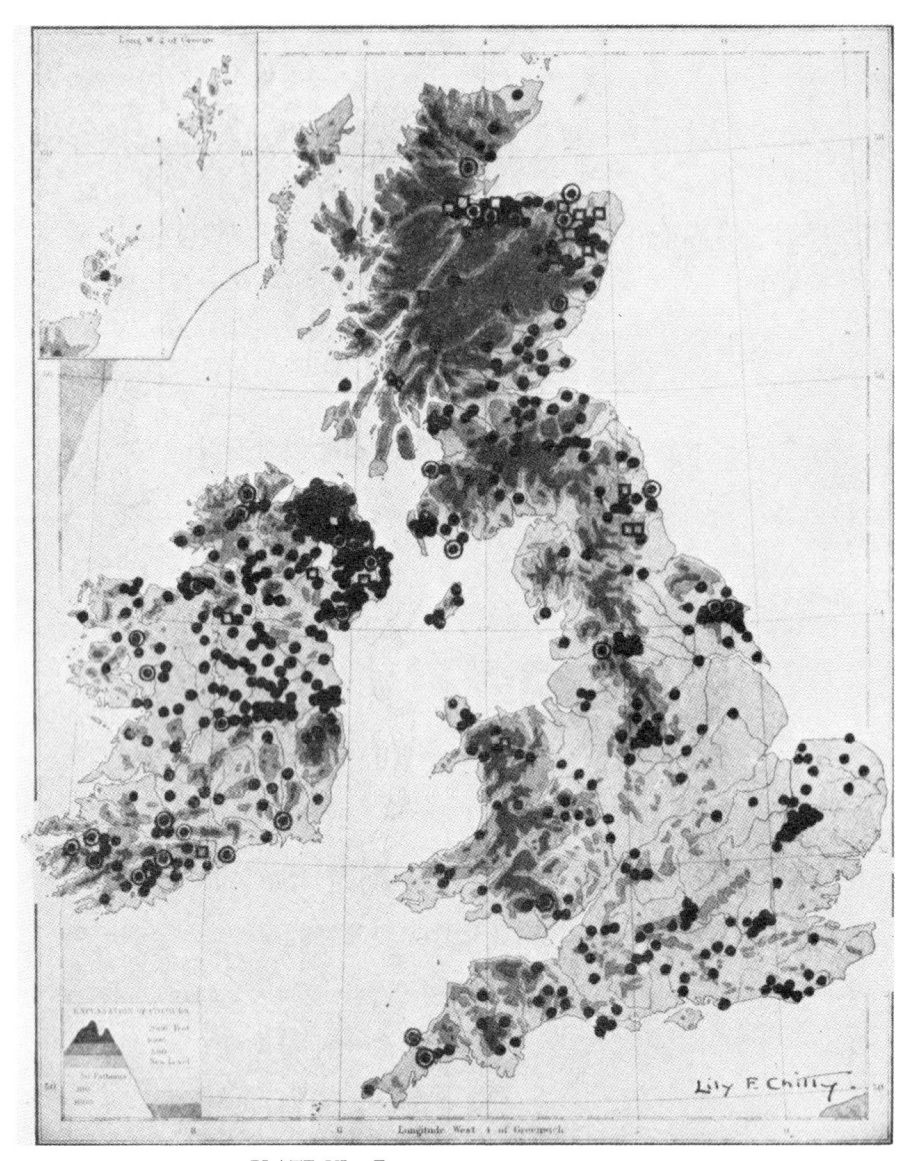

PLATE VI.—FLAT AND HAMMER-FLANGED AXES.
(Pages 45, 70, 73. Illustrations, Fig. 40, 1 and 3.)

By L. F. Chitty (1938), using, *inter alia*, The Catalogue of Bronze Implements, British Museum Crawford, *Geog. Journ.*, XL (1912) 184–203, 307–317 ; Childe, *Proc. Roy Soc Edin.*, 50, 1930, Map II ; Armstrong, *Proc. Soc. Antiq.*, XXVII (1915), 253–5, Map ; and List published by National Museum of Ireland, Dublin, 1915, Nos. 1–51.

● Axe.   ⊙ Hoard.   □ Mould.

PLATE VII.—CAST-FLANGED AXES. (Page 48. Illustration, Fig. 40, 2.)
By L. F. Chitty (1938), using, *inter alia*, The Catalogue of Bronze Implements, British Museum.
Omitting those with hammer flanges (rudimentary) and with bar or developed stop ridges (palstaves).
● Flanged axe.   ◊ Long Continental type.   ⊚ Hoard.

PLATE VIII.—CORDONED URNS. (Pages 41, 42. Illustration, Fig. 38, 8.)
By L. F. Chitty (1938), based on, *inter alia*, Abercromby, *Bronze Age Pottery*.
● Urn of Cordon series, including transitional forms.   ⊙ Several found on site.   O Degenerate form, apparently derivative.

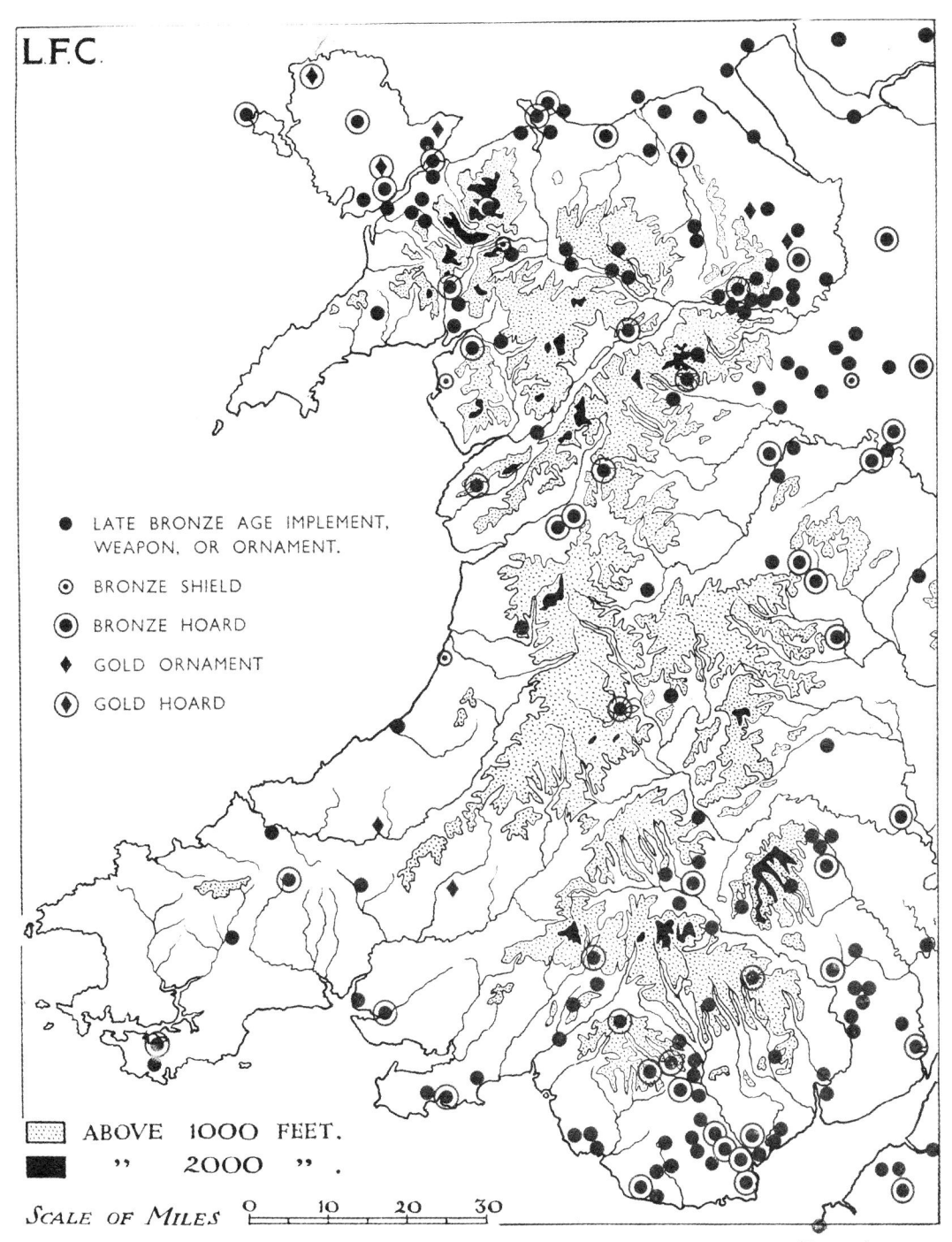

PLATE IX.—Distribution of finds of the Late Bronze Age in Wales and its borders. (Page 73.)

By Lily F. Chitty (1943), based on, *inter alia*, R. E. M. Wheeler, *Prehistoric and Roman Wales*, Fig. 112, and W. F. Grimes, *Guide to the Prehistoric Collections*, National Museum of Wales. In addition to the Late Bronze Age types generally recognised, hoards containing indigenous advanced forms of looped spear, palstave, tanged chisel, etc., are mapped. "Tara" gold torcs are excluded.

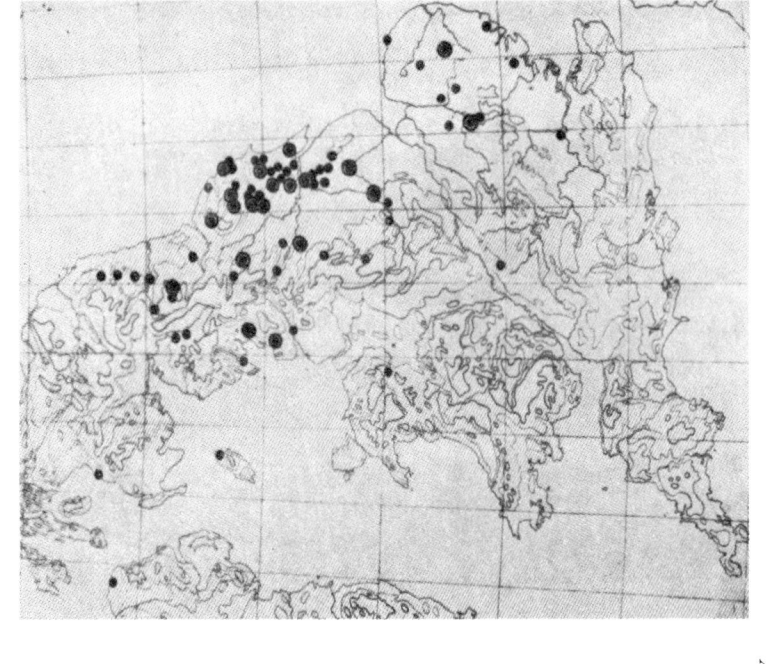

PLATE X.

(a) SOCKETED AXES, BRETON TYPE, IN BRITAIN.
(Page 23. Illustration, Fig. 40, 6.)

(b) SOCKETED AXES, YORKSHIRE TYPE, IN BRITAIN
(Page 71. Illustration, Fig. 40, 7.)

After L. F. Chitty and C. Fox, in Fox, "Distribution of Man in East Anglia," *Proc. Prehist. Soc. E. Anglia* (1933), p. 104, Pl. IX.

● Single axe.　⊙ In hoard.

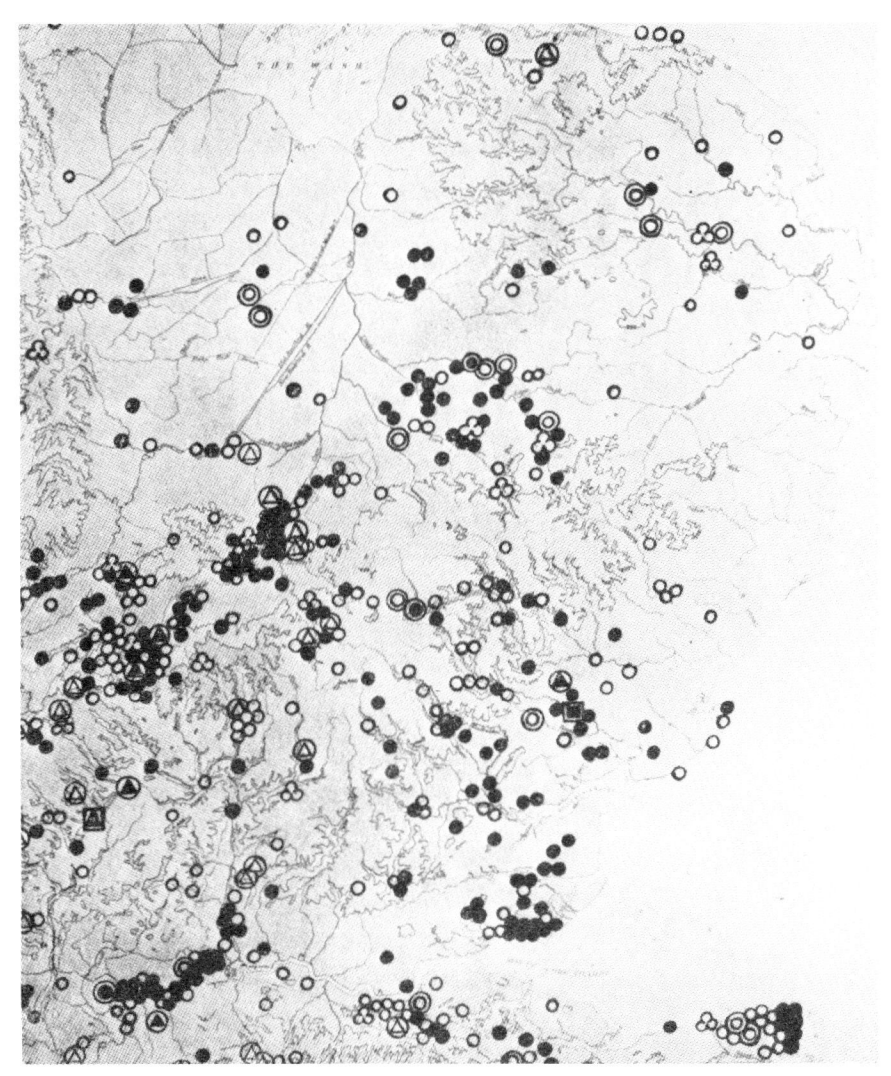

PLATE XI.—Distribution of objects of early iron age "c" in East Anglia.
(Pages 19, 79.)

After L. F. Chitty and C. Fox, in Fox, "Distribution of Man in East Anglia," *Proc. Prehist. Soc. E. Anglia* (1933), p. 158, Fig. 7.

● Finds other than—   O Coins, ◉ Coin hoard, ⊕ Prolific coin site,   ⊙ Hoard,   ⬤ Fort. La Tène III, no previous evidence.   △ Fort occupied in La Tène III.   ⊕ Fort, period of construction not known.   ▲ Vervlamivm.   ■ Camvlodvnvm.

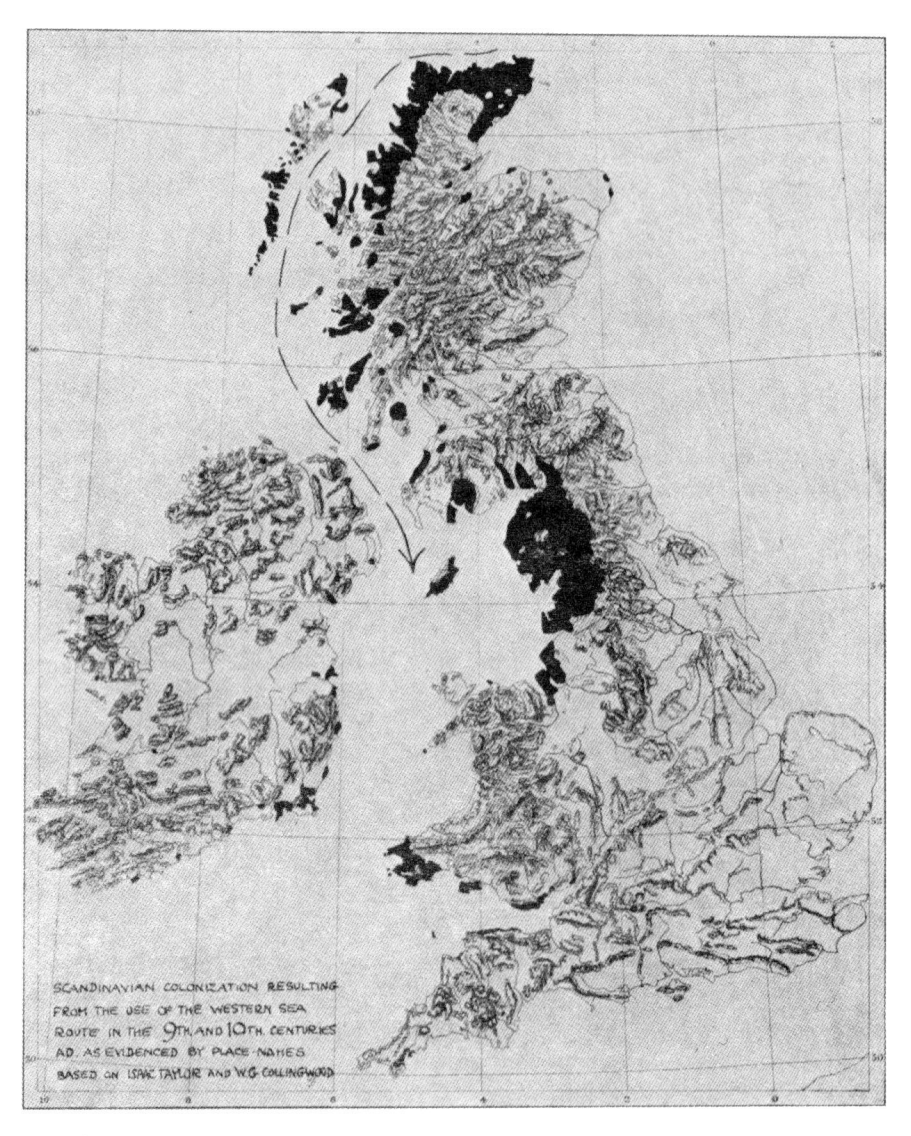

PLATE XII.—Distribution of viking settlements in northern and western Britain.
(Pages 22, 42.)

Based on Isaac Taylor, *Words and Places*, 2nd ed. map, p. 1, and W. G. Collingwood, *Scandinavian Britain* (1908), Map, p. 1.

Note.—The distribution in Eastern Britain is *not* shown.

PHYSICAL MAP OF SOUTHERN BRITAIN.

The overprint shows the distribution of antiquities of the Bronze Age, *circa* 1900-500 B.C. Monuments, settlements, bronze implements, certain stone implements, and precious objects are included. A blue dot represents either a single find, a group of associated objects or a barrow of the Bronze Age with its contents. By L. F. CHITTY and CYRIL FOX.

PERSONALITY OF BRITAIN, MAP C.

INDEX

In order to keep the Index within due compass, a number of purely topographical references, and all names of persons, have been omitted. It is suggested that the Index should be used in conjunction with the Table of Contents (pp. 5, 6).

Aegean, 10
agriculture, agricultural, 10, 11, 57n, 65, 67, 77n, 79, 80, 82, 84
Aire Gap, 45n, 69, 71, 72
alder, 51, 54
alignments, stone, 11n, 20
All Cannings Cross, 19
alluvium, 68, 80
Alps, alpine, 17, 20, 22, 86, *see also* West Alpine
altitude, 53, *see also* elevation
amber, 44, 45n, 85
    coast, region, 10, 24
    route, 11, 87
Anglesey, 45, 58n, 69, 70
Anglo-Saxon(s), 14, 17, 19, 28, 33, 61, 79, 80, 81, 82, 83n, 89, *see also* Saxon
animals, domestic, 63, 65
    wild, 62, 63, *see also* horse, lynx, etc.
ash, ashwoods, 53, 55
"Atlantic" climatic phase, 51, 77, 78, *see also* "sub-Atlantic"
Atlantic coast, zone, etc., 21, 34n, 50, 51, 53n, 85
    ports, route, seaways, etc., 10, 22, 27, 42, 43, 45n, 87
Aunjetitz, 10, 47, 83, 85
Aurochs, 63
Avebury, 20, 32
axe, cast-flanged, 47, 48n
    flat, 45, 49, 70
    hammer-flanged, 45, 49
    socketed, 23, 71-2
    stone, 57n, 70n, 84
    winged, 15

Baltic, 15, 27, 45
barrows, barrow burial, 40, 42, 54, 55n, 56, 68, 73, 76
    long, 11, 20, 41
Barry, 26
beads, faience, 49
beaker(s), 14, 16, 19n, 28, 54, 64
    A, 27, 62
    B1, 26
    B2, 27
    culture, 41, 42
    period, map, 9n, 55, 66, 68, 69, 78
beaker-folk, 19, 32, 40, 42n, 65, 85
    A, 14, 16, 20, 28n, 44, 45n, 87
    B1, 14, 19, 20, 45n
    B2, 14, 16, 20, 28, 87
bear, 62, 64
beaver, 63
beech, 51, 53, 55
Belgae, Belgic, 58n, 79, 83, 86
Belgium, 15, 86
Berkshire, 66, 67n, 79
Berwyns, 29, 70
bilberry, 54
biotic factors, 53, 54
birch, 51, 53, 54, 55
birds, 63
Black Mountains, 32, 58n
Blackamore, 76n, 78
Blaenrhondda, 74
Bleasdale, 58n
boar, 63, 64
boats, *see* dug-outs, curraghs
Bodmin Moor, 54
Bodvoc, 83
bog moss, 54
Boreal, climatic phase, 26, 51
boulder clay, 56

box, 55
bracken, 55
brambles, 53, 56
Breckland, 55, 56, 65, 68
Breiddin, 37n
Bristol, 61, 67
Bristol Channel, 22, 23, 26, 48n
Brittany, 15, 19, 20, 22, 33, 34n, 49, 50, 84, 85, 87
Broch culture, 22, 41
Bronze Age, 9, 55, 58, 70, 83
    chronology, 9
    climate, 51
    metal working, 20, 21, 45, 47, 49, 57, 68, 88
    settlement, 56, 64 ff, 77, 78, 82n, 89
    subsidence in, 9, 26, 27
    summary, 85, 86
    see also barrow, urn, foodvessel, beaker, etc.
Bronze Age, Early, 11n, 14, 27, 41, 43, 44, 45, 49, 58n, 62, 70, 73, 78n, 87
    Middle, 20, 40, 44, 49, 58n, 62, 87
    Late, 15, 17, 19, 20n, 23, 42, 48, 49, 50, 66, 67, 68, 71, 73, 76n, 77, 78n, 84, 86
bronze dagger folk, 50
brooches, La Tène, 35n, 36n
Brythonic, 41
Bugeilyn, 76n

Caernarvon, 69
Caesar, 15, 63n, 84
cairns, 14, 55n, 58n, 76n, *see also* Megalithic
Caithness, 22, 29, 32, 45, 73, 85, 87
Calleva, 38
Calluna vulgaris, 53, 54, 55
Cambridge region, uplands, etc., 54, 56 ff, 66, 67, 79, 81-2
Cambridgeshire, 65
camps, *see* hill forts
Camulodunum, 58n, 83, 86n
Canterbury, 67
Cardigan Bay, 28
Carmarthenshire, 45, 73
carnivores, 62
castle, 41
cauldrons, 42, 48
causewayed camps, 14, 15
Celtic agriculture, 77, 80
    art, 35, 36, 63
    bronzes, 62n
    Church, 40
    language, 40, 41
    pony, 63
    saints, 70
Celts, 19, 38n, 50, 76, 84
chalk, formation, 29, 31, 32, 58, 67, 79, 88
    occupation of, 54, 55, 56, 64, 65, 66, 68, 77, 78, 82, 83
    vegetation of, 53, 55, *see also* downs, North Downs, etc.
Channel zone (English), 15, 19, 34n
charcoals, 55n, 57
charioteers, 36
Cheshire, 37n, 58, 59
Cheviot Hills, 29, 69, 76
Chilterns, the, 31, 40, 65, 66
Christchurch, Hants, 15
Christianity, Christendom, 40, *see* Early Christian
Church, Celtic, Roman, 40
cinerary urn, *see* urn
circles, of stone, wood, 11n, 58n
Cissbury, 82
civilization, in Britain, 19, 28, 40, 45, 49, 87, 89

95

civilization, Celtic, 86n
　　European, 11, 45, 86, 87
　　Mediterranean, 11, 84
　　Roman, 86n, 89
　　sources of, 10
Clacton, 27
clay (clay-lands), 53, 54, 55n, 56, 57, 58, 59, 65, 68, 78–9, 81, 82, 83n, 86n, 88
Cleveland Hills, 65
cliff castle, 33n
climate, 51, 53, 54, 86, *see also* Atlantic, Boreal, etc.
climatic change, 77, 78
"climatic climax," vegetational, 53, 54
Clyde, river, estuary, 44, 45n, 71, *see also* Forth-Clyde isthmus
coastline (of Britain), 15, 24–5
coinage, 38, 83, 85
Colchester, 89, *see also* Camulodunum
commerce, commercial, 11, 17, 20, 87, 88, *see also* trade
communications, prehistoric, 67
Constance, Lake of, 22
continent of Europe, 15, 19, 20, 25, 34n, 50, 89
continental, 15, 34n, 50
copper, 10, 19, 44, 45, 47, 50, 70, 85, 88
Corbilo, 84
cordoned urn, *see* urn
Cornwall, Cornish, 22, 32, 33, 34n, 41, 44, 49, 69, 88, *see also* tin
Cotteswolds, 32, 33, 45n, 57n, 64n, 65, 68
cotton grass, 54
culture(s), chronology of, 9
　　continental, European, Mediterranean, 11, 17, 19, 21, 22, 34, 40, 43, 85, 86, 87, 88
　　continuity of, 40, 88
　　diffusion of, 15, 17, 19, 20, 33, 87
　　duality of, 42, 44, 86
　　expansion of, 19, 37, 40, 42, 85
　　fusion of, 9n, 40, 85
　　Highland, character of, 21, 40, 70, 88
　　Lowland, character of, 33, 38, 40, 67, 88, 89
　　province, Irish sea, 44, 88
　　resurgence of, 40
　　Roman, 37
　　successive, 20
　　unique, 29, 41, 88
　　unity of, 41, 67, 88
Cunobelinus, 83
curraghs, 70
currency bars, 38, 86
Crete, 10, 11

daggers, flat, 44, 45
　　flint, 45
　　grooved, 49
　　tanged, 19, 45, 85
damp oakwood, *see* oakwood
Danes, 19
Dark Ages, 9, 55, 58, 66, 75n, 82, 86n, *see also* Early Christian
Dartmoor, 29, 54, 73, 76
Dee, river, 59, 72
deer, 63
Denmark, 26, 85
depopulation, 78n
Derbyshire, *see* Peak district
Dervacus, 83
Derwent, river, 69, 73
Deverel-Rimbury, 17, 20n, 49, *see also* Late Bronze Age
Devon, 22, 26, 32
diseases, 63–4, 94
distribution, factors governing, 14, 15 ff, 28 ff, 33, 56 ff, 63, 64 ff, 73, 77 ff
　　maps, limitations of, 68
Dobuni, 38n
dog, 63
Domesday, 28, 82
Dorset, 17, 34n, 77n

Dove, river 69, 73
Dover, *see* Straits of Dover
downs, downland, 29, 54, 55, 65, 66, 77, *see also* North Downs, etc.
dry oakwood, *see* oakwood
Dublin, 44, 45n, 69
dug-out boats, 67
Durham, 29, 62
dykes, 58
　　Offa's Dyke, 33, 58, 80

eagle, 63
Early Bronze Age, *see* Bronze Age
Early Christian period, 41, 44, 73, *see also* Dark Ages
Early Iron Age, 17, 19, 26, 37, 41, 42, 51, 54, 55, 58, 62, 66, 73, 76, 77
　　"A," 19, 33, 37n, 78n
　　"B," 22, 33, 34, 36–7, 38, 42, 49
　　"C," 15, 38, 79, 86
　　chronology, 9
East Anglia (East Anglian), 14, 15, 16, 19, 31, 40, 49, 54, 55, 58, 64n, 65, 67n, 68, 71, 79n, 83, *see also* Cambridge region
East Moors, Cardiff, 26n
economic factors, outlook, power, etc., 82, 83, 84, 85, 86n
edaphic (soil) factors, 53
Eddisbury, 37n
Eden, valley, 69, 71
Egypt, 10, 83, 85
elevation, relation to settlement, 73–6, 88–9
Elk, Irish, 62
elm, 51, 55
English Channel, 15, 17, 23 24, 27, *see also* Channel, Straits of Dover
erosion, 27, 28, 87
Essex, 17, 27, 68, 81, 84, 86
estuaries, 15, 17, 19, 22, 28, 32, 33, 39, 67, 86, 87, *see also* ports, rivers
Europe, 10, 17, 24, 40, 44, 45, 46, 47, 53, 87
Exmoor, 29

false crests, siting on, 55
fauna, birds, 63
　　carnivores, 62
　　domestic, 63
　　rodents, 63
　　ungulates, 62
Fen(s), 27, 40, 54, 55, 56, 58, 64n, 65, 66, 67n, 68
Fenland(s), 14, 15, 32 34
Ffos Ton Cenglau, 54
Ffridd Faldwyn, 38, 41
Finistère, 22, 85, 87
fishing, 66, 67
flint, flint mining, 45, 65n
flora, factors governing, 53, *see* vegetation
foodvessel, 33, 41, 42, 44
　　culture, 9n
forest, 52, 55, 56, 58, 59, 61, 65, 68
　　succession, history of, 51, 52, 54
forests (ancient), 25
　　avoidance of, 63, 68
　　clearing of, 80, 81, 82
　　disappearance of, 54, 55
　　occupation of, 57n, 58n, 68, 72, 82
　　submerged, 25, 26
　　varieties of, 53, 54, 55, *see also* oakwood
Forest of Dean, 24, 29, 38n
Forest Ridge, 31, 78
Forestian, Upper, 54
Forth-Clyde isthmus, lowland, 41, 71
forts, *see* hill-forts
fowling, 67
France, 11, 22, 45, 49, 85
　　Atlantic, Western, 10, 22, 24, 42, 85
　　Northern, 10, 15, 17, 36n, 84, 86

Gaelic, 44
Galloway, 32, 45n, 69
Garonne, river, 84
gault, 56
Gelligaer Common, 75n
geology, of Britain, 28 ff, 61, 68, *see also* Jurassic, limestones, sandstone, etc.
Germany, 15, 24
glacial drift, 58n, *see also* soils, impervious
Glamorgan, 24, 26, 54, 57n, 62, 69, 74, 75n, 76n
Glastonbury, 26, 33, 63
Gloucestershire, 62, 82, 86
goat, 63
gold, 10, 44, 45, 49, 69n, 73, 83, 85, 88
gorse, 55
grassland(s), 53, 54
gravel(s), 56, 58n, 65, 66, 78, 82
    vegetation of, 53, 55
gravel terraces, 83, 88
Greece, Greek, 11, 49, 84
greensand, lower, 66, 68, *see also* soils, pervious
grenz horizont, 51

Hafod 74
halberds, 45, 46
Hallstatt culture, influence, 23, 42, 48
harbours, harbourage, 15, 22, 23, 28, 34n, 39, 42, 83, 84, 88, *see also* estuaries, ports
hare, 63
hawthorn, 53, 55
hazel, 51, 53, 55, 56
heath(s), 54, 55, 56, 88
heathland, 53, 54, 65, *see also* soils, pervious
Hebrides, Hebridean, 14, 22, 32, 63, 86n
hendre, 74
Hengistbury Head, 67
Herefordshire, 58, 81
Hertfordshire, 79, 86
Highland Zone, a barrier, 33, 38, 40, 44
    character of, 29, 33, 40, 87, 88-9
    climate, 51, 53
    culture in, 32, 37, 40, 44, 48, 88
    lowland in, 29
    occupation, settlement, 37, 58n, 62, 69-76, 79n, 82
    traffic in, 70-2
    vegetation in, 52, 53, 54
Highlands, gold trade in, 49
hill-forts, 32, 33, 36, 38, 50, 54, 73, 77, 82, 83
hinterland (in relation to ports), 71
hoards, 49, 76
Holland, 15, 20
holly, 53, 56
horse, 63
horse-bits, 35n, 36n
Humber, 15, 32, 33, 65, 66, 67n, 68, 87
hunters, 62, 64

Iberia, 85, *see also* Spain, Portugal
Icknield way, 66
Ictis, 84
igneous rocks, 28
impervious soils, *see* soils
intrusions, 42, 49n, 59
invaders, 19, 39, 42, 51, 53, 67, 77, 78, 88
invasion, aspects of, 10, 11, 14, 19, 20, 33, 40, 41, 82, 86, 87
    sources of, 15, 17, 42
Ireland, 14, 23, 34n, 85
    duality of culture in, 42, 44
    external relations, 42-4, 59
    influence on Britain, 45-8, 49, 73n, 88
    see also trade, gold, copper, etc.
Irish Sea, 22, 42, 44, 59, 69, 71, 88
    trade, *see* trade, Irish
iron, 24, 38n

Iron Age A, B, C, *see* Early Iron Age
Isle of Man, *see* Man
Italy, 84
Itchen, river, 67

juniper, 55
Jurassic outcrop, rock, etc., 32, 33, 35, 36, 58, 65, 66, 71
Jutland, 10, 85

Kent, 15, 16, 24, 27, 36n, 64n, 66, 68, 84, 87
kinship, 40

La Tène, 9, 17, 35n, 63, 82, 83, 89
lake villages, 26, 33, 63
Lancashire, 58, 59
land bridge, 25
land-fall, in Britain, 22, 28
Land's End, 22, 33, 49, 69, 85, 87
land sinkage, *see* subsidence
Late Bronze Age, *see* Bronze Age
limestones, 32, 53, 54, 55, 57n, 58n, 64, 65, 69, 78, 88
Lincoln Edge, Wolds, 32, 58, 65, 66
Lincolnshire, 11, 20, 32, 41, 71
liver-rot, liver-fluke, 63, 94
Llantwit Major, 62
Lleyn, 69
Llynfawr, 24, 76n
loams, 53, 79, 83n
Loire, river, mouth, 22, 84, 85
London, 66, 86
long barrows, *see* barrows, long
lowland, in Highland Zone, 29, 88
Lowland Zone, character, 29-32, 87, 89
    climate, 77
    cultural aspects of, 40, 41, 42, 71, 88
    cultural chronology in, 9
    distributions, 32, 33, 45
    importance of, 38-9
    romanization of, 38
    settlement in, 58n, 64-8, 82, 83, 86
    settlers from, 62
    vegetation in, 53
Lowlands, gold trade in, 49
Luce Bay, 69, 70
lunula, 49, 69
Lydney, 63, 82
lynchets, 77
lynx, 62, 65

Maglemose culture, 26
malaria, 64
Man, Isle of, 14, 44, 70
maps, symbols on, 14, 64, 68
Margam Mountain, 83
marshlands, 11, 54
Massilia, 84
Meare, 33
Mediterranean Sea, cultures, etc., 10, 11, 22, 43, 44, 49, 83, 84, 87
megalith builders, 57n
Megalithic culture, folk, tombs, etc., 11, 22, 24, 27, 28, 32, 40, 44, 45, 73, 78, 85, 87, *see also* barrows, cairns
Mendips, 29, 32, 55
menhirs, 11n
merchants, 45, 48, *see also* trade
Mercia, Mercians, 33, 58
Mersey estuary, 59, 69, 70, 71
Merthyr Mawr, 26n
Mesolithic times, period, folk, 10, 15, 27, 44n, 51, 78
metal, metalwork, metallurgy, 10, 11, 34, 35, 36, 44, 45, 49 85, *see also* gold, copper, tin, etc.
Middle Ages, 67
Middle Bronze Age, *see* Bronze Age
Midland Gap, 29, 59

Midlands, the, 58, 68
migration, seasonal, 74
mining, flint, 65*n*
moorland(s), 53, 54, 74, 75, 76, 78
moose, 62
Morbihan, 22
Morvah, 49
mosquito, 64
mountains, mountainous country, 29, 33, 54
    settlement in relation to, 37, 70, 73, 75–6, 82
Mycenae, Mycenaean, 11, 49, 83

Nene, river, 15, 65, 67
Neolithic Age, 9, 11, 77, 78, *see also* Megalithic
Neolithic "A" pottery, culture, etc., 9, 14, 15, 19, 27, 28, 65*n*, 87
Neolithic "B" pottery, culture, 9, 14, 15
Neolithic culture, folk, man, times, etc., 40, 43, 44, 45, 51, 54, 57*n*, 62, 63, 67*n*, 85
New Forest, 54
Norfolk, 26, 32, 55, 65*n*, 66
Norman, 41, 82
North Channel, 42
North Downs, 29, 65, 66
North Sea, 15, 17, 22, 24, 25*n*, 26, 27, 28*n*, 51, 87
Northampton, shire, uplands, 32, 38*n*, 65
Northumbria, 33, 44, 69, 71
Norway, Norsemen, 22, 70
Norwich, 67

Oak, common, 53
    Durmast, 53, 54
oakwood, "damp," 53, 54, 55, 56, 57*n*, 58, 64, 72, 78*n*, 79, 81, 88, 89
    "dry," 53, 55
occupation, character, range, etc., 55, 58*n*, 76, 77, 78
    intermittent, 74, 78, *see also* settlement
Offa's Dyke, *see* dykes
Ogham stones, 44
Orkneys, 14, 22
Orwell, river, estuary, 15, 55, 67

Padstow, 69
Palaeolithic Age, 10, 62, 63
Palaeozoic Age, rocks, 28, 29, 33
palstave, double-looped, 23
Parisii, the, 18, 34
parkland, 55, 88
Peacock's Farm, 26–7
Peak district, 29, 32, 33, 54, 71, 73
peat, 25*n*, 26, 52, 54, 56*n*
pedestal urns, *see* urns
pelican, 63
Pembrokeshire, 26, 28, 32, 41, 58*n*, 69
Pen Dinas, 37, 41
peninsular routes, 22, 69
Pennines, the, 29, 41, 54, 58*n*, 59, 69, 71, 72
Pentland Firth, 24
Penwith, 49
pervious soils, *see* soils
Peterborough, 65, 67
Pictish culture, 41, 73
pig breeding, 79
pine, 51, 53, 54
place names, 82*n*
plateaux, 83, 89
    occupation of, 77, 78
ploughs, 77*n*, 79
Plumpton Plain, 77*n*
Plynlimon, 70
pollen analysis, 52
population, character of, 19
    concentrations of, 65, 66, 67
    distribution of, 53, 64, 65, 69, 82, 88
    increase of, 78, 79, 82

population and trade, 71
ports, 67, 71, 83, 84, 86
Portugal, 10, 21
pottery, 37*n*, 38*n*, *see also* urns
poverty line, level, of settlement, 58*n*, 78

Quercus petraea, 53
    Robur, 53

Rabbit, 63
rainfall, 51, 53, 78, 88
rapier, 48
reindeer, 62
religion, 10, 84–5
revolution, economic, 82
    industrial, 84
Rhayader, 73*n*
Rhine, river, 17, 20, 44, 83
Rhineland(s), 10, 16, 85, 86
Rhine-mouths, 15, 87
Rhône, river, 20, 84
Ribble, river, 45*n*, 71
Richborough, 15
ridgeways, 66, 67*n*, *see also* trackways
Rillaton, 49
rivers, as highways, 72
    in relation to settlement, 19, 32, 65, 67, 79, 87
rocks, igneous, metamorphic, 32, *see also* geology
rodents, 63
Roman age, period, times, 9, 41, 42, 45, 50, 51, 63, 77, 79, 80, 82, 83, 84, 86, 89
    civilization, 38
    conquest, 15
Romanization, 19, 38
Romano-Celtic agriculture, 80
round barrows, *see* barrows

St. Albans, 58*n*, 89, *see also* Verulamium
St. George's Channel, 22, 42, 44, 88
St. Just, 49
St. Samson, 70*n*
Salisbury Plain, 29, 32, 54, 65, 66, 67, 70*n*, 77*n*, 83, 85, 86, 89
sand(s), 53, 55, 68, 78, 82
sandstone(s), 32, 54
sarsens, 32
Saxon, 15, 40, 42, 58, *see also* Anglo-Saxon
Scandinavia, 15, 24
Scilly, 14
Scotland, animals in, 62, 63
    continuity of culture in, 40, 41
    cultural connections, 44, 45*n*, 69
    distributions (settlement) in, 11, 14, 36*n*, 37, 73
    seasonal migrations in, 74
    structural character of, 28–9
    trade connections in, 49, 85
    vegetation in, 53, *see also* Caithness, Clyde, etc.
sea route, western, 22, 23, 51, 86
    -ways, -road, 22, 24, 32, 42, 48*n*, 49, 70, 87, *see also* Atlantic
seafarers, -men, 10, 15, 42, 43
Secondary formations, deposits, 28, 29
sedge, 54
Seine, river, 15, 17
settlement, areas of difficult, 78 ff
    areas of easy, 78 ff, 82
    coastal, 70
    expansion of, 19, 78
    factors governing, 15, 28, 32, 55, 62, 65, 66, 67, 68, 69, 70, 71, 72, 82
    geological structure and, 65, 68
    influence of elevation on, 73, 76
    seasonal, 74, 76
    water supply of, 66

Severn, river, valley, estuary, 29, 33, 45, 61, 70, 72, 73*n*
shales, 54
sheep, 54, 63
Shetlands, 22, 63
shields, bronze, 48
Shropshire, 29, 45*n*, 70
sickle, bronze, 22
    socketed, 48*n*
Silchester, 38
situlae, 42
Skye, 11, 32
Snowdonia, 70
societies, Mediterranean, continental, 11
soil characters, 32*n*, 53, 55, 89
soil(s), impervious, wet, water-holding, heavier, richer, 56–9, 68, 78, 79, 82, 83, 88, 89, *see also* claylands
    pervious, well-drained, light, 55, 65, 66, 67, 78, 79, 80, 88, 89, *see also* chalk, gravel, etc.
    rich, exploitation of, 83
Solway, 71
Somerset, 22, 26, 33, 62, 86
Somme, river, 15, 17
South Downs, 29, 65
Southampton Water, 32, 67
Spain, 10, 19, 21, 22, 23, 42, 49, 50*n*, 83, 84, 87
stock-raising, 10, 11
stone, hog-back, 62
Stonehenge, 32
Stour, river, 15, 67
Strabo, 63
Straits of Dover, 15, 27, 84, 86, 87
Strata Florida, 63
structure, geological, 28 ff, 68, 87, *see also* geology
sub-Atlantic, 51, 54, 77
sub-Boreal, 51, 54, 77, 78
submerged land surfaces, 27
subsidence, 9*n*, 26, 27, 28, 51, 87
Suffolk, 55, 65, 84
survival(s), cultural, 40, 75–6
Sussex, 36*n*, 54, 65, 68–9, 77, 78, 82, *see also* Weald
sword, striking, 20

Taff, estuary, 69
Talbenny, 58*n*
Tasciovanus, 83
terrets, 35*n*
Tertiary formation, rock, etc., 28, 29, 32, 68
Thames, river, 15, 72
    estuary, 45, 64*n*, 87, 89
    importance of, 66, 86*n*
    lower, 27*n*, 34, 86, 89
    upper, 33, 65, 66
    valley, 32, 55, 58, 84, 86
tide, tidal, tidemarks, 25, 26, 27, 28
tin, 10, 24, 33, 44, 45, 49, 50, 69, 84, 85, 86, 87, 88
torcs, gold, 49
Towednack, 49
trackways, 70, *see also* ridgeways, etc.
trade, 70, 72, 83, 84
    Armorican, 89
    Atlantic, 89
    coasting, 67
    continental European, 11, 45, 48*n*, 84
    entrepôts, 45, 48, 67, 69
    export, 47
    gold, 49
    Irish, 7, 24, 48*n*, 69, 70, 72
    northern, 44
    oversea, 23, 62*n*, 69–70, 84, 86, 89
    relation to population, 71
    river, 67
    routes, 11, 73*n*
    southern, 24, 83, 84
    tin, 33, 49, 50, 86

traders, 23, 39, 43, 67, 84, 86
traffic route, way, 67, 68*n*, 69, 89
transport, sea, 19, 28
Trent, river, 15, 72, 79*n*
Tre'r Ceiri, 38, 73
Tyne Gap, 71

Ulster, 42, 69
undergrowth, 53
urn, cordoned, 41, 42
    encrusted, 41, 42, 70
    overhanging-rim, 9*n*, 42
    pedestal, 15
Urus, 62

Vaccinium Myrtillus, 54
valley, settlement, 37, 69, 80–2, 83
valleyward movement, 83
vegetation, 53–61, 63, *see also* forest, varieties of
Veneti, 23, 34, 84*n*
Verulamium, 58*n*, 83, 86*n*, *see also* St. Albans
Viking Age, culture, 22, 42
villa, Romano-British, 62, 83*n*

Wales, animals in, 62, 63
    beakers in, 20, 62
    continuity of culture in, 40–1
    cultural relations with Ireland, 44, 45, 69, 70
    cultural sources, 73*n*
    forests bordering, 58
    frontier of, 33
    geological structure of, 28, 29
    in Bronze Age, 73, 73*n*
    inaccessibility of, 68
    rivers as boundaries in, 75*n*
    Roman villa in, 62
    sea route to, 34*n*
    seasonal migration in, 74
    settlement, distribution of, 11, 32, 37, 70, 73, 75*n*, 76, 78, 82
    trade to, in, across, 23, 45*n*, 48*n*, 49
    vegetation in, 53
    "Wessex" culture in, 22, *see also* Glamorgan, Pembrokeshire, and many place-names: and under "Welsh"
Wash, the, 15, 27, 32, 67
Weald, the, 31, 38*n*, 58, 69, 81
wealth, 29, 83, 86, 88
Welsh Marches, 29, 37, 82*n*
    mountains, sea-plain, etc., 41, 62, 70, 75*n*
Wessex, 14, 15, 19, 20, 22, 41, 49, 54, 57*n*, 68, 73*n*, 89, *see also* Salisbury Plain and Wiltshire
Wessex culture, 9, 40, 45*n*, 49, 83
West Alpine, 10, 15*n*
Weymouth, 15, 29, 67
White Horse Hills, 29, 65
Wicklow Mountains, 45
Wight, Isle of, 33
wild cat, 62
Wiltshire, 45*n*, 65*n*, 77*n*, 79, 83
Winchester, 67
Witham, river, 34, 65
wolf, 62, 64, 65
woods, woodland, 54, 55, 63, 65, *see also* forest
Worcester, -shire, 72, 81
Wrekin, 70
Wye, river, 72

Yew, 53, 54, 55
York, 44, 67*n*
Yorkshire, 20, 35*n*, 36, 41, 45*n*, 58, 62, 67, 68*n*
    east, Wolds, 14, 19, 32, 33, 34, 42*n*, 54, 65, 71, 73*n*
    north-east, 66*n*, 76*n*, 78
    west, 37
Ystradfellte, 83